THE ROMANCE
OF ARCHAEOLOGY

THE ROMANCE OF ARCHAEOLOGY

A handsome youth in bronze at Pompeii rising from the ashes with which Vesuvius covered him in the eruption of 79 A.D. This magnificent statue is perhaps the original of a Ganymede by a famous Greek sculptor, which, after being carried to Italy, was bought by a Pompeian and transformed into a candelabrum.

# THE ROMANCE OF
# ARCHAEOLOGY
### *Formerly* MAGIC SPADES

BY
## R. V. D. MAGOFFIN

PRESIDENT OF THE ARCHAEOLOGICAL INSTITUTE OF AMERICA
PROFESSOR OF CLASSICS, NEW YORK UNIVERSITY

AND

## EMILY C. DAVIS

ARCHAEOLOGICAL STAFF WRITER OF SCIENCE SERVICE

GARDEN CITY PUBLISHING COMPANY, INC.
GARDEN CITY, NEW YORK

PRINTED IN THE
UNITED STATES OF AMERICA

TO OUR MOTHERS
ELIZABETH VAN DEMAN MAGOFFIN
AND
BIRDIE CLEVELAND DAVIS

NIHIL HUMANUM AB ARCHAEOLOGIA ALIENUM EST.

NOTHING THAT CONCERNS HUMANITY IS ALIEN TO ARCHAEOLOGY.

# AUTHORS' PREFACE

THIS book is written with the hope of helping to diminish the once rather widespread notion that Archaeology was the unnecessary and fatuous excavation of the broken remnants of a bygone, and therefore superseded, antiquity. It tries to tell the story of the unexpected resurrection of the past into the liveliest and most fascinating form of modern science.

There is in this book no pretense to the meticulous scholarship that must document every statement, but due and willing acknowledgment is made herewith to the hundreds of archaeological books and journals in English — especially the *American Journal of Archaeology* — French, German, and Italian in which the initiated know most of the facts are to be found. The book therefore contains no long bibliography and no thousands of confirmatory or unduly explanatory footnotes. It tells the truth and aims to tell it in a way that is popularly readable and entertainingly instructive.

The authors make no pretense to an exhaustive treatise on archaeology; not to exhaust their reading audience has rather been their intent.

The chapters dealing with the Mediterranean and Asiatic civilizations have been prepared by Professor Magoffin. He wishes to thank the museums of this country and their directors for courteous assistance both with facts and illustrations. He makes due acknowledgment to the *New York Herald Tribune* for permission to make use of the articles under his name which have been appearing in the Sunday edition of that newspaper. He is most grateful to Associate Curator Ambrose Lansing of the Department of Egyptian Art of The Metropolitan Museum of Art, and to Professor James A. Montgomery of the Philadelphia Divinity School and the University of Pennsylvania, and Chairman of the Managing Committee of the American Schools of Oriental Research, for the critical help they gave on the chapters in their special fields, which they were kind enough to read. He is under special obligation to his former colleague, Professor David M. Robinson of Johns Hopkins, who read the entire manuscript with his customary acumen.

The chapters dealing with Britain, Scandinavia, and the American continent have been prepared by Miss Davis. She wishes to extend her sincere thanks to the many archaeologists, particularly those working in the American field, who have personally given her in connection with her work with Science Service the latest information on their discoveries, and who, in many cases, have been kind enough to read portions of this manuscript. Many of the progress reports of the delvings into America's past here described were reported to the newspapers served by Science Service and in its weekly magazine, the *Science News-Letter*. It is fascinating to see the explorations begin, grow, and finally take such form that their achievements can thus be preserved in book form.

# TABLE OF CONTENTS

# LIST OF ILLUSTRATIONS

# THE ROMANCE
# OF ARCHAEOLOGY

CHAPTER ONE

## THE SPADE IS MIGHTIER THAN THE PEN

THE combined elements of surprise and satisfaction meet in archaeology more often perhaps than in any other modern science. In the first place, people are always expressing surprise that Schliemann knew enough to look for the ancient high-walled city of Priam under the modern Turkish hills of Hissarlik. Then they are even more surprised that Troy (to which fair Helen went because she wanted to be the first woman in the world — as she was — to get her gowns from Paris) is only one of nine cities built through the ages one above another.

A visitor always expresses surprise when he is taken to the Roman Forum, and at the ancient Senate corner is shown more than twenty levels, visible one above another, of stratification which date the history of part of that greatest small spot on earth from about 600 B.C. to 1870 A.D. But one who visits or reads about Troy or the Forum gets entire and immediate satisfaction from the information that in ancient times builders did not clear away what was left of a place after a fire, earthquake, or post-war destruction, but knocked in and levelled over what walls could not be used for rebuilding. It should therefore no longer elicit surprise that, when the archaeologists go to work, thousands of such smaller objects as coins, vases, trinkets, and even pieces of statuary are found in the strata.

One reads that the ancient world was alive with statues. To refute the charge of having begot an Irish bull, it is only necessary to point to the millions of visitors in the museums of the world whose lively admiration is excited by the beauty of the ancient statues, few and shattered though they be. If, then, statues were so numerous in the ancient world, where are they now; and of those we have, why are practically all so badly shattered or battered or mutilated?

3

It is written also that in ancient Greece and Rome there were nearly as many statues of bronze as of marble.  The value of the metal to the early medievillains will easily account for the disappearance of most of the bronze statuary.  The mode of the dissolution of the marbled forms of sculptured beauty is attested by scores of extant lime pits.  Long-continued wars with the barbarians, and ensuing poverty and degradation, rendered the remnants of Romans insensible to all forms of beauty.  It was a pitiable age of crass necessity.  Marble made wonderful lime for mortar; houses and fortifications had to be built.  So into the lime pits were dumped marble marvels of inestimable and irreplaceable value.  Priceless creations of Phidias, Scopas, Praxiteles, and Lysippus, once so deliciously alive in sculptured reality, are now dead strips of dirty mortar in crumbling, useless walls.

National Museum, Rome
Courtesy of Comm. R. Paribeni

A DISARMED DIANA

A statue found at Ostia, the ancient seaport of Rome.  The sculptor has carved the lovely huntress, Diana the goddess, but his model was clearly a young Roman girl.

The bronze Hercules of the Vatican is flatheaded because he was toppled off his pedestal and, alighting on his head, stayed there, covered with rubbish and hidden between walls, for more than a thousand years.  Agrippa decorated the fountains in Rome with three hundred statues of marble and of bronze.  The stories in ancient authors of the shipments of statues, in one case of as many as 6,000 in a single lot, and of the dedicated or acquired thousands of statues at Luxor, Delos, Delphi, and Olympia, or in the temple of Apollo on the Palatine, in Vespasian's Forum of Peace, or in the temple of Fortune at Praeneste, authenticate the wildest possible statement of the ubiquity and the number of ancient statues.

### PALESTRINA, THE ANCIENT PRAENESTE

In central Italy there is a mountain the western slope of which faces toward the Mediterranean, visible twenty miles away, through the eight-mile gap between the Volscian mountains and the Alban Hills. From the citadel top of this Monte Glicestro one can see to the northward across the Campagna the noble dome of St. Peter's Church and, still farther beyond, the lifting summit of Mt. Soracte. Southward the view carries sixty miles along the Sacco valley toward Naples. It was not only the most beautiful but also the most strategic site in Latium, and was therefore chosen by a group of the settlers of the second millennium B.C. for their stronghold. It became a powerful and wealthy city before the settlers on the Tiber, at a place later to be known as Rome, constituted more than the quarrelsome denizens of a military outpost. This is proved by the discoveries at Praeneste, for such was its name, of the Bernardini and Barberini tombs with their buried funeral treasures of gold and ivory and bronze.

Praeneste wilted before the rising sun of Rome. In the first century B.C. the younger Marius took refuge behind its strong walls, but the army of Sulla captured it and razed it to the ground. The terraced streets of Palestrina (*Praeneste*) have beneath them great rock-cut reservoirs in which in ancient times the city hoarded water for its use, especially against a siege. Several parts of the ancient temple of Fortune the Firstborn have always been visible. On the floor of one of the lower caves, where priestly responses were asked or given, was found the best and largest of Roman mosaics which in its pictorial beauty, portraying a stretch of the Egyptian Nile, is the pride of the municipal building in which Palestrina has housed it. But it was not until about 1906 that the local archaeologists were able to obtain the funds to start a real exca-

vation.  Good sense said that the ancient open city square
was directly below the open area of the modern piazza or plaza.
It was.  The pavement of ancient Praeneste of Republican
days was about twelve feet below the modern flagging.

Digging in the pit one day in the stratum just above the
ancient pavement, old Pietro came upon three terra-cotta cups
filled with hard-packed dirt.  An American student working

A COLUMBARIUM

The covers of the cinerary urns, in which the ashes of the dead were, have
been left in their dove-cote shaped recesses.  Note the floor mosaic showing
the charioteer and the heads of his four horses.  The excavation is near Porta
Portese at Rome.

at Palestrina at the time said they looked like what in the museums were called dice boxes.  The dirt was carefully picked
out of the cups.  At the bottom of each one were two bone
dice exactly like ours, and a number of colored glass (faïence)
counters.  Well, what of it?  Such cups, such dice, and such
counters had been found before.  Never had all been found
together, however, in such a way as to give an idea what sort
of game was played with them.  Here in each of three small

terra-cotta cups were two dice and twenty-four colored counters, six of each of four colors. Parchesi has gone somewhat out of style as an indoor sport, but plenty of people there are who, if these ancient cups, dice, and counters were put before them today without their knowing anything about the discovery, would get a parchesi board and start to play. They might perhaps have what the doctors of the old school used to call a "conniption fit," if they were told that those dice and counters had been buried since at least 80 B.C. Three out of the four at the least would exclaim in unison, "Well, as my old friend Solomon used to say, 'There's nothing new under the sun.'"

*Photograph by R. V. D. Magoffin*

PICKING ON THE OTHER FELLOW

Pietro of Palestrina had no idea that the next stroke of his pick would hit a beautiful marble head at the corner of the eye and knock off his nose.

Another day Pietro was swinging his pick. He was not yet deep enough in the pit to need to be careful. As he swung a mighty blow he must have slipped, because the point of his pick struck in the black earth at about the level of his eyes. Out from the black wall came a sudden glint of white, accompanied by the "ping" that marble gives back to a blow from steel. Through volleys of execrations, poor Pietro was pulled from the pit, and the director of excavations, Capitano Felice Cicerchia, took his place.

The piece of marble, after being dug out and washed at the nearby fountain, disclosed itself as the head of a young Roman. But horror of horrors! The nose was gone. The break, however, was fresh. So down into the pit went the Captain, scratched about a moment in the loose dirt, and found the nose. After it was washed it was put back where it belonged. Now, except for a small abrasion, where the pick had struck at the corner of the eye, and a faint line down the side of the nose and across the upper lip, the features of this handsome Roman youth are restored and preserved to us forever.   The next day the King of Italy drove the Superintendent of Public Instruction out in his car to Palestrina, and after examining the newly discovered head, said that Palestrina had a prize indeed, and should not lack for a reasonable appropriation with which to continue so fruitful an excavation.

Roman antiquity is the gold mine of Italy, but the Italians, although this stratum of antiquity is deservedly theirs in lieu of veins or mines of ore and coal, despite the monetary value of their heritage from Rome, appreciate it  even more because of its artistic and historic value.   More honor to them!

### The Modern Making of Ancient History

Some years ago the students of the School of Classical Studies of the American Academy in Rome, on their annual two-months visit to Greece, arrived late one night at a certain city in Euboea, that island lying like a breakwater along the east coast of Attica and Boeotia.   The Professor-in-charge, after getting his charges fed and to bed, went out to look for a means of conveyance by which to take the students to an excavation some distance away which they were to visit the next morning.   Walking along a narrow street, he saw interesting things in the dimly lit window of an antique shop, but, thinking it shut, was about to go on.   A man came hurrying up the street and turned into the shop.   The professor, after a moment of hesitation, followed him, to be met, as one can well imagine, by two very much surprised Greeks.   After successfully identifying himself not only as not being an agent of the law, but as being a safe and sane foreigner in search of purchasable antiquities, he was taken into a back room.   The Greek who had preceded him into the shop had made a discovery late that afternoon while digging a foundation trench over near the very excavation, long since abandoned, where the members of the American School were to go the next morning.

He had found a small terra-cotta pot which he had lifted from its place.   In it were sixty-seven silver coins.   As soon as possible he struck across the mountains to his cousin in town, who was a dealer in antiquities.   The professor took the finder back in the morning and saw the cavity in the bottom of the trench in which the pot had stood.

ATHENA AND HER OWL

The typical silver coin of Athens.   The Greek letters in front of the owl are the first three letters of the name of the city Athens (Athenai).   A reproduction of the design on the right has long been used as the colophon of Henry Holt and Company.

After considerable bargaining the professor bought the sixty-seven coins.   Several days later in Athens he identified them.   They ran in date from 456–455 to 412–411 B.C.   A half dozen of those dating 412–411 B.C. were as bright and new as if they had been struck the day before.   And now the stage is set for a demonstration of the modern making of ancient history.

The great and the suicidal war of Hellas was the Peloponnesian War, 431–404 B.C.   The Athenians and Spartans were both ready after ten years of warfare, 431–421 B.C., to agree upon a peace, which, we feel sure, was understood by both parties as only an armistice.   During the ensuing years, however, whenever the military service of soldiers was up, Athens paid and discharged them, and as a sort of bonus, gave to many of them a two-acre patch of ground in the island of Euboea. In 412 B.C. a certain veteran received his discharge pay, and went over to Euboea to settle on his bonus property.

Some months later there came an announcement from Athens that an expedition was to be sent to Sicily.  Private rumor said it was really aimed at the capture of Syracuse, the largest and wealthiest city in the Greek world.  It was allied to Sparta.  Everyone saw the point.  The plunder would be tremendous, and Sparta, the great protagonist in the war against Athens, would be stabbed mortally under the fifth rib, and yet the Peace of Nicias would not be technically broken.

The recall of the veterans to arms was sponsored by Alcibiades, handsome, aristocratic, very rich, and very clever, and quite the most gifted in effrontery of any Athenian of that time; and in the sequel he proved to be the most debonair of all the plausible rascals of history.  The soldiers, and boys under military age, and the discharged veterans all leaped to the call of opportunity.  Our veteran in Euboea got together what little he needed, and then, before he left his new little house, he buried in a terra-cotta pot under his floor the balance of his money, among the pieces being a number of the new coins that had been minted that very year and paid to him when he was discharged.  He hurried to Athens, was enrolled, and sent on board the fleet which was so eager to go that the ships raced one another down the Saronic gulf, as all the women of Attica on top of the houses at Piraeus waved them *bon voyage*.  The expedition was the greatest debâcle of history.  The entire force was killed or captured.  The pot of coins, after 2,333 years, turned up accidentally by a spade in 1921, is one of the thousands of pitiful mortalities of that ill-starred expedition now archaeologically authenticated.

### The Inside Story of a Crocodile

Some years ago a gentleman bought a number of Egyptian papyri, which in his presence were put in tin cylinders and carefully sealed.  The amusing *caveat emptor* of the transaction — the disappearance of about one-fourth of the papyri from the tins without a seal broken, and the subsequent repurchase of the missing ones at a price greater than had previously been paid for the entire lot — has nothing to do with the story, other than as illuminating comment.

Five illicit diggers for spoils came upon a cemetery of crocodiles. (They were as much surprised doubtless as Grenfell and Hunt had been at Tebtunis when they found a cemetery of crocodiles whose throats were stuffed with papyrus.) The five men were in a quandary as to how to dispose of their discoveries. Every night for the best part of a year they carried the crocodiles several miles off to the rocky edge of the desert and burned them in a dark and deep natural cave. The cemetery was finally exhausted. Then quite accidentally a spade struck upon something hard. It was the concreted dome roof of a small sanctuary. A hole was made in the roof and three of the men were lowered through it. In the center of the small room on a cubical stone lay a mummified baby crocodile. The diggers did not touch it until they had turned over every bit of the floor dirt down to virgin rock. Not a thing of value — to them — was discovered. They were absolutely enraged. One of them picked up the baby crocodile and smashed it on the cubical stone where it had lain so quietly for more than two thousand years. As it fell apart out rolled a lot of papyrus. The crocodile had been stuffed with the waste paper of Egypt. The writing and the figures were the accounts of overseers, but all of it was valuable from the point of view of the economic history of the time. The papyrus from the baby crocodile was sold to the gentleman above mentioned for a good round sum. It may be left to the imagination to picture the staggering realization of the illicit diggers who had so carefully burned nearly a hundred big crocodiles all stuffed with papyrus, as well as on the wistful exasperation of papyrologists who bemoan the irreparable loss of certainly important records and possibly invaluable literature.

### Why America Has One Venus Less

The Venus of Cyrene in her marbled perfection, in the judgment of connoisseurs of art, almost approaches the exalted plane of rank held by the unrivalled Hermes of Praxiteles. The

Archaeological Institute's School of Classical Studies at Rome was carrying on an important excavation at Cyrene in northern Africa under a permit from the government of Turkey. Part of the indemnity from Turkey after Italy's successful war

*Courtesy of the National Museum of Rome*

THE VENUS OF CYRENE

The famous Venus found by the Italians eleven days after work had begun in the excavation which our American School had to resign, having had the permit from Turkey. The most beautiful female statue in the world, perhaps.

in 1911 was the Cyrenaica. Italy purchased from the American School its archaeological tools and properties. After some years it began to excavate at Cyrene where, after the declaration of war, the Americans had left off. Not many days after the excavations had been resumed, a guard stumbled over a piece of embedded stone. The stone was marble, and the marble was one of the sculptural wonders of the world. It was the Venus of Cyrene.

Reasonably authentic rumor ran the prices that were offered for her by foreign museums and individuals into the millions of dollars. But her value was, and is, such that more than one Italian of official consequence has declared that if some foreign person, museum, or government, should offer to Italy for the Venus of Cyrene the amount of the Italian national debt — over a billion dollars — that dream-reality of sculptured beauty would stay right where she is. As someone said, after being convinced that the statement had been made and that its tenor was indubitably true, "Let the modern — even if unregistered — descendants of Croesus put that in their pipes and smoke it!"

One day, not long after this Venus of Cyrene had been inducted into her new home in the *Museo delle Terme* in Rome, so the story goes, her guard, who had gone out of the room for a few moments, on his return saw to his consternation and horror a strange man running his hands up and down over the contours of this sacrosanct statue.  He bade the stranger desist and begone, in tone and language not fit even for a lady of marble to hear.  The stranger put up an argument, saying that he was not hurting the statue, would not injure it for worlds, was by way of being something of a sculptor himself, knew that he could obtain something from such a marvel of art by manual contact that visual, mental, or sympathetic contact could not touch, etc.  But the guard was importunately, even rudely, obdurate.  The stranger stepped over the rope, but before leaving made, in a mild and persuasive way, other excuses for his conduct in such interesting but unintelligible language, that the guard's curiosity overcame his rage. He accepted the excuses, regretted his orders, and then exclaimed, "Who are you, anyhow?"  The stranger said, "My name is Rodin."

### An Archaeological S.O.S.

The Fayum in Egypt is the sandy basin left by a prehistoric Nilotic overflow which through the ages has in great part trickled or been absorbed away.  In the seventh or sixth century B.C., Greeks, who had earlier been allowed to found Naucratis as a commerical seaport on the Egyptian coast of the Mediterranean, wanted other sites on which to settle.  Presumably, the only place they could get was the sandy waste of the Fayum.  There was subsoil, however, and with either water or fertilizer a good return from crops was usually sure. More than twenty Greek towns soon arose.  After a few hundred years the Greeks were overlaid with a stratum of Hellenistic inhabitants, then that by a Roman layer, and it by a stratum of Coptic Christians.  The westward sweep of the Arabs overwhelmed all these towns.  The men were doubtless all killed, the women and children made captives, and the buildings either partly demolished or entirely knocked down.  It would seem, however, that most of the objects of personal and household use were left untouched; perhaps, being Christian, they were saved by a taboo. During succeeding centuries the blowing sand covered these four-ply settlements until they were nothing to the eye but scattered mounds of sand.

For many years there has been desultory digging at the bases of these sand-covered mound cities. Grenfell and Hunt of Oxyrhyncus fame found some good papyri in one or more of them, but left and moved on up the Nile to better hunting grounds. Some years ago, local pashas who either owned or began to get concessions of extensive tracts of land in the Fayum found that the best and most easily obtainable fertilizer for their potential fields of tobacco was the four times inhabited towns of long ago which under the sand had disintegrated into four good strata of Greek, Hellenistic, Roman, and Coptic fertilizer. The plan of economic attack is to strike the ground rim of the mound with a narrow-gauge track and dig straight through it, hauling little train loads, mostly by gravity power, of its débris out to their fields where it is scattered in regulation fertilizer fashion. Rather a sad commentary on the internationally understood code on the obligation to care for antiquities!

An American traveller in 1926 was being introduced to the Fayum. He and a friend were walking along the inside crest of the divide through one of these fertilizer-split towns. When they came opposite some stone ruins across the divide, the friend suggested that rather than walk all the way round they do a shoe-sole ski down the slope of the cut to save time even at the expense of getting their shoes full of sand. No sooner said than done. Arriving at the bottom the American happened by good chance to look back at his parallel sand tracks. From one of them, at about the height of his eyes, protruded something that looked like a long stogie. He pulled it out of the sand. His friend said, "Keep it, and when you are back in your hotel in Cairo, get some towels, water, and a hot iron; then dampen, unroll, and press it out very slowly and carefully. The chances are you will have something." He did so, and found he had a magnificent piece of papyrus with several lines of ancient Greek writing on it in two different hands.

Some days later the American traveller was visiting a physician to whom he had presented a letter.   During dinner one night the Egyptian servant brought in a man whose daughter had been under the care of the doctor.   He reported on her condition and listened attentively to the doctor's directions. He then bowed, and produced from his shirt a bandanna handkerchief which he shook out on a tray.   The jingle of the black objects was that of silver coins.   He told the doctor he was trying that evening to finish turning under the fertilizer that had been spread from the last train load from the mound. It was already dark, and he had no light.   Suddenly he had heard a crack at the point of his plowshare, and had investigated.   He had broken a little terra-cotta pot, and, scratching about, had found the score of coins which he had just poured out on the tray as payment of the debt he owed the doctor for the care of his daughter.   The physician thanked him and bade him good-night.   After he had gone, the doctor said to the American, "Do you want those coins?   I get lots of them, you know."   "I certainly do," was the reply.

Shortly thereafter the traveller went on board his boat at Alexandria bound for the Piraeus, the seaport of Athens.   He at once gave the black coins a preliminary bath and then threw them into a tin cup half full of lemon juice.   Late that afternoon he told a fellow traveller the story of the coins.   Out of his chair leaped his listener with a strong exclamation, followed by the suggestion that the two go down together to look at the find.

After a few hours in lemon juice, the dirt, with a little vigorous rubbing with a stiff tooth brush, comes nicely off silver coins.   The coins bore on the obverse, pictured heads of Roman emperors from Domitian to Marcus Aurelius (84–166 A.D.). The lettering around the edges was in Greek.   On the reverses were various things of a pictorial or commemorative kind. On three of the coins, however, were the representations of the *uraeus* cobras of Egypt, the same serpent that erects itself above the Pharaonic crown. On one coin a male cobra stood erect upon his tail; on another a female was just as erect on hers; and on the third coin both male and female cobra stood facing each other, isocephalic if not beatific. Thus, a chance American traveller becomes heir to some Roman who, having settled in the Egyptian Fayum, was for some reason forced to leave, but who before going had buried his current wealth in a terra-cotta cup under his floor. These silver coins were within an ace of being turned under to fertilize a crop of Egyptian tobacco. The moral seems to point to the fact that it is more sensible and much better to do as the University of Michigan Near East Expedition under Professor F. W. Kelsey did at Kom Washim and salvage the thousands of valuable antiquities from the mounds, where both provenience and chronology can be definitely established, rather than let rushing materialism salt a tobacco field into a future gold mine with antiques which, like arrowheads before plows in New Mexico, are turned up practically without their scientific value.

### Bringing the Past to Light

In 1902 Commendatore Boni discovered in front of the temple of Antoninus and Faustina in the Roman Forum, and by the side of the Sacred Way, a prehistoric cemetery. There were found in it fifty-two graves, partly cremation and partly inhumation burials. Although the inhumations seemed to be somewhat the earlier, the fact that they were at the same level proved that the then inhabitants of the Palatine hill were living amicably together, although they were of two distinct peoples, the one being of the inhuming (earth-burying) Ibero-Ligurians and the other of the incinerating (cremating) Terremare or Villanovans. This fact is probably the basis for the old story of the coalition of the Romans and the Sabines which came about through the intercession of the girls who figure in the so-called "Rape of the Sabines."

Buried with the dead in the prehistoric cemetery were hundreds of small funerary objects of terra-cotta, bronze, glass, amber, and ivory. They were clearly much earlier than anything that had been found in Rome before.  How were they to be dated?  Of course, the traditional history of Rome had the city founded in 753 or 754 B.C.  But even that seemed not to be an early enough date for these cemetery burials and objects.  Besides, it was known that the custom in interring the dead was to begin just outside a gate, on both sides of the roads, leading out of the towns.  The gate in the Palatine wall from which the Sacra Via emerged, although not exactly located, was certainly up the hill some little way from the present Arch of Titus.  It would therefore have been a century or more before the burials could have reached the spot where Boni had found the cemetery.

Two or three years later workmen were drilling into the bottom of a lava stream below Marino in the Alban Hills to break off enough of that wonderful material to pave the streets of their town.  Lo and behold! they came upon a cemetery under the lava stream.  With the burials were found objects like those in the prehistoric cemetery in the Forum.  Geology said the lava stream had broken out of the side of Monte Cavo (*Mons Albanus*) about 900 B.C.  The cemetery was already there, of course, when the lava stream ran over it.  Therefore, by the help of a sister science, archaeology could date quite closely the objects found in both cemeteries.  As a result the date of the settling of Rome was thrown back, quite incontestably, more than 200 years.

### A LIGHT-FINGERED GREEK IN POMPEII

Digging along one of the newly opened streets in Pompeii in 1926, the excavators came to a doorway leading back into a house that looked prospective.  The workmen with spade and pick rapidly cleared out the large central room (*atrium*) of the house.  The tops of the two door posts leading out at the back were already in sight.  A laborer struck a hard blow with his pick and down rolled a small avalanche of ashes (*scoriae*).  Out popped a beautiful bronze head.  Everyone nearly went mad.  The big pick yielded to the tiny trowel.  The greatest care had to be exercised to free, without a scratch, inch after inch of the bronze body of the Greek ephebe (*i.e.*, youth of earliest military age). When he had been uncovered down to the knees, the truth was no nearer than at the beginning of his disinterment.

Finally, the wonderful bronze statue stood clear on his small pedestal. But his mystery was still unexplainable. There were still some ten inches or so of ashes over the floor at the foot of the statue. While removing them, two beautifully decorated spiral pieces of bronze were found. Each had on it four socket points. The pieces were put into the hands of the statue. They fitted exactly the apertures between the thumbs and the fingers. Then, and not till then, the marvelous bronze stood out as a life-like candelabrum in bronze. The money that has been offered for that statue would stagger the most skeptical. We must revise our opinion of the small proprietor of Pompeii who had culture enough to decorate his reception room with a candelabrum which in that day

*Courtesy of A. Maiuri*

FLAMING YOUTH

A Greek statue in bronze, after being shipped to Naples, was probably bought at an auction sale by a Pompeian living on Abundance Street. The new owner turned his statue into a hall light and probably told his visitors, jokingly, that he had elevated Ganymede, the cup bearer to the great god on Olympus, to an Apollo, the bearer of light to man.

was costly and which today under like circumstances would be wholly impossible.

If the German Amelung is right, this splendid bronze is either the original or a copy of the Ganymede (with Zeus) which was dedicated at Olympia, and which Pausanias saw and attributed to the sculptor, the younger Aristocles of Sicyon. Both the head and the body are of fifth-century type, although different in style.   Some authorities say the statue is of Hellenistic date; others, of whom Robinson of Johns Hopkins is one, think it may be a good Roman copy of the head of one, and the body of another, Greek work of the fifth century B.C.

Is it to be wondered why the whole world this past half hundred years has so suddenly become alive to its ancient dead, and why every civilized nation is trying to outdo the other in financing excavations, in exploring sites where tradition has said were ancient cities, and in preserving and exhibiting the wonderful finds that have been made?

Archaeology is undoubtedly succeeding in giving the human touch to inanimate things of long ago, and thereby quickening the dead past with a vitality that makes our inheritance of the ages a living possession of priceless worth.

*Photograph by R. V. D. Magoffin*

WHERE CICERO SAT

Sheepskins are often awarded nowadays in open air theatres.  The little theater at Tusculum, back of Frascati in the Alban Hills, near one of Cicero's villas, offers preliminary sheepskin exercises.

## A ROYAL PROCLAMATION

Babylonian Cylinder with a lengthy proclamation, written in cuneiform characters, by King Nebuchadnezzar. Found at Marad, a suburb of Babylon.

CHAPTER TWO

## THE MODERN TONE OF ANCIENT TIMES

MOST people have to dig to make a living; archaeologists seem to dig for fun. Archaeology has been at times a sport for kings; now it is the royal sport of scientists. Things that

ANCIENT LIFE BROUGHT TO LIGHT

A chamber of the tomb of Meket-Re at Thebes, as it was found in its topsy-turviness by The Metropolitan Museum's Egyptian Expedition.

were fun to do ought to be interesting to read about. By the nature of the case, archaeological finds are exciting entities; the unity of science is their connecting link.

What fun it has been to make the points of the pyramids invert themselves, as it were, and trace history on the Egyptian sand! Over seventy of those stupendous monuments to slave labor have survived. To be sure, they were built to entomb Pharaonic royalty, but the irony of fate was as heavy as their architectonic granite, limestone, and alabaster. In one pyramid only has the body of its royal builder been found. Tomb robbers in ancient times were not journeymen, they were adepts; but even at that, luckily they missed a plenty.

It is so easy now to read statistics about the great pyramid of Cheops (Khufu) across the Nile from Cairo. The red granite on the inside came from Syene, the limestone coating from Mokattam, some miles away across the river. It is 481 feet high, it has a slope to its sides of 75 degrees, it occupies an area of thirteen acres, its equilateral sides now measure fifteen feet less than they did 4,000 years ago, its four sides lie squared with the cardinal points of the compass, it contains some 2,300,000 blocks of stone, averaging two and a half tons to the block. But it has taken a long time to find out all those facts. And more are to come. In fact, one more new one came not long ago. Petrie discovered that the granite blocks of the great pyramid had been cut with the help of tubular drills with points of hard stone.

### Pots Full of Money and History

The coinage of Cyrene in Africa was stamped on one side with the likeness of a plant called silphium. Had there been no written statements that Cyrene owed its prosperity to the raising and shipping of silphium, it would nevertheless have been archaeologically possible to have reached that conclusion from the pieces of money minted there.

It is, however, the coins that are sold without proof as to the site of discovery which retard the conclusions their stamped faces carry. In 1909 four thousand *denarii* (silver pieces worth 20 cents each) of King Juba II were found at El Ksar, southwest of Tangiers. The information gleaned from eighty-one of the pieces secured by the French Bibliothèque Nationale raised a great longing for the others which were scattered who knows where. Some time before 1887, and somewhere near

Sidon, a pot was found containing over 8,000 coins of Philip and of Alexander the Great.

A hoard of gold and silver coins was found not long ago near Keneh in Upper Egypt. The coins came into the hands of dealers, whose letters about them to various collectors brought a small hegira at once to Paris. In this hoard were forty-five gold and over two hundred silver coins, all in magnificent condition. The proof that they had lain together and were found as a hoard appeared on the surfaces of the gold coins where here and there were tiny patches of grey silver oxide which had come from the disintegrating surfaces of the silver coins. An examination made of them by Newell of the American Numismatic Society, America's best judge, shows that the hoard was buried very shortly after 144 B.C.

*Courtesy of the Royal Ontario Museum of Archaeology, Toronto*

A POT OF MONEY

The ancients buried their money in jars, because there were no banks in which to deposit while they were away from home. That fact accounts for most of the finds of hoards of coins.

Upon the death of Philometor, several powerful factions in Egypt, particularly the Greek and the Jewish, had come out for his widow and young son in opposition to the claim on the throne set up by Philometor's brother Euergetes on his return to Egypt in 147–146 B.C. The army sided with Euergetes and by its aid he made good his claim to the throne. He at once put into practice the good old policy of assassination and banishment of the opposition. Portable treasure naturally sought cover, and many a pot of coins went into the earth to wait for safer days. This Keneh hoard, from its date, may well have been one of those hidden treasures.

The pictorial value of these coins is very great.   Their un-rubbed condition brings out the heads of the Egyptian rulers and their consorts, sharply cut in profile.   Queen Arsinoë has not quite so true a Greek profile as Berenice whose beautiful face can be seen on several coins from the "Delta Hoard" found in the same year as the coins from Keneh.   One may lay a straight-edge along the face of Berenice from the top of her forehead to the tip of her nose and get no daylight under the edge of the rule.   But the Ptolemaic Pharaohs were all very proud of their Macedonian profiles.   The point of the nose is long and sharp; the project-ing chin turns up a little as if to meet the end of the nose; the lips are firm and straight; and above the eyes the brow bulges in the famous Ptolemaic manner.

*Courtesy of the Boston Museum of Fine Arts*

A PTOLEMAIC PROFILE

A Greek head of the Hellenistic period. It is probably a portrait of Queen Ar-sinoë II.   Note the long pointed nose so characteristic of the Greek Ptolemies of Egypt.

The most famous of the Ptolemaic coin designs is the center piece on the reverse of the majority of their issues.   It is the living image of the Mace-donian eagle, standing erect in a lordly fashion, its claws hold-ing a bundle of thunderbolts, as it, the bird of Zeus the Thunderer, should do.   Its feathers pantagraph its splendid neck, breast, and wings, and pantalet its legs.   This is the eagle that seems to have furnished itself as a model for the eagle on our latest ten-dollar gold pieces.   Much to our humiliation, the work on our coins is not so well done as that by the artists and die cutters of twenty-two hundred years ago.

In 1887 an Englishman presented to the British Museum a decadrachm, *i.e.*, a Greek silver coin about the size of a silver dollar, which had been dug up at Bokhara in India. It has been accepted generally as one of a series of coins struck to commemorate the expedition of Alexander the Great to the Punjab. When it was struck, the flan was not in its proper place on the die: therefore, several important details were missing. Numismatists and historians have been waiting for forty years for a second coin of the same series to turn up, or, to be more exact archaeologically, to be turned up. The second eagerly awaited decadrachm has been acquired lately by the British Museum, due to the kindness of three British gentlemen who dug more deeply to purchase the coin than did the man who found it not far beneath the surface of the soil of India. This is a coin that really talks.

The style of work is Greek, but it was done by a Greek who had never seen an elephant, because the legs of the beast on one side of the coin are rendered incorrectly. The coin was issued shortly after the death of Alexander, as is proved by the fact that the figure on the reverse of the coin is rendered as a god. It was issued at Babylon, or thereabouts, as the monogram BAB on the reverse suggests.

On the obverse of the newly acquired coin a regal figure on horseback is attacking with a lance a warrior on an elephant; the driver, who sits in front of the person attacked, has turned around and is launching a javelin at the king on horseback. On the reverse of the coin is an upright figure girt with a sword who holds a thunderbolt in his right hand and rests with his left hand on a spear. The thunderbolt is enough to proclaim the figure as a king represented after death as a god. But the coin has yet more to say. On the head of the god is a Persian headdress (*kyrbasia*), but bearing a Greek helmet-crest between two tall plumes.

Plutarch records the fact that Alexander the Great was conspicuous at the battle of the Granicus for his shield, and especially for the crest of his helmet and the long white plumes that stood erect on either side of it. To be sure, the artist meant to tell on these coins the story of the battle of the Hydaspes between King Porus of India and Alexander the Great. It is perhaps too much to say that Alexander ever came near enough to Porus to have a thrust at him on his elephant: but the reputation that Alexander had as an impetuous hand-to-hand fighter makes even such a claim worth consideration. It is certain, however, that the new coin, which gives the entire figure with the crested helmet — as the earlier coin does not — proves that after Alexander had won the empire of the East, he transferred the plumes and crest of his Greek helmet to a

*Vatican Museum, Rome*

TOMBSTONE ADVERTISING

The baker, Publius Nonius Zethus, utilized part of his sepulchral monument to advertise his business. On one side of the inscription is carved his flour mill; on the other, a sifter, a basket, containers and molds.

Persian *kyrbasia*. It can now be seen that the figure on horse-back is also Alexander the Great, because he wears the same headdress, crest, and plumes as the deified king on the reverse of the new coin.

On an issue of Roman coins are to be seen the instruments used in a Roman sacrifice. On other coins we have temples and public buildings which have entirely disappeared, pre-served thus for us in miniature. On coins one sees altars smoking with incense, the wreaths that were awarded to those who saved the life of a fellow-citizen in battle, the standards of different army legions, a stretch of the arches of an aqueduct long since gone, the folding *curule* chair with its seated magistrate, ancient wagons, ships, triumphal arches, prize vases for athletic victories. We know that the Romans had elections and voted for candidates, and that they had laws proposed to them, and voted on their passage. But we should not know how they did it if the descendants of a man, who had passed some popular laws, had not issued, when they were mint officials, several series of coins that showed the two sets of ballot boxes and the two kinds of ballots used.

When Lake Copïas in Boeotia in Greece was drained some years ago, 1,549 bronze coins of great historical value were found, and by good fortune were kept together as a collection. The point is obvious.

### THE LURE AND LORE OF THE RESURRECTED PAST

There is a story told by an ancient author that has in it a naïveté which can hardly be matched in the art dealings of whatsoever buyer of today. A Roman general had captured some Greek cities in which were hundreds of ancient statues, many of them the works of the greatest sculptors of the best Greek period. The statues were to be shipped to Rome. There were no marine insurance companies, but the hard-headed Roman general thought he knew his business. He drew up a contract with the owners of the ship which stipulated that if the boat went down and the statues were lost, they had to be replaced with as many others *of equal value*. It is known that many ships which were carrying antiquities from the east to the great new market at Rome did founder, and especially along the dangerous North African coast. A sunken cargo of bronze and marble sculptures was located off Mahdia in Tunis in 1909. Divers brought up many objects. In Rhodes and Delos, between 1900 and 1910, several inscriptions had given the date of birth and the birthplace of the sculptor Boëthus of Chalcedon. None of his work was identifiable. What should come up in 1909 from the sunken ship but a fine bronze herm of the god Dionysus *signed* by Boëthus himself!

It was believed even in ancient times that the rocky isle off Cape Kepháli in Corfu (Corcyra) was the petrified ship of Ulysses. In 1913 Dr. Doerpfeld, the German archaeologist, discovered a prehistoric settlement on that cape which dated as early as 1100 B.C. The chances are excellent that he will soon prove his contention that the Phaeacians of the Homeric story of Ulysses really existed and lived on the island of Corcyra. Although additional proof is no longer needed to authenticate Homer and his stories of Troy and the heroes both on the Trojan and the Greek sides, the location of the Phaeacians on that beautiful island, the halfway point between Greece and Italy, will be a delightful confirmation of one of the world's best tales of travel and adventure.

It has only been of late, due to the excavations and to the comparative standards of artistic judgment, that a statement of the Greek archaeologist and historian Pausanias has been verified. That writer said that the Greek theatre at Megalopolis was the largest, that the theatres of the Romans in general excelled those of the Greeks in decorations, but that the theatre at Epidaurus surpassed them all both in harmony and beauty. That statement was as true 1,700 years ago as it is today, but our scientists feel better now that it has been proved.

Sculptors of a century ago made some of the worst possible restorations of the shattered figures of ancient art. They had not been trained on ancient canons and relied often upon their own over-puerile academic interpretations. The now famous sculptures from the temple of Aegina were found in 1811. Cockerell made a number of hasty sketches of them from which Thorwaldsen restored the pedimental (gable-end) composition, both figures and groups. He did it most unhappily. But the restored figures were set up in the museum at Munich. They were copied and published everywhere. Some new fragments were found in 1901. The German archaeologist Furtwaengler thereupon began a new study of the grouping of the figures in the gable ends of the temple. To his amazement, he found that Thorwaldsen's former grouping was so entirely wrong that every figure had to be changed except the Athena in the centre of one pediment. It will take fifty years more to get those figures unscrambled in the popular books and mind. So much for even scientific work when done in a field not the scientist's own.

### NEW LIGHT ON ANCIENT LIFE

It is both strange and amusing how slowly an established fact travels from one type of mind to another. The foundations (*podia*) of many Roman temples are built of big oblong blocks of tufa. To hold them from shifting, they were keyed together with various sorts of bronze clamps in countersunk holes. When the temple of Castor in the Roman Forum was enlarged in the days of the early empire, a contract was let for furnishing the bronze clamps. Some years ago, when a few layers of the foundation were removed, the clamps were found holding the outside blocks to the next row within, but nowhere else was there a clamp found. The

SYMBOLS OF THE LABYRINTH

A great divinity of Cnossus in Crete was worshipped by the symbol of the double axe. With plants and rosettes these double axes form a beautiful decorative *motif* for the giant jars which took the place of storage bins in Minoan days. Note the handles for the ropes by which the jars were lowered or raised.

clamp holes were all there, ready and waiting, but they were as empty as they had been for 1,900 years. There must have been a nice little "graft" arranged between the contractor and the inspector.

One of the rooms in the palace at Cnossus in Crete was dedicated to the worship of the double-bitted axe. The Greek word *labrys* means *axe*. The word *labyrinth* is from the Greek word, and *the* Labyrinth is the famous one in Crete where the Minotaur, Theseus, Ariadne, and a ball of yarn are the basis of a good story. At all events, the double axe was worshipped in Crete as the symbol of some divine person or idea, and as a symbol belonging to religion that double axe had cleft its way into certain scientific minds. The men who were asked to interpret the holes in the shape of a double axe in certain foundations of ancient Roman buildings were hipped on religious significances. They were neither builders nor stone masons. When they saw that so many of these double-axe shaped holes were empty, their own minds being full of the Cretan worship of the symbol of the double axe, their wits hewed true to a preconceived line. They declared that the holes were sacred.

TWO GREEK COINS

Upper: Artemis with bow and quiver; the eagle of Zeus (coin of Abydos).

Lower: Janiform head of Zeus and Hera; a double bitted axe (coin of Tenedos).

But the holes, instead of being hidden receptacles for the disembodied souls of the double axe, were really the unfilled mortices for double clamps of bronze. Such, however, is the perversity of the human mind, clamped fast to preconceived ideas, that it may well be doubted whether the first interpreters have yet admitted their religious aberration. They are probably as unchanged as are said to be the present descendants of the aboriginal, antediluvian, even preadamite autochthones of Malta, Gozo, and the other islets of that group of intellectual negativity.

When Arthur Evans began work on the island of Crete, there was an unbridged gap in eastern Mediterranean history between the mature civilizations of Mesopotamia and Egypt and the rudely beaten national amalgam from which was fashioned later the stunning figure of Hellenism. The excavations of Schliemann completed one span of the desired bridge. But it was Crete that furnished the material for the great central span and the approaches on the far side. The historical world has hardly ceased yet to gasp at the stupendous structure that rose up almost over night. Perhaps the discoveries in Crete and the proof adduced to guarantee the correctness of spanning with three new Minoan periods an unbridged space of 2,000 years is the *chef d'oeuvre*, the *ne plus ultra*, of the modern science of archaeology.

*Photograph by Mary Gay, Winsor School, Boston*

TWO MODERN CRETANS

Sir Arthur Evans shows his excavations at Cnossus to Harriet Boyd Hawes, joint author of "Crete the Forerunner of Greece," and the other members of the Mary Chapin Marcus Expedition.

With Crete recognized as the head of a sea-power, the dates of which ran along contemporaneously with those of Egypt, its three zeniths matching the VI, XII, and XVIIIth high-spot dynasties of the Nile kingdom, developments in comparative sciences became as momentous as they were momentary. A number of the unexplained myths and traditions of early Greece were illuminated by the new light from Crete. Mycenean civilization could now be seen to be the mainland exotic of which Minoan island civilization had been the stem and the flower. The story of Theseus and the Minotaur was no longer a labyrinthine maze for speculation; it was the open book of the payments of Athens' prehistoric tax to an overlord. Crete had been the fabled Atlantis until its discovery had compelled propriety to move Atlantis westward beyond reach. The Kheftiu in Egyptian hieroglyphics were early Cretans, and the carven presentments of visitors and ambassadors of the Kheftiu in Egyptian tombs and mastabas tallied exactly with the paintings in color of the Cretans on their own home and palace walls. Verily an archaeological triumph.

*Courtesy of the Minneapolis Institute of Arts*

### THEY KNEW THEIR LIONS

This crouching lion of Pentelic marble, a Greek work of the IV century B.C., shows in its technique of pose and muscle the hand of a master sculptor. The United States is fortunate to possess so magnificent a specimen of ancient art.

Answers to hitherto unsolved problems of antiquity came every day; and every day also came new finds that resolved themselves into a succession of question marks. Immense hoards of pottery furnished masses of data for comparative chronology. Basins decorated with lion-headed serpents and painted sphinxes, a carved roaring lion holding a bowl between its paws, and with a fountain hole gaping in his breast, offered similarities to farther eastern art. The find at Phaestus in 1906 of an olive press of the Middle Minoan period salved the feelings of the economists. Statuettes and paintings of horses' heads, owls, all kinds of birds, antelopes, ducks, cats, and fish furnished an amazing drive for the hunters of pre-

historic fauna.  Almost the only quieting thing in all the
thousands of objects or artistic similitudes that thronged the
archaeological offing was a design on the long neck of a one-
handled jug.   It was a painting of a handsome Cretan youth
chucking a lovely Cretan girl under the chin.   Somehow, that
had not only a more or less familiar look, but it could have
been suspected.

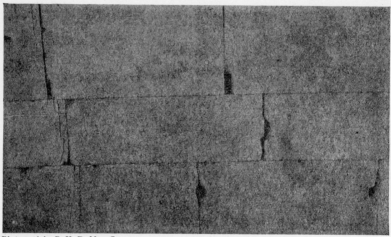

*Photograph by R. V. D. Magoffin*

A GREEK LAW CODE ON MARBLE

A famous code of early laws was found at Gortyna in Crete cut on the face of
a wall of stone blocks that had been used for a mill dam.   The water had been
running for centuries over the inscription which was discovered by accident
when the water was diverted to enable workmen to repair the dam.

In 1857 M. Thenon found an inscribed stone — now in the
Louvre at Paris — in the wall of a mill on the bank of a river
at Gortyna in Crete.   In 1878 M. Breal read the Greek of the
inscription as having something to do with the adoption of
children.   In 1879 Fabricius found in a house near the same
mill a stone fragment the Greek of which, being translated,
referred to the rights of heiresses.   In 1884 Professor Halbherr
visited Gortyna.   It happened that the water at the time had
been mostly sluiced off during some repairs to the mill dam.
Some Greek letters were shown to him that were near the top

of a wall over which, a little below the mill, a channel of water was running. The wall was part of a circular construction, which, if the curve were complete, would have been one hundred feet in diameter. The letters on the wall were quite too provocative for an archaeologist. It was arranged to sluice all the water away from the wall. When it was cleared and cleaned, there was an inscription indeed. It turned out to be the original, in two parts, one older than the other, of the code of laws of Gortyna, the longest and best code of early Greek law.

Atlantis-like, let us now move westward.

Archimedes is acclaimed as their own alike by modern mathematicians, philosophers, and chemists. He invented a sun-glass that set on fire the ship of the Roman admiral Marcellus who was besieging Syracuse in Sicily. Archimedes seems, however, to have been too much absorbed in working out mathematical theorems to have had time to concoct a poison gas or some other chemical agency which would have discomfited, nauseated, or hors-de-combatted the Romans. Syracuse was captured. Some Roman soldiers, looting about, entered his house, and, according to the ancient authorities — as read — after perplexedly watching him as he drew circles and figures in the sand on the floor with a stick, demanded that he tell who he was. Archimedes was so intent on his work that he neither noticed nor answered them. When they drew their swords and threatened his life, he said with fine philosophic calm, "Don't disturb me. I'm thinking." Whereupon they killed him. Now along comes archaeology to correct and elucidate a good story by not only verifying it but by making it better as well. A mosaic bought at the sale in the Palazzo Bonaparte in Rome in 1860 of things which had been found in the excavations of Joseph Napoleon and Joachim Murat at Pompeii and Herculaneum from 1806 to 1815, is now in the possession of a lady in Wiesbaden, the widow of a German colonel of infantry. This authenticated mosaic portrays a Roman soldier who, with his sword drawn, advances upon a seated figure, clearly Archimedes. Before the seated mathematician, on a three-legged table, is a board. It is an *abacus*, the ancient computation board, on part of which was spread sand or wax in which geometrical designs could be drawn with a *stilus;* on the other part were strung counters for numerical calculations. Archimedes was therefore working in the natural and approved fashion on a proper abacus. Archaeology has thus rescued Archimedes from an unnatural scientific method and an untidy immortality.

It would not be correct, however, to say that Archimedes invented the magnifying glass. He made a larger one, or combined several, to produce a sun-glass powerful enough to set a ship on fire. In the Ashmolean museum in England there is a round magnifying glass found in Egypt, which, if not predynastic, is certainly no later in date than the first Dynasty. In 1928 there were found in Crete two lenses of crystal that date between 1600 and 1200 B.C.

The widespread interest in origins of whatsoever sort has been fostered by archaeological discoveries. Oral and written language has come in for a large share of that interest, because in language inheres the most noticeable and quite the most important difference between man and beast. "Tracking the alphabet to its lair" has come to be one of the most exciting indoor sports of the philologist. But he gets many of his best spoors from the outdoor discoveries of the archaeologist. Palaeographical and epigraphical evidence found by the archaeologists, and run through the gamut of the scientific repertory of the comparative philologist, has done wonderful things in helping to follow language back toward the cradle from which issued the first weird utterances of the Indo-European race.

It would not be wise to push too far the purposely naïve statement of the facetious philologian who explained the origin of language as the appreciative oral bias of the esthetic *homo antiquissimus.* This pre-everything man painted and drew on cave wall or face of an inviting rock, pictures of his environmentally visualized flora and envisaged fauna. As he and his friends gazed upon these more or less artistic productions, their grunts of appreciation or disdain were rapidly incorporated into prehistoric language. Back of this illuminating erudition lies the as yet unsolved universal "did the hen or the egg come first" query. Did early man draw, or make signs, or talk, when he first found it necessary to communicate with someone else? In this country, locally understood grunts and pictures had to be disseminated abroad by the universally understood sign language of the North American Indians. But the Indians did not develop an alphabet as we understand it. Picture writing, however, in several places in or near the east Mediterranean did develop from a drawing that, let us say for example, represented a man, and had for it a word which meant *man*, into a sort of shorthand symbol that may have had the sound *m*. In some such way the letters of an alphabet were born. Then came the different languages of different peoples. Archaeology has discovered the materials which philology has subjected to scientific cross-examination.

The agents of Lord Elgin in 1802–1804 excavated a burial mound in the Attic plain near Piraeus, the seaport of Athens. They found, among other things, a large marble jar in which was a small cinerary urn of bronze. They were put in the British Museum. Not long ago, after more than a century, the bronze urn was taken out to be cleaned. Around the rim an inscription in punctured letters came to light. It read, "I am one of the prizes of the Argive Hera." The form of the letters created the greatest interest, because they were of Argive type, a style that had died out of use during the Peloponnesian war. A similar inscription on a beautiful fifth-century bronze hydria (for which $40,000 is said to have been paid) in the Metropolitan Museum has been published lately by Miss Richter.

It will seem stranger yet to learn that archaeological discoveries of words and sentences carved on stones or painted on walls have proved to us even how the ancients pronounced certain of their letters and syllables. A late study, by Leon of the University of Texas, of the inscriptions in the Jewish catacombs of Rome is to the point. Three-fourths of these inscriptions are written in Greek, the rest in Latin. Many of the words are misspelled in such characteristic ways as to make clear that the epitaphs were written by Jewish people using languages foreign to them and therefore often confusing words with similar sounds. These misspelled words therefore give a clue both to the language of that day of the Jews, and to the common pronunciation both of Latin and Greek.

More important yet is the discovery of a bilingual or trilingual inscription. The best known such find is that of the Rosetta Stone, now in the British Museum, a stone discovered in 1799 by Napoleon's soldiers while digging a trench at the Rosetta mouth of the Nile. On it are three inscriptions: one in Greek; one in hieroglyphic, the official and priestly method of Egyptian writing; the third in demotic, a shorthand and more common variety of the hieroglyphic. The way to read Greek had never been lost; the way to read hieroglyphic or demotic had never been found. In the hieroglyphic text an elliptical line called a *cartouche* is drawn round certain characters. Champollion in 1822 guessed that the words in the cartouches were the names of the potentates, Ptolemy and Cleopatra, mentioned in the Greek text. The story reads like a novel: how from deduction and trial there followed the decipherment of the entire inscription, and the solution of the mysterious Egyptian writing. Both the hieroglyphic and the demotic texts were found to be translations of the Greek. Another example of the same kind was the decipherment of the Babylonian cuneiform of the Behistun inscription, carved high on a cliff on the border of Persia, which came about, after Rawlinson's publication of the alphabet and translation of the Persian part of that inscription, through the discovery that a part of the Behistun inscription was a Babylonian translation of the Persian part.

Before the Roman emperor Augustus died he had his autobiography engraved on bronze tablets which were placed in front of his tomb. This inscription was copied *verbatim et litteratim* on dozens of temples of Rome and Augustus throughout the realm. Out in the Greek east, however, the people could not read it. Therefore, just as is done in many European countries for shop and street-car signs, the original was also translated into the local language. Nearly the entire inscription, both in Latin and Greek, was found by archaeologists years ago at Angora (Ancyra) in Anatolia. Fragments of other copies have been discovered, such for example as the Latin one at Pisidian Antioch and elsewhere, so that we have the inscription almost complete. The spelling of the Greek not only translates the Latin, but also transliterates it; that is to say, the Greek spelling reproduced the pronunciation of the Latin.

The best examples of this kind, however, that have come from epigraphical archaeology are those of the transliterations of the names of the three Roman litterateurs with whom those of us who have studied Latin in High or Preparatory schools have come very closely in contact, namely Caesar, Cicero, and Vergil. Their names, carved in Greek letters which give the exact sound of the Latin pronunciation, were pronounced Kaisar, Kikero(n), and Ouergilius, as the spelling shows. That is to say, in the best Latin of the first centuries B.C. and A.D. the *c* in Latin was pronounced like *k*, the *ae* like *ai*, and the *v* like *w* (i.e., *ou*).

One never knows what is coming out of an excavation, and never what will be the most important part, say, of a newly found inscription. Not long ago the French were excavating some tombs at Byblos in Phoenicia. Among other things they found a beautifully decorated sarcophagus supported by four lions. On the sarcophagus was engraved an inscription in Phoenician letters which was some two hundred years older than any Phoenician inscription thus far found. The proud record of the King Hiram who had been buried in this splendid casket ended with the sort of admonitory curse which even to this day is sometimes used by unprogressive sentimentalists. The translation goes, "if any one shall uncover this sarcophagus, may his sceptre be broken, may his rule be overthrown, may peace forsake him in Gebal; and may he himself, if he deletes this inscription, be carried into captivity." The artistic value of the sarcophagus and the recovery of another boastful and yet timorous curse inscription vied for a time with each other in archaeological estimation. But it was soon agreed that the writing was the more important, because it gave to scholastic science Phoenician writing of the thirteenth century B.C.; and better yet, it shed considerable light on the antiquity and derivation of our own alphabet, which, as Ullman of Chicago has lately said, may revive belief in the old Greek tradition that their alphabet was introduced by Cadmus in 1313 B.C. Butin, in 1928, announced that inscriptions found near the ancient turquoise mines at Sinai were written by Phoenician miners in their own alphabet, and could be dated as of 1900 B.C.

In 1921 at Anzio (Antium) on the coast below Rome there were discovered some remains of the only calendar thus far known that dates prior to the calendar reform made by Julius Caesar. The dates and the concurrent festivals and commemorative occasions were painted in black and red on a white wall. The calendar shows that the year was one of thirteen months, a fact that will be of significance to the proponents of the present agitation for a reformed calendar into one also of thirteen months. The name of the extra month, one of twenty-seven days, was Merkedonius. It came at the end of the year, and was intercalated only in alternate years, at which time either four or five days were taken away from February to insure accuracy.

Scientific archaeology does not dig at random, however fortuitous many of its finds may be. But there are many archaeological finds that are wholly accidental. A guard stubbed his toe on a stone that turned up as the Venus of Cyrene. The new kneeling Niobid of Rome was found at the bottom of a trench which was being dug for the foundation wall of a building. Much of Caesar's trench and fortification works in Gaul was found by the Allied soldiers in digging their trenches during the World War. Ancient fortifications and houses were found in the same way in the Balkans and at the Dardanelles. The temple at Olympia in Greece was partly above ground and its site was certain, but the discoveries of the Hermes of Praxiteles and the Victory of Paeonius were both accidental and unexpected. Perhaps half the score of major digs now under way in England are the result of accidental finds. The workmen on the railroad outside the Porta Maggiore at Rome nearly fell into the sudden cavity which opened beneath their picks, and thus discovered the so-called underground basilica, the purpose of which is not yet conclusively determined. A famous excavation of the Pacific School of Religion near Jerusalem, and the identification of the site as that of the Biblical Mizpah, was predicated on a chance photograph made by a German army flier. Thousands of visitors to the Roman Forum have stood in and commented upon certain shallow places in the travertine pavement in front of the basilica of Julius Caesar near the column of Phocas. It was not until an air picture of the Forum was taken in 1905 and the photograph made from the developed film that those shallow places showed up as depressions cut two thousand years ago in

*National Museum, Rome*

APOLLO FLESHES A VENOMOUS
SHAFT

Niobe boasted that her seven daughters and seven sons were more beautiful than Diana and Apollo, the two children of Latona and Jupiter. The jealous Latona bade her children kill the entire Niobid family, which they did with their arrows from the sky. The most beautiful of the many Niobid statues, which ancient sculptors loved to carve because of the many opportunities to portray emotions, was found by the workmen of a Roman bank while digging a foundation trench in Rome, back of the Janiculum hill on which the American Academy in Rome is located.

which to embed the huge bronze letters of an inscription of a certain Lucius Naevius, a court official or praetor, who had paved that part of the Forum, and whose tribunal was near by.

The value of the metal letters easily accounts for their disappearance. The complexity of the buildings at Ur of the Chaldees can be appreciated somewhat from the top of the *ziggurat*, or Babel-like tower, but the pictures taken from the air clear up at once many difficulties which the workers on the ground do not see at all.

SLAYING OF THE NIOBIDS

Relief sculpture of II century A.D. on side of a marble sarcophagus. The arrows of Apollo and Diana have already struck down several of the Niobids. The rest look with horror upward at the cruel deities bent on their destruction.

Shakespeare may have been the first to mention the fact that the world was his oyster, but it is clear that he got no such succulent rewards in opening the world as do the archaeologists. Is it any wonder that archaeology has become the most ubiquitous of present international, national, and individual pursuits?

## TUTANKHAMEN'S PRIVATE SECRETARY AND GENERAL

A prized possession of the Metropolitan Museum is the seated statue of Haremhab, general of the armies of Tutankhamen (*circa* 1355 B.C.). He is here represented as a scribe. Haremhab later became the first king of the XIX Dynasty of Egypt.

## CHAPTER THREE

## THE GLAMOR OF THE GIFT OF THE NILE

EGYPT was ancient before Greece was born. Pyramids pointing Pharaohs toward immortality antedated the Rome changed by Augustus Caesar from brick to marble by as many centuries as his Altar of Peace antedates King Victor Emmanuel's Altar of Italy. The race backward now on between Egypt and Mesopotamia, with India a possible third, is a strange one. Progress by retrogression sounds weirdly antithetical. Science is groping nobly forward into the jumbo of the "substance of things hoped for"; archaeology is spading splendidly backward into the limbo of the forgotten realities of the past.

Man and beast have run a similar course, starting back to back, as it were. The retrogressive discoveries in the animal kingdom have run backward through elephantine, mastodonic, and megatheriumptious colossalities; bodily bulks with pinhead brains. From the beginning, man has held his size in body, but his enlarging brain made him able after a while to erect a pyramid against which the mightiest pterodactyl would have beaten his wings in absurd futility.

It is by that very massive solidity and indestructible longevity of material structure that Egypt has held an archaeological priority which the discovery of merely earlier objects in Mesopotamia or India will challenge in vain.

Even before any proofs were forthcoming, it ought to have been a certain guess that the earliest civilizations in mass would have been found in the valleys and deltas of the great rivers in the warm countries. The gap now existing between the early cultures in the Nile and Mesopotamian valleys and the scattered finds of much earlier Old Stone Age sites, will be filled in due time. Five thousand years B.C. will soon be pushed back to ten or fifteen thousand B.C., not only in the two valleys named,

43

but also in the valleys of the Indus, Brahmaputra, and Ganges in India, and the Hoang-ho and Yangtze in China.

A romance in astronomy has been made from one of the many theories advanced in connection with the building of the pyramids; and no wonder. The exactitude of the measurements of the pyramid of Cheops (or Khufu), the careful orientation to the four cardinal points of the compass, the slope of the door passage in the north side: these, and other architectural niceties, coupled in the mind to the traditional amplitude of the Ptolemaic system of astronomy, and to the widespread belief in the accuracy of Mesopotamian astrology, to say nothing of sun-worship, made a tenable theory quite difficult to break down.

Later, several of the pyramids of the Sakkareh group gave to the world their series of religious texts, dating approximately 2825–2644 B.C. Then came the discovery among the hieroglyphs in mastaba tombs of a score of the same symbols which had been in use in symbolic Masonry long before the discovery of the mastabas. These touched the mystery of that perceived and yet indefinable relation between a supreme power and its astronomical attributes. The intuitive certainties of the human soul and mind seemed in some way almost inevitably to be linked with those most stupendous, and at the same time most minute, of all extant human constructions.

Archaeology with its magic spades uncovered the fallacy. The pyramid of Cheops belonging to the Fourth Dynasty was the best of a series of pyramids of which the smaller and cruder step pyramid of Zoser was the earlier prototype. The pyramids, all seventy of them, — for those across the Nile from Cairo are but three in a great series — were found to be only the more aspiring part of a gigantic plan. First comes the pyramid itself with its passages and sarcophagus chamber; secondly, the temple outside for the worship of the deified occupant of the pyramid; thirdly, the causeway that ran to the Nile; and fourthly, the portico temple at the river's brink, where, after landing, the anniversarial processions formed to pay their ceremonial dues to the deified Pharaoh.

Again, the pyramid stage seems, both archaeologically and historically, to fit in between the earlier grave, and the later tombs cut in the cliffs. The predynastic types of simple graves; then the larger graves of sun-dried brick with limestone roofs; and those still larger ones with corbelled vaults at Abydos, belonging to the First and Second Dynasties; these are the pre-pyramid group. The post-pyramid rulers to display their power, covered the land with temples, but meanwhile they

*Courtesy of the Metropolitan Museum of Art*

DIGGING UP HISTORY

The Egyptian Expedition of The Metropolitan Museum is here shown clearing the forecourt of the XI Dynasty temple at Deir el Bahri at Thebes.

honey-combed with rock-hewn shafts the beetling cliffs of gorge and valley in the hope — destined to be vain — of securing final resting places against the hands of vandals.

The pyramids can be more easily explained in the light of Pharaonic pride, wealth, and power, and by the amazing progress in architectural skill, than by any theory of mystical design. It is clear that they were built by the Pharaohs as their own tombs. Of all the structures ever raised by the hand of man, the pyramids are the most impressive conceptions of the persistence of the human race's hunger for immortality.

Because its outer casing was painted red, the Greeks named a great stone head protruding from the sand near the pyramids of Gizeh, Rhodopis. (Although it has been known from the time that statues were first found in Egypt that they were painted, nevertheless, we know more about the technicalities of their painting since Winlock of the Metropolitan Museum published his discoveries of the paint on the statues of Queen Hatshepsut.) Then the Greeks said that the head was that of the famous courtesan Rhodopis. Perhaps it was not for nothing that Shaw lets his Julius Caesar find Cleopatra perched up under the ear of the Sphinx.

At all events, the Sphinx has been called "she" for many years, and some sentimental traditionalists still persist in calling this silent head that of a woman. Of course it is not. The sphinx was a symbol of the sun god Horus, whose earthly representative was the Pharaoh. The great Sphinx head of Gizeh is a portrait of Khafra (Chephren) whose pyramid stands next to that of Cheops. The Sphinx has been freed from the encroaching sand, and now crouches there showing his animal body, and reaching out fifty feet before him with his huge paws, between which is a sacrificial altar. It is simply an outlying part of the pyramid concept.

Probably the majority of people, until Tutankhamen suddenly leaped from the tomb to the picture sections of the world's press, still thought of Egypt as the "Bride of the Nile" (which they think means the "gift of the Nile"), as a country teeming with lotus buds, papyrus, cats, and crocodiles, as the place where Cleopatra and "Cleopatra's needle" were in some occult way connected with a thread more elusive than the one which Theseus unrolled against the Minotaur, and finally and especially as the land of the three pyramids of Gizeh. There *are* certain misconceptions in those views.

The chief pyramid field begins on the west side of the Nile opposite Cairo with the three pyramids of Khufu (Cheops), Khafra (Chephren), and Menkaura (Mycerinus). It extends, however, southward for sixty miles to the Fayum (where the crocodile was especially worshipped). But there are two other fields in the Sudan, one at Gebel Barkal, near the Fourth Cataract, and one at Begarawiyah (Meroë), between the Fifth and Sixth Cataracts, about a hundred miles from Khartum.

THE SPHINX AS IT WAS

THE SPHINX AS IT IS

It is not entirely amazement when objects are discovered which were made several thousand years ago and which foreshadow so many of the things we had supposed were unknown until only yesterday or today; it is something more than that.

Daedalus and Icarus made themselves into flying machines thousands of years B.C. The Germans were only good classicists when they remembered that an early Greek airplane was called The Dove, and so called one variety of their war planes *Die Taube.* We can read in writing of long ago that Heron of Alexandria invented a hodometer (*hodos* is Greek for *road*) that worked with cogwheels and marked off distance. Such a modern invention loses much prestige when one reads of the sale of the effects of the Roman emperor Commodus, among which were some carriages equipped both with hodometers and waterclocks.

"It is wizardry," said one of the visitors to a certain "dig," after the archaeologist in charge had reconstructed an episode of a morning some 4000 years earlier. The visitors had come to see the excavation of an ancient town site. The battered walls had been built of sun-dried brick. One of the visitors said, "Well, where do we go from here?" His tone was that of a very petulant scoffer and his scorn touched the archaeologist on the raw.

"Would you believe that a score or so of these bricks could tell a story both true and charming?" "No! I wouldn't," was the reply. The director said a few words in Arabic to one of his workmen who gathered up a score of bricks and started off on a trot. The visitors followed the director about a quarter of a mile to the place where the workman stood with the bricks spread out on the ground before him.

"One day about 4000 years ago," began the archaeologist, "some twenty laborers were here on this spot molding bricks of mud and spreading them out to dry in the hot Egyptian sun. It was nearly time for lunch, so after laying out the last batch, the laborers stopped work, got their little baskets of food and sat or squatted down to eat. The seven-year-old daughter of one of the men, perhaps of the foreman, had just brought her father's lunch basket over from where they lived. She had a pet gazelle which had followed her, like Mary's little lamb. Suddenly a dog sprang from somewhere, and the little gazelle jumped out among the newly made bricks, and then stopped either from fright or because the dog had seized it. The little barefoot girl was no less quick than the dog. She leaped after it and caught it just as it reached the gazelle and pulled or slapped it off."

"I'll say that really would be a wonderful story, if there was a word of truth in it!" said the scoffer.

The director then showed satisfactory evidence that they stood on the site of a small sun-dry brick yard. He had also two of the brick molds which had been found the day before. The bricks fitted the molds, and the mud was that of the bricks. Then, at a word from the director, the workman turned over the bricks he had carried out. There on the bricks were three tracks of the naked feet of a little girl, one the shallow track of a speeding foot, and two deeper tracks close together as if she had been straining at something. There were the four tracks of a standing gazelle. Just behind them were the two tracks of a dog's hind feet, showing that his two fore feet were on the gazelle's back. To the left on another brick was one track of the right hind foot of the same dog, but turned at right angles to the other two, showing that he was "going away from there" on the jump. "You win," said the doubting Thomas, "you're a wizard."

As the magic spades of archaeology dig up the artifacts of the past, history recovers the facts it needs to warrant the phrase *the modern making of ancient history*. Ancient royalty and wealth could not conceive the possibility of proper burial apart from the funeral trappings that would authenticate their rank at the judgment seat of Osiris or in the life beyond the grave. Tombs therefore came to be mines of treasure, and as archaeological discovery has shown, successful grave robbery became a science. History also saw at once why the Pharaohs had resorted to every possible device of concealed entrances, hidden tomb chambers, and pitfalls along the rock-hewn shafts. But the lure of buried gold was stronger than the tricks of mere man's mind. There is no belief in the world as strong as that in hidden treasure, and the tradition of the few great finds has eclipsed the many failures.

When the modern scientific archaeologist reads about Belzoni, of Beelzebubish memory, who in 1817 began the search for buried Pharaohs across from Thebes, he becomes a human chameleon.  He turns absolutely green with envy, then red with shame, then white with rage.

On October 17, 1817, Belzoni entered a great tomb and was so overcome by its contents that for three weeks he wandered about in it like a man in a trance.  It must have been quite that, for Belzoni himself says, "Every step I took I crushed a mummy in some part or other."  He missed the date of the tomb by 700 years; but Schliemann misdated Troy even more than that.  Later, the tomb was found to be that of Seti I, but the magnificent alabaster sarcophagus was a cenotaph, (*i.e.*, had purposely been left empty).  When Belzoni set a candle inside the beautiful coffin engraved within and without, the light shone through the two inches of solid alabaster sides not as if these too solid sides were translucent, but rather partook of a delicate transparency.  One can see it for oneself when next he visits the Soane Museum in London.

That Italian circus performer, Belzoni, with his battering-ram technique in excavation, was after all a man of parts.  In 1815 he brought from Luxor to Alexandria the famous bust of Ramses II, now in the British Museum.  He dropped an obelisk into the Nile, but fished it out again.  He trod on the acres of mummies in the Theban tomb, but he could do naught else, for they lay "as thick as leaves in Vallombrosa."

Approximately the length of the blade of a spade on the same level will turn up a stratum one hundred years thick.  In a stratified site the deepest layer is the oldest, but in a shafted cliff, the oldest tomb may be the farthest or the nearest up the valley, the highest or the lowest on the cliff's bare face; which is to say that it is the part of wisdom neither to generalize nor to specify.

The story of the excavation of the royal tombs of Egypt began at Abydos, the sacred city of Osiris.  There the First and Second Dynasties held court.  But had the excavators set up the claim that the smaller graves lined with sun-dried brick or the larger ones with vaulted ceilings were either the earliest or the best or the largest of the Pharaonic burial places, they would have been very foolish. From the contents of the tombs, however, they were enabled to say that tools and implements of copper were already in use, that necklaces and bracelets of gold were in fashion, that vitreous glaze had already been invented, and, because of the very primitive figurines, that the art of sculpture was about to begin.

*Rhode Island School of Design*
*Gift of Mrs. Gustav Radeke*

A PORTRAIT

A head from a mummy case. Graeco-Egyptian of the II century A.D. Note the archaistic work on the hair. A valuable original in the Museum of the Rhode Island School of Design in Providence.

The later discovery of earlier predynastic graves of smaller size with simpler funeral accessories was no less valuable from the historic point of view. The objects buried with these most ancient dead were doubly illuminating. Not only did they give a glimpse at the religious hope of immortality, but they also pictured the state of domestic art. Simply made objects of adornment proved late stone and early metal culture, the pottery and the woven articles were a contemporaneous moving picture of the simple home life of the time.

If the capital was moved from Upper Egypt to Memphis at the beginning of the Third Dynasty and the Pharaohs of the Old Kingdom (III–VI Dynasties) had built for their tombs such stupendous structures as the pyramids, anyone would be justified in saying there had been a change of government, an enlargement of territory, and a tremendous increase in wealth. After philology, epigraphy, and palaeography had deciphered the hieroglyphs of the Rosetta stone, history had still to wait until archaeology had found the material on which to apply the newly won knowledge. It was archaeology which first traced the blocks of limestone, granite, basalt, and alabaster to their quarries, and in so doing enlarged our knowledge of the sphere of influence or the spread of territory of the rulers who could command the sources of such constructional material. Archaeologists with their magic spades scientifically moved the sands which the winds of the Sahara had driven in drifts across the valley. They thus uncovered the mastaba tombs of the nobles who in death had ranged themselves around the pyramids of their lords. On recovered Pharaonic rock-cut tombs and temples were spread, often in beautiful colors, the pictured and written story of the forgotten past. The panoplied ruler driving his chariot over his fallen enemies revealed his military exploits in language somewhat over-boastful; the noble proved his loyalty in no less vigorous phraseology; the slaves served their masters for ever and for ever, carved everlastingly in their varied tasks. Every type of daily act, regal and menial, every function of the household in palace, on the farm, or on the river, every beast and fowl stood, stalked, or fluttered in lasting glyph, and even the menu in graven letters tempts eternity.

Chaos, in scientific hands, soon came to order. History rewrote itself as its facts were served up on the archaeologist's spade.

Thirty miles south of Cairo lies a pyramid field at Lisht. The Metropolitan Museum of New York, by its archaeological discoveries there in connection with the first and second kings of the XII Dynasty, set the Middle Kingdom (XI–XIV Dynasties) of Egypt in its correct place and proper perspective. It was easy to see the advance in technical skill. It was possible to posit an extension of available source territory from the use of such new stones as amethyst, haematite, and jasper. There were innovations, among which the scarab, the spiral design, and fluted columns were the most noticeable. But in general the art was the same. Its technique showed advance in experience, but its spirit seemed to have frozen in the ancient tracks of old Kingdom tradition. Nothing but comparative archaeology could have recognized the reversion to archaism and been secure in stating that art in Egypt had hobbled itself by a blind adherence to tradition and fixed canons.

Carnegie Museum, Pittsburgh                                    Gift of Andrew Carnegie

AN EGYPTIAN BOAT

From a crypt at Dahshur placed there at the time of the obsequies of the Master of the Royal Craft. It had been buried there six hundred years before Abraham left Ur of the Chaldees.

It would be easy to say that a coalition of princes in Upper Egypt, directed by the ruling family of Thebes, having chafed intolerably against the yoke of the Hyksos invaders who ruled Egypt from the Delta, threw off that foreign yoke, and set up their capital at Thebes. But dynastic, or military, or institutional, or political annals are the barest of all skeletal frames. They must be fleshed with the accretions of experience; social convention will be their cuticle, religion their soul, ambitious idealism their heart, philosophy their breath of life, archaeology their food; comparative science must sit in their crania and pull the levers that coördinate their functions; art will glorify their countenance or gross materialism flatten it into ugliness. Civilization, that is to say, must be looked at in the round, and the first great law of progress is to understand a convention well enough to break it not iconoclastically, but idealistically. The discoveries of archaeology have demonstrated that original tendencies in sculpture did not develop until sculpture in the round inaugurated their possibilities. Then a broadening of the imagination is sure to produce a naturalistic school of art such, let us say, as developed at Tell el-Amarna. An extension on the religious side may change, as it did in Egypt, the contracted posture in which the prehistoric dead were buried on their sides, to a straightened supinity that demands first an anthropoid coffin, then the perfection of mummification, and then the lavish expenditure of every possible type of adornment.

One genius fires another. A Schliemann is unthinkable without a Homer; Strabo was the inspiration of Mariette. That French archaeologist dug and dug again. His 141 sphinxes drove him beneath their feet — into the vaults where the dead bulls of Apis had been buried; they in turn postulated a third gallery, where Mariette found twenty-four granite coffins, $13 \times 11 \times 7\frac{2}{3}$ feet in dimensions, and each weighing sixty-five tons.

How little would we know of the great religious "heresy" of Amenhotep IV beyond the fact that he abandoned Thebes and transferred his capital to Tell el-Amarna, changing his name coincidently from Amen-hotep to Akhenaten, if a fellah woman hunting phosphate in the rubbish heaps of Akhenaten's capital had not sold for fifty much needed cents some tablets she had found? For thus the cuneiform tablets known so famously as "the Tell el-Amarna tablets" came to light.

Someone said it was a "ghoulishly reluctant tribute to archaeologists to call them grave robbers." As a matter of fact, present excavations are done in the name of science, with the official permission of the governments concerned, and with the general approbation of civilized mankind. The robberies were carried out, almost without exception, within a few years of the ancient burials. Two famous papyri, the Abbott and the Amherst, give us the facts about the robberies at Thebes which were discovered in the reign of Ramses IX (about 1100 B.C.). One of the eight robbers at the trial made the following confession:

"We opened their coffins, and coverings. We found the august mummy of the King. There were numerous amulets and ornaments of gold at his throat; his head had a mask of gold upon it; the mummy was overlaid with gold. Its coverings were wrought with gold and silver within and without, and were inlaid with every splendid and costly stone. We stripped off the gold, which we found on the august mummy of this king, and the amulets and ornaments which were at its throat, and the coverings in which it rested. We found the queen likewise and we stripped off all that we found on her in the same manner. We set fire to the coverings, and carried away the funeral furniture which we found with them, consisting of gold, silver, and bronze. We divided the booty, and made the gold, amulets, ornaments, and coverings into eight parts." (Shortened from Breasted, *Ancient Records of Egypt*, IV, 538.)

Look where the two colossi of Memnon sit on eternal guard across from Thebes on the west bank of the Nile! They are each sixty feet high and each weighs 1,000 tons. The nails on their middle fingers have an area of 35 square inches. One of them was damaged in 27 B.C. by an earthquake. Soon thereafter, because of a noise that issued from it after sunrise — now known to have been due to the rapid expansion of the stone under the heat of the rising sun — it was identified as the statue of Memnon, son of Dawn.

One might have thought these gigantic figures could have protected the tombs and temples behind them in that arc of Libyan cliffs in which are the shattered remnants of the temples of Amenhotep III, of Deir el-Medineh, and of Deir el-Bahri, and, still farther back, the burials in the rugged and rocky ravines of the Valley of the Kings and the Valley of the Queens.

Following the appearance in 1876 of papyri and funerary objects dating in the XXI Dynasty, the French archaeologist Maspero had a suspect arrested. Third-degree methods were necessary before he was ready to lead Brugsch Bey, of the Service of Antiquities, to a certain hole in the cliff not far from the temple of Queen Hatshepsut. Brugsch was as fearless as he was enthusiastic. He had himself lowered by a rope for forty

SENTINELS OF THE AGES

The two great statues of Memnon, made of sandstone conglomerate, dominate the plain across the Nile from Karnak and Luxor.

feet down a dark shaft. He began by stumbling about among a lot of gold-covered mummy cases and found he was in a "catacomb crammed with Pharaohs."

It is easy to imagine the inward gnashing of teeth of the three hundred hired Arabs, all probably professional tomb robbers, and some of them certainly the very men who for six years had been plundering the *cache* and selling their spoils, who at a few cents a day were now compelled to help hoist the sarcophagi, pack and sack them, and carry them to a steamer at Luxor. From the description of the wild gesticulations and cries of joyful adoration made by the thousands of natives who lined both banks of the Nile all the way down to Cairo, we can get an approximation of the same sort of scene thousands of years ago when the cortege of a dead Pharaoh was ferried down the river to his tomb.

James Baikie has made a nice comparison between the Elizabethan age as the period of the discovery of new worlds and our own age as the period of the resurrection of the ancient world.   In that resurrection it has not been the colossi, the overpowering pyramids, and the extensive temples that have been of the most value; it has been rather the "unconsidered trifles," the potsherds, the objects with no intrinsic money value, which have bulked the larger.

Nevertheless, the temples which extended from Heliopolis near the Delta, particularly those at Karnak, Luxor, Deir el-Bahri, and Edfu, as far as those at Philae, have more than justified themselves to archaeologists, sculptors, architects, and historians.   It may well give pause to the modern clamor for haste when the temple at Karnak is considered.   It was building from 2000 to 30 B.C.   Architects as well as tourists gasp at its proportions.   The walls of the front gate are 49 feet thick; the first court inside is 275 × 338 feet, or 8,000 square feet more than the entire area of St. Paul's in London. Twelve of the columns in the hypostyle hall are 69 feet high and 33 feet around, with capitals on top of which a hundred men can stand without crowding.   Each column is twelve times as large as the column of Trajan at Rome, or the Vendôme column in Paris.   The Paris cathedral of Notre Dame can be put, with room to spare, in the hypostyle hall alone. It was able to house, under water, more than 700 statues that were fished out during the years 1903–1905.   One of them was the pink granite head of Senusert III, one of the finest pieces of the art of the XII Dynasty.

Nothing short of a visit will convey a satisfactory impression of the temple of Queen Hatshepsut.   It was discovered as long ago as 1798 by two French savants who had accompanied Napoleon's expedition to Egypt.   Work at laying it bare was continued at intervals, but it was not finished until the Egyptian Exploration Fund completed the work (1893–1908).   At least, they thought they had.   But in 1928 there were discovered 299 scarabs, the most beautiful lapidary pieces of the XVIII Dynasty, which had been deposited on the day the queen's temple had been founded.

Queen Hatshepsut's temple architect, Senmut, seems to have been this Egyptian Elizabeth's Essex.  In building the temple for his queen, he introduced his own portrait *behind* various doors in it.  In the season 1927–1928, the Metropolitan Museum's Egyptian Expedition found he had also dared to start a tomb for himself deep down and directly beneath her temple.  Only one room of his tomb had been decorated before his downfall.  Its ceiling represents a chart of the heavens, the best, and one of the earliest astronomical charts thus far found.  Senmut also brought down from Assuan to Karnak two granite obelisks 97½ feet high for the Queen's jubilee.  They were the tallest obelisks ever made with the one exception of that erected at Heliopolis by her enemy (and also her half-brother and nephew), Thothmes III, which was 105 feet high, and which is now in front of St. John Lateran at Rome.  The so-called Cleopatra's Needle in London, and its twin in Central Park, New York City, lack twenty feet of being as tall as those of Queen Hatshepsut.

The first Pharaoh ever found in his own tomb was the mummified Amenhotep II, the son of Thothmes III, who was discovered in 1898 by M. Loret.  It was, however, through the funds provided by an American, Mr. Theodore M. Davis, and given through the Egyptian Service of Antiquities, that archaeological work in Egypt received its greatest impetus.  In 1905 Messrs. Davis, Maspero, and Weigall found the tomb of Yuaa and his wife Tuaa, father and mother of Queen Tyi.  Its contents were extraordinary : magnificent furniture, enamelled blue (an Egyptian secret) couches, a chariot, cushions still soft with the down with which they had been stuffed 3,000 years earlier, alabaster vases, mummified meats for the dead, two gilded coffins in which the dead lay in a repose so calm and life-like that it seemed they were just on the point of awakening.

Mr. Davis was early on the trail of Tutankhamen.  In 1906 he found in an uninscribed tomb chamber a number of articles bearing the names of that Pharaoh and his queen.   In 1907 he and Mr. Weigall found the body of Tutankhamen's father-in-law, Akhenaten, the so-called heretic, in the tomb of Seti I.   Then in 1908 Mr. Davis discovered the tomb of Haremhab, the general who usurped the throne after the short reign of King Ay who followed Tutankhamen.   There were bones, but so crushed as to be unrecognizable, in the great sarcophagus (8 feet 11 × 3 feet $9\frac{1}{2}$ × 4 feet).   Haremhab's statue in gray granite is in the Metropolitan Museum, having been presented by Mr. and Mrs. V. Everit Macy.

The most imposing tomb found in Egypt that has come to a museum in another land is the tomb of Perneb, an official of high rank under a Pharaoh of the V Dynasty.   It was acquired from the Egyptian government in 1913 and presented to the Metropolitan Museum in New York by Mr. Edward S. Harkness.   This massive and dignified tomb was originally in the cemetery of ancient Memphis, and was found only 250 yards north of Zoser's step pyramid at Sakkareh.

In 1914 Flinders Petrie discovered the "Treasure of Lahun." It comprised the complete jewelry outfit of Princess Sat-hathor-innut, probably the daughter of Senusert II of the XII Dynasty. The articles in part were: vases of alabaster and obsidian for cosmetics; toilet articles of various kinds; collars, a diadem, a pair of copper razors with handles of gold, a large mirror of silver, girdles, beads of carnelian and green feldspar, and an amethyst necklace.   This wonderful collection was purchased for the Metropolitan Museum.

Perhaps the best example of a proper return for an "act of archaeological conscientiousness" was the discovery in 1920 of the tomb of Mehenkwetre (2000 B.C.) at Thebes.   This tomb of the XI Dynasty had been worked over twenty years before, but no plan of it had been published.   The Metropolitan Museum people had little expectation of a find, but simply decided to clean up an unfinished job.   They were nearly done when a workman called Mr. Burton's attention to the way the limestone rubbish trickled away from his hoe at a crack where the wall met the floor.   Electric torches showed that beyond that crack was a rock-cut chamber full of brightly painted figures of men, animals, models of Nile boats, etc. These miniature objects constitute the best find ever made to authenticate house and farm economy. Among them are a stable with cattle, a slaughter house, a bakeshop, and home-brewing establishment, traveling and pleasure boats (in the Metropolitan); women spinning flax and weaving cloth, a

*Courtesy of Metropolitan Museum of Art*

NEW KNOWLEDGE OF OLD TIMES

A traveling boat on the Nile and its kitchen tender. One of the wooden models of the XI Dynasty (*circa* 2000 B.C.) found in the tomb of Meket-Re at Thebes.

carpenter shop, etc. (in Cairo). These mannikins in their usual dress and the boat models fully rigged and equipped, were divided equally between the Museum in Cairo and the Metropolitan Museum in New York.

Tutankhaten was a young noble who married the third daughter of the "heretic" Akhenaten, who had flouted the Egyptian priesthood by moving his capital from Thebes to Tell el-Amarna and changing the state religion from the worship of the Theban sun god (Amen) to that of the supreme sun god (Aten). When Tutankhaten succeeded, somewhat unexpectedly, to the throne, he recanted from the faith of his father-in-law, moved his capital back to Thebes, and changed his name to *Tutankhamen*. His reign was short. His queen was left a young widow. She knew she had few friends, so she decided to marry a husband who had military resources. By good luck we know all about her diplomatic attempt to marry a prince of the Hittites, because papyri found not long ago contain the correspondence  Unsuccessful though she was in the matter of a new husband, she was so successful in burying her first husband that he remained unfound among his marvelous funerary trappings until almost the other day, when he, the last of the Pharaohs unaccounted for, turned up as the ancient wonder boy of modern archaeology, inside the first intact royal tomb chamber ever found in Egypt.

The American, Theodore Davis, held his concession in Egypt from 1902 until it reverted in 1914 to the government, at which time it was secured by Lord Carnarvon and Howard Carter.  They knew that the tomb of Tutankhamen had to be somewhere there in the Valley of the Kings, but for six long years their labors were unrewarded.  It was to be their final season, and like Davis, they were ready to admit defeat, despite the fact that just below the tomb of Ramses VI the workmen's huts were built on masses of flint boulders that marked the proximity of a tomb.

On November 4, 1922, there came to light under the first hut that was removed, a step cut in the rock.  It was only thirteen feet below the entrance to the tomb of Ramses VI, who, as we know now, dying about 1157 B.C., cut his tomb where it is, not knowing of the existence of the tomb of Tutankhamen, who had been buried 201 years earlier.  At the bottom of sixteen steps, Carter came upon a door with nameless seals, but there was also a well-known necropolis seal bearing the jackal and nine captives.  Had Carter examined a few inches below the necropolis seal he would have found a seal bearing the name of Tutankhamen, but he hurriedly filled in the steps and rushed off to cable Carnarvon in England the message which swept the world, with him, into a fever of excitement: "At last have made wonderful discovery in Valley; a magnificent tomb with seals intact; re-covered same for your arrival; congratulations."  He secured also as soon as possible the help of Mace and Burton from the staff of the Metropolitan Museum, and of Breasted of Chicago.

On November 26, a second sealed doorway was found, thirty feet below the first. Carter poked a hole and with a candle took the first glimpse; then with an electric torch Carnarvon had to content himself with a peep. But it had been enough. Both men went crazy, and the world followed them.

THE TOMB OF TUTANKHAMEN

The entrance of Tutankhamen's tomb in the Valley of the Kings is seen at the bottom of the illustration. Its location escaped excavators so many years because it was not suspected that the tomb of Ramses, which opens just above it, could have been dug so near.

Tutankhamen was wise to avoid discovery until real archaeological science was ready to handle him and his treasures. Fifty years ago his tomb would have been plundered; the gold and gems would have been highly dispensed and widely dispersed. A hundred years ago the best efforts of the excavators of that day would have failed dismally, tragically indeed, to preserve the beautiful fragilities of many of the exquisite objects, for the archaeologists had not yet learned how to measure, to photograph, to record, to interpret, and to preserve, all at the same time.

The world has not stopped marveling at the magnificent mass of tumbled household articles that stupefied by their profusion of richness and artistry not only those first intruders upon three thousand years and more of Pharaonic privacy, but that still tongue-tie every visitor to the Cairo Museum. The sarcophagus of pink granite, the gilded beds, the walking sticks with curved handles of alternate ebony heads of Ethiops and ivory heads of Caucasian captives, the glut of gold and gems, made King "Tut," the resurrected Son of the Sun, a household word.

Inside the "store chamber" and facing the door, his paws barely protruding from a shawl over his jackal figure, crouched Anubis, the deathlessly vigilant god of the dead. Near by stood treasure chests full of personal jewelry for the Pharaoh's use in his future life beyond the tomb. His writing materials and palettes, his hunting chariots and decorated bow-cases for use in future hunts, the fully rigged barques in which the King would accompany the great Sun God across the sky and back below the world through pitch-black caverns to the next day's starting point: these and scores, yes, hundreds, of other objects appropriate to Pharaonic burial lay scattered about in wild confusion.

At the back of another chamber stood the gilded carved shrine in which were four jars containing the viscera of the dead Tutankhamen. Before the beautifully decorated faces of the shrine stood, like guardian angels, lovely statuettes of the tutelary goddesses Isis, Nephthys, Neith, and Selkit. They face the shrine and stand with outstretched arms in upright loveliness. Above the heads of each is a row of fourteen gilded solar cobra heads. From the top of the canopy rise on each side thirteen other large cobras, the head of each surmounted by the golden disk of the sun.

When finally Tutankhamen's mummy was found and unwrapped, for the first time the ritual known from the "Book of the Dead" was exemplified in all its complexity. Royal mummies were wrapped in a way to symbolize Osiris, the god of the dead. As the linen bandages, the necessary sheets and pads, were removed from Tutankhamen's mummy, one hundred and forty-three pieces of jewelry of various religious import were discovered. On his thorax were found five gold collars and a resin scarab all hung with gold wire. In the sixth and eighth layers of linen were found the golden dagger in its belt. Over the thighs and shins were the ceremonial apron, a sheathed iron dagger, an anklet, the Buto serpent, and the Nekhebet vulture; in the eleventh and twelfth layers of the bandages were the Kheper beetles, the Uzat eye, the solar hawk, and the lunar crescent. Bracelets covered the mummy's arms from wrist to elbow. The most beautiful of the pieces of jewelry was the gold pectoral representing the bird that was the spirit of the king. Its outstretched wings are inlaid with turquoise, carnelian, and lapis lazuli. The collar of Nekhebet is a flexible pectoral of indescribable beauty. It has the form of a vulture whose outspread wings covered Tutankhamen's breast. Two hundred fifty-five gold plaques inlaid with semi-precious stones compose the outspread wings. Red jasper and lapis predominate. Of the five pectorals on Tutankhamen's mummy, probably the most wonderful is that of three Kheper beetles, which support solar and lunar discs, and hang from ten strings of gold beads suspended from a clasp above of an inscribed cartouche.

The fourth room to be cleared (1927–1928) was piled six feet high in topsy-turviness, a perfect example of a hurried robbery. All containers had been emptied on the floor by the robbers in order to find gold, silver, and copper. One of the containers was a casket, the ivory veneer of which is carved in beautiful bas-relief. Its front panel depicts Tutankhamen and his consort Ankhesenamen standing and facing each other. They are dressed in court costume, but as if at a floral fête. Both wear garlands and collarettes of flowers, and the young queen hands to Tutankhamen a bouquet of papyrus and lotus blossoms. Carter calls this ivory panel the "unsigned work of a master — a Benvenuto Cellini of the period, and perhaps the finest specimen of Theban art found among this hoard of art treasures."

A nest of anthropoid coffins, the outermost being thirty inches long, was found. Inside the second coffin was a smaller coffin of wood, 8½ inches long, inside of which was a tiny coffin that had on it the titles and name of Queen Tyi, the grandmother-in-law of Tutankhamen. Inside this innermost tiny coffin, five inches long, was a plaited lock of Queen Tyi's hair.

Important also, as are the objects of art, is a small wooden chest which had been emptied except for sixteen small ritual implements, clearly models, not real tools, of *iron* fixed into redwood handles. In addition to these sixteen model tools of iron, an amulet headrest of iron, also a small model, was found under the head of Tutankhamen; and most interesting of all, a dagger with gold haft and rock crystal knob head, which was on the right thigh of Tutankhamen's mummy, has a blade of *iron* that is still bright and has the appearance of steel.

Late in 1928 several black wooden chests with vaulted lids were opened. In them were portrait statuettes of Tutankhamen about 15 inches in height. These so-called *shawabtys* (or *ushabti*) were to substitute for the king in the lower world, should he be called upon to do any hard work, or as the text from the Book of the Dead has it, "even as a man is bounden to cultivate the fields, to flood the meadows, or to carry sand of the East to the West." These statues are important because they are *simulacra* of the deceased Tutankhamen, because they show the correct Osiriac mummification in linen, with the hands crossed and holding the flail and crozier, and particularly because with each shawabty was a complete set, in copper or blue faience, of model vessels and implements for agricultural work in the future world.

The fineness of technique, the lavishness of gems and gold, the unique designs, the brilliance of color, the *tout ensemble* of Pharaonic tomb display is well nigh incredible.

There are four rooms in the tomb of Tutankhamen. The first has been called the antechamber. There was found the gold-overlaid throne-seat with the king and queen on the back panel. Beyond it to the left is the Annex. At the end of the antechamber, to the right, is the sepulchral hall, where the great gilt shrine (17 × 11 × 9 feet) was found, and to its right, but extending back toward the entrance passage, is the Store Chamber, in which was the cobra-corniced shrine containing the viscera jars.

Such a splendid find raised many difficulties. A rider to the excavation agreement says that objects found in an *untouched* tomb go to the Cairo museum; otherwise the finds are to be divided half and half. Examination of the seals showed that a thief or thieves had entered the tomb, for it had been sealed again later by the inspectors of Ramses IX. In the two outer chambers the objects were all heaped up in the utmost confusion. There being no inventory, however, of all the objects, it is easy to see why a question might have arisen over whether any object had been *touched* (in the sense of *taken*). At all events, Egypt claimed the entire contents of the tomb.

American tourists who have been jolted by camels around the pyramids have for the past two or three years ridden with curious eyes around the wire fence inside which they were told Reisner of Harvard was excavating. What he found has turned out to be a discovery of unique importance. An intact tomb belonging to the early period has for the first time given an opportunity to study the burial of a great personage. The tomb is that of Hetepheres, the mother of Cheops, the Pharaoh of the great pyramid.

When Julius Caesar and Marc Antony successively and successfully courted the lovely Cleopatra, this regal queen mother of Cheops had been lying a hundred feet below the shifting surface of Sahara sand 1,000 years longer before their time than the 2,000 years that have since elapsed. Hetepheres would have been nearly as much an archaeological find for Tutankhamen or for Moses as she is for us, for she had been buried so long before their time that it had been entirely forgotten.

Under the avenue which led to the pyramids of the queens of Cheops two openings were found. The one first discovered had over it a layer of plaster beneath which were found closely packed limestone blocks. When these were removed, twelve steps were found which led into the main shaft, which on down for nearly a hundred feet had been also packed with limestone blocks. Finally the entrance to a chamber was reached. From the fact that five tools, stone chips, and rubbish boxes were found on the floor, it was clear that the tomb was not quite finished when the burial was made.

Reisner believed from the first that he had discovered, not a burial, but a reburial. Pharaoh Sneferu had made a tomb for his queen Hetepheres near his own pyramid at Dahshur. Sneferu died and was entombed. When Hetepheres died, her son Cheops placed her mummy in the prepared tomb, as is proved by inscriptions. Thieves broke into Queen Hetepheres' tomb, but were discovered, and of course killed, before much treasure, if any, had been carried away. Cheops, seemingly, was having a secret tomb prepared near his own pyramid, but did not wait for its completion, but removed his mother to it at once.

Inside the tomb chamber was a marble sarcophagus, over which lay a number of faïence-inlaid sheets of gold. On the floor were several chairs overlaid with gold, and a set of eight marvelous toilet jars of alabaster. On what was left of a palanquin and bed were four identical inscriptions which, when translated, say: "the mother of the King of Upper and Lower Egypt, the Follower of Horus, the guide of the ruler, the favorite one whose every word is done for her, the daughter of the god of his body, Hetepheres." Inside a gold-encased box, on the lid of which an inscription said "the mother of the King of Upper and Lower Egypt, Hetepheres; box containing *deben* rings," were found two sets of ten anklets. These rings for the legs are inlaid with dragon flies of malachite, lapis lazuli, and red carnelian. They are of different diameters, graduated in size to fit the leg. On the floor also were discovered three cups of gold, two gold and five copper razors, three gold and four copper knives, as well as several flint knives and many pieces of pottery and alabaster. To the dismay of the excavators, when the lid of the sarcophagus was raised, no mummy was inside. It must have been hidden somewhere else.

The French have recently made known the results of the excavations in Egypt about which visitors in Cairo have heard so much gossip. The French Institute of Eastern Archaeology, which is financed by government grant, has made a half dozen splendid "digs," of which three are of first importance.

The farthest north of the pyramids across the Nile from Cairo is Abou-Roach, the tomb of Tetf-Re or Didoufri, the successor of Cheops, one of the Pharaohs of the Fourth Dynasty (roughly 2850–2700 B.C.). Near this, and about five miles from the pyramids of Gizeh and only eight miles west of Cairo, the French archaeologists have unearthed an intact cemetery, a necropolis containing some twenty mastabas of the Fourth and Fifth Dynasties, and some fifty tombs which considerably antedate them. Many of the bodies are buried from forty-five to seventy-five feet below the surface of the ground. Most of them were found in sarcophagi, on which were carved, in some instances, the façades of dwellings. They give also, so far as is now known, the earliest examples of the "false door," so well known in Egyptian tombs.

But the most important fact in connection with the find is that the type of burial is inhumation, thus proving that burial, as we understand it, preceded the practice of mummification in early Egypt.

The second important find, made by the French Institute of Cairo, was of a temple with the same dimensions as that of Hathor at Denderah. It is a temple of the Theban god of war, Montou, incarnate in a Sacred Bull. It has been supposed that the country near Thebes, where Karnak and Louqsor (if we recognize the French for Luxor) stand unrivaled, had been excavated completely. This new temple is important because of its continuity. On the walls are inscriptions with the names of the Roman emperors Domitian and Trajan, inscriptions of Ptolemaic dates, and others on back to 2000 B.C.

On the west side of the Nile only a few miles away from the newly discovered temple there came to light the third find, at Deir el-Medineh. It is the best of the three. It was the village in which lived the artists, painters, sculptors, and builders of the great necropolis of Thebes, the capital, from 1500 to 945 B.C. The inscriptions give the names and genealogies of the mummies. Up to the present time more than sixty tombs have been examined. In the tomb of Nakhton-Amon (or Amen), the sculptor and cult priest of Amenophis I, on the entrance wall to the mummy chamber are splendid painted figures

*Courtesy of the Oriental Institute of the University of Chicago*

A TEMPLE FROM THE AIR

The Egyptian temple at Medinet Habu as seen from an airplane. This is one of the sites at which the Oriental Institute of the University of Chicago is revealing and preserving the glories of ancient Egypt.

of the royal artist and his wife. On the wall of the tomb of Pashed is painted a wonderful Anubis. In the tomb of the scribe Nefer-Abt, male and female dancers in lively action adorn in beautiful colors the walls of the provision chamber. From one rifled group of tombs were taken twenty-seven mummies, all of one family, stripped, however, of their rich vestments and precious ornaments.

These new French finds do not rival Tutankhamen, but they give us much new and important material to add to our growing knowledge of the life of ancient Egypt.

Firth of Oxford, digging in 1927 about the base of the step pyramid at Sakkareh, uncovered a temple said to be the oldest stone building in existence. It was the funerary temple of Zoser, his daughters, and his court. A statue of the Pharaoh was found in one chapel, and in a lower chamber was found much of the furniture entombed with Egyptian dead. The architect who built the Step Pyramid has attained to greater

*Vatican Museum, Rome*

LEO THE SILENT

A sacred lion of Egypt dedicated by the Pharaoh Nectanebo II to the god Thoth.

fame than Zoser himself. Imhotep used fluted columns in his work, and thus takes priority over the Greeks in that regard. He was also a physician so famous that he was later deified as the god of medicine.

The extreme scientific care of the modern archaeologist is seen in the treatment of the objects from the tomb of Tutankhamen. It will be many months before all of them will have been examined. The "Lion Gardant" vase for unguents, the alabaster boat probably for Tutankhamen's celestial journey, and the wonderfully carved head-rest of ivory, representing Shu, the god of the air, who supports the "pillow," are three of the finest of the things cleaned and put on exhibition in the late summer of 1925. The head-rests, of which four were found in the Annex of the tomb, are ritualistic. All of them are different in certain characteristic ways, but all are varieties of the *Urs*-pillow which is prescribed by the *Book of the Dead* to "lift up the head of the prostrate one."

The country known so well as the "Gift of the Nile" will be giving an admiring world thousands of other marvelous objects of artistic glory and historical value, lo! these many years to come!

STEPPING DOWN THE AGES

The northern flight of stairs of the Ziggurat, or Babel-temple, at Ur of the Chaldees in Mesopotamia.

## CHAPTER FOUR

## THE RECOVERY OF NEAR EAST ANTIQUITY

ROME has held captive the imagination of the world because it is the first outstanding phenomenon of world empire based on law and order, backed by military preparedness; it has been emulated because of its municipal architecture, its engineering triumphs in bridges and roads; in a word, Rome was great because of its all around effectiveness. Greece holds us enthralled by its original genius, still unsurpassed, in the field of the fine arts. Egypt has kept us astounded with its colossal monuments. But the Near East (Palestine, Syria, Asia Minor, and Mesopotamia), certainly because of Old Testament story, and probably because of the vaster and less known territory involved, has kept itself hidden until now in fascinating mystery. The lure of its past could never have been explained had not the magic spades of archaeology come to the rescue.

History inclines to set national peoples and territorial governments inside of fixed boundaries. Archaeology, however, has shown how unsatisfactory hard and fixed lines are. Civilization in certain favored spots in the Near East rose to very high levels. But the influences of those civilizations extended over the entire Near East, and each acted upon the other in ways never dreamed of before archaeology brought the proofs to light.

For centuries the Near East has been dominated by the anti-foreign Turk. It was only a little more than a hundred years ago that the first archaeological work there could begin. The discovery and the copying of the inscription on the Rock of Behistun (1835–1845) not only led to the decipherment of the wedge-shaped writing known now as cuneiform, but it was also the opening wedge for the entrance of archaeological scholars into Turkish territory.

Beginning in 1838 with the work in Palestine by the American, Edward Robinson, discoveries in the Near East began to multiply. With the establishment of the Palestine Exploration Fund in 1866, the discovery of the Moabite Stone in 1868, and the publication by George Smith in 1872 of the fragments of the Babylonian Flood Story, Palestine became a sensation.

*Courtesy of the Oriental Institute of the University of Chicago*

A MANGER IN PALESTINE

A stone manger found in the Stables of Solomon at Armageddon (Megiddo)
by the excavators on that important site.

Nimrud and a few places in Mesopotamia had been excavated before Schliemann visited the supposed Homeric site at Hissarlik. His discovery that it was Troy added to the fuel that set the world on fire with determination to explore the Near East. It was not long before English, French, Germans, and Austrians were swarming over the delectable ground. The discovery at Sidon in 1887 of the sarcophagus portraying in relief the battle at Issus with the figure of Alexander the Great overtopping the scene created the wild excitement it deserved. The next year, Americans entered the Near East and began to excavate Nippur in Babylonia. It may not be far from the truth to say that till about 1865 the excavations in the Near East had been conducted rather with the hope of finding spoils with which to enrich public and private collections than with the intention of increasing historical knowledge by scientific excavation. Since about 1870, however, there has been very little excavation other than scientific, due in part to an international demand for honest and careful work, and in part to mutually satisfactory arrangements as to proper oversight and a reasonable division of the objects found.

When the late George Smith made the sensational finds at Kouyunjik in the Euphrates valley of certain tablets now known as the "Creation Tablets," and the "Deluge Tablets," the Near East past rose from the dead. The synthetic thunder produced by archaeology and the revivifying lightning forged by scholarly Vulcans, after blowing the ashes of the forgotten past off the glowing facts below, heralded the Aurora which today would be screened in the vivid words: "Came the Dawn" of Biblical archaeology.

The Deluge of which Scripture tells used to be denied even by the exponents of the so-called Higher Criticism. But now we know the Indian, the Persian, the Greek, and the Chaldean versions of a Flood. The date of this Chaldean epic, as found in these Babylonian copies on the tablets, is about 2300 B.C. Quite apart from the well-nigh universal tradition of such a Flood, we now have the literary account in the Bible authenticated by the Pir-napistim story, and these two are sufficient to establish without question the fact of a great Deluge in the Mesopotamian valley in prehistoric times. And now in 1928 along comes Woolley and discovers in lower Mesopotamia the stratum of river deposit many feet thick which was left by a great flood somewhere about 5400 B.C.

A story told by the Roman poet Ovid that Zeus and Hermes had appeared in a Phrygian valley to found a temple for their joint worship was used to discredit the story in the Book of Acts that Paul and Barnabas had been saluted as Zeus and Hermes when they arrived at Lystra in Asia Minor.

Inscriptions referring to, and statuettes of, these deities found by Buckler and Calder in the region near Lystra (while travelling under the auspices of the American Society for Archaeological Research in Asia Minor) is sufficient evidence of their prominence there to give a solid historicity for the Bible story.

Excavation by the American School in Jerusalem and the Xenia Seminary of a mound known as Tell Beit Mirsim some thirteen miles from Hebron in Palestine has laid bare in successive strata the pottery and other objects of a place that became a town about 2000 B.C. It was burned. Then about 1700 B.C. it was reoccupied by a people whose polygonal, revetted walls prove them to have been Canaanites. The ruins show that the city was again destroyed about 1225 B.C. This date tallies with the Israelitish invasion of Palestine. In II Chronicles (XII, 4) one may read that Shishak, king of Egypt, "took the fortified towns of Judah." This was about 923 B.C., a date which is confirmed by the Shishak list found at Karnak in Egypt. The Palestinian town of Tell Beit Mirsim shows clear evidence in its ruins of having been destroyed, but not by fire, about 925 B.C. By comparisons of pottery it is clear that the town was burned about 600 B.C. Chaldea conquered this territory in 588–587 B.C. Study of the fifteenth chapter of Joshua when compared with the facts as now known has made it possible for Albright of the American School in Jerusalem to identify Tell Beir Mirsim with the chief town of the sixth district of Judah, namely Kirjath-sepher. Thus another long-lost town of Biblical record rises almost magically to bear witness to the value of archaeology.

It was about two hundred and fifty years before the wooden horse was pulled into ancient Troy that Joshua brought the sun to a halt upon Gibeon and the moon in the valley of Ajalon. Joshua's military successes against the Amorites and the kings of Jerusalem were so astounding that Jabin, the King of Hazor, sent word to the Canaanites, Hittites, Jebusites, and Hivites to mobilize against the upstart newcomer and his Israelites. But at the waters of Merom Joshua and his forces "smote them and chased them into great Zidon . . . until they left them none remaining." Then Joshua returned and took Hazor, "the head beforetimes of all those Kingdoms," and burned it alone of all the cities he captured; the rest he destroyed, but not by fire.

About twenty miles above the sea of Galilee the river Jordan widens out into the small Lake Huleh. West of the lake there is a mound known as El Kedah, which bestrides the junction of two main roads, one from Damascus to Egypt and the other from Sidon to Bethshan (Beisan). A site that could control these two main roads would be one of great strategic importance. But when it is seen also that El Kedah is the center of five radiating roads that run to the advanced string of fortresses of Bethshan, Taanach, Megiddo, Dor, and Harosheth that defined the Canaanite frontier along the ridge flanked on the west by Mt. Carmel and the sea at Acre, and by Mt. Gilboa on the east, it is at once evident that here was an ancient "railhead." The Tell el Amarna letters and the story in Joshua connecting Sidon with Hazor, and all the other pertinent literary and Biblical records point to El Kedah as Hazor.

According to II Kings (XV, 29), Solomon repaired Hazor; in a hieratic papyrus of the thirteenth century B.C., Hazor is associated with a navigable river; in I Maccabees (XI, 67–68) Jonathan is said to have camped by the Sea of Galilee and then in the morning to have led his troops to the plain of Hazor; Josephus the Jewish historian, says Hazor overlooked the lake.

Garstang, for many years Director of the British School at Jerusalem, has certainly found Hazor, the great central strategic site of the leader among the upper Jordan Kingdoms before the time of Joshua.

Archaeology has overturned tradition by locating Mizpah, the city of Benjamin, at Tell en-Nasbeh seven miles north of Jerusalem. Badè of the Pacific School of Religion, now Director of the Palestine Institute, by examination of an airplane photograph made by a German aviator during the war, saw walls on this hill. His excavation has laid bare the Israelitish sanctuary with its Temple and High Place, and also a sealed cistern which is probably that into which Gedaliah and his murdered companions were thrown, as related in Jeremiah (40–41). In clearing out two tombs, among the things found were two animal toys of clay lying beside the skeleton of a child, and a terra-cotta head of the Babylonian goddess Astarte, with bobbed hair.

*Courtesy of the Museum of the University of Pennsylvania*

BETH–SHAN OF THE BIBLE

Looking east, toward the Jordan valley, at the "Mound of the Fortress" (*Tell el-Hosn*, or Beisan, the Beth-shan of the Old Testament). Nine city levels have been found on this *tell*, that of the earliest period being of the time of Thothmes III, and of the latest, that of the Arabic.

Beisan, the Biblical Beth-Shan, is, like Troy, a city of nine levels. From the center of a field of ruins rises a mound known as the Mound of the Fortress, commanding the strategic site where the angle of the plain of Esdraelon touches the valley of the Jordan. The mound was the acropolis or stronghold of successive inhabitants for over 3,300 years.

The Arabic city, the remains of which did not extend far below the present surface of the mound, was first cleared under the direction of Fisher, and then of Rowe, of the Museum of the University of Pennsylvania. Then successively were laid bare below the Arabic the Byzantine, the Hellenistic, the Israelitish, the Philistine, the Assyrian, and two clearly defined Egyptian levels, the lowest, thus far, belonging to the time of Thothmes III.

Beneath an Egyptian temple in the eighth level (from the top) were found a Syrian dagger, a unique Hittite axe head, and a Cretan chair and table, showing interesting trade relationships. In the Early Seti (Egyptian) level a room contained a quantity of grain and a hollowed-out stone in which the grain was to have been pestled into flour. In the lowest level, of about 1500 B.C., were found beautifully decorated pieces of pottery, part of a bronze trumpet like the silver one found in Tutankhamen's tomb, and a splendid lapis lazuli scarab with the name of Sesostris I (1970–1935 B.C.) inscribed within a cartouche.

During 1928 a migdol — or Canaanitish fort-tower — was laid bare. Among the finds of interest in it were a pottery model of a war chariot, with the two horses, the pole, and the yokes (recalling at once the passage in Joshua XVII, 16), and a brick silo with a content of 9,270 gallons. The latest discovery (1929) is that of a stepped altar, 16 × 12 feet, in the temple of Mekal, dating about 1500 B.C.

It has been said often that Palestine is a poor site in which to excavate. It is true that the district was small, that it was the corridor through which the armies of Egyptians, Hittites, and Mesopotamians had to pass in their marauding or punitive campaigns, and that it was "a land of comparatively low material culture." It may be that no such treasure will be found as Troy, Mycenae, Tutankhamen, and Ur of the Chaldees have afforded, but each new discovery adds to the great historical value of Palestine. The foundation of Palestinian ceramics was laid by Flinders Petrie during the excavation of Tell el-Hesy (Lachish), and thereby the possibilities of comparative ceramics were enhanced. The discovery by Americans (Harvard expedition) of inscribed *ostraca* (pieces of broken pottery) at Samaria belonging to the age of Ahab, about 850 B.C., has fixed several points in Biblical history and archaeology.

Excavation during the last few years has gone through the Israelitish stratum and discovered much about the peoples who lived in Palestine in very early times. The early inhabitants of Gezer of about 3000 B.C. had rude pottery, flint knives, burned their dead, and were not Semites.  Miss Garrod, under the British School of Archaeology, has recently (1929) discovered in caves on Mt. Ephraim the bones and tools of men of the Old Stone Age.  The date of the very early Galilee Skull found in 1925 is still under discussion.  It seems to be a Neandertal type.

Courtesy of the British School of Archaeology in Jerusalem

ANCIENT SAMARIA

The columns of the Basilica in the foreground show plainly where the ground level was before the excavations began.

From 326 A.D., when the Empress Helena excavated for the Holy Sepulchre, Jerusalem has always had the lion's share of archaeological interest in Palestine.  To mention the Crusades, and the existing rivalries of Jew, Christian, and Mohammedan for the sacred site, may be enough.  But excavations have not been made easier in Jerusalem itself by such adventures as the one in 1911, when a certain unauthorized group, foreign to Palestine, opened a natural shaft near the Virgin's fountain, cleared out the rock tunnel cut by Hezekiah, and opened a tunnel that led toward the Haram enclosure, and were discovered and stopped.

We know that the site of Solomon's temple is now covered by the Haram-esh-Sherif; that Hezekiah's tunnel was to connect the Virgin's fountain with the Pool of Siloam, in anticipation of the impending siege by the Assyrians; that it was Simon Maccabaeus and his family who destroyed the fort on

*Courtesy of the British School of Archaeology in Jerusalem*

IN KIDRON VALLEY

Two of the tombs in the famous Kidron valley below Jerusalem. The one at the left is the tomb of St. James; that at the right the so-called tomb of Zachariah.

the Ophel; that Mt. Zion is the rocky spur between the Kidron and Tyropoeon valleys, and that on its south end is Ophel, the elder city of Jerusalem, which David named after himself, David's City. In 1925 the Palestine Exploration Fund people excavated the eastern wall of the Jebusite city, dating it by pottery belonging to the Late II and III Bronze Age (1600–1400 B.C.). In 1928 Crowfoot of the same Fund found at Ophel a necropolis probably that of the tombs of the Kings of Judah. He also discovered near the Pool of Siloam, ten feet below the present surface, a Byzantine street on which bordered a number of interesting houses, under an arch in one of which was found a long-lost gate in the western wall of the City of David.

Stone Age men, Jebusites, Canaanites, Hittites, and Egyptians, all ruled in Palestine before the Israelites made it their historic home, as archaeology now proves to us.

We begin to understand Ezekiel (XVI, 3) when he says of Jerusalem, "the Amorite was thy father, and thy mother a Hittite," and Genesis (X, 15–17), where Jebus (= Jerusalem) is a brother of Heth; and why Uriah the Hittite lived at Jerusalem. These are true reminiscences of the temporary Hittite occupation.

Archaeology has converted both laity and clergy. No longer do they fear that archaeological investigation will overturn Biblical statements. Thus far the finds have confirmed them, or have opened confirmatory possibilities.

The ever backward leaps of history excite an interest greater than do any of the fabulous feats attributed to seven league boots. The Hittites, from having been one of the numerous, ubiquitous, and unimportant -ites of Palestinian ethnography, suddenly a few years ago arose full grown from the mountain cairns and ruined city sites of Asia Minor. With the discovery in 1906–1907 of the royal library of the Hittites at their capital, Boghaz Keui in central Asia Minor, there began what was almost a rush to dig in this philological Eldorado. Here in the valley through which from time immemorial a great trade route to and from the mysterious East had taken the same logical path that surveyors for the Berlin-to-Bagdad railway took not so long ago, in the ruins of a second Hittite capital, there came to light thousands of pieces of broken tablets. When pieced together, they made some eight hundred fairly complete tablets in cuneiform writing that dated in the thirteenth century before Christ.

There was some help to be had from fragments of the trilingual dictionaries compiled by the Hittites themselves to help them in their linguistic Babel, and there were the two Hittite letters from Tel el-Amarna in Egypt which had been partially interpreted in 1902. It was finally found that these

Hittite texts were in eight different languages. The literary value of the inscriptions is not so great as their historical value. They disclose that central Asia Minor supplied silver and copper to Egypt and Mesopotamia; they give also considerable supplementary help to the political history of the Hittites.

Among the inscriptions is some correspondence between the widow of one of the Pharaohs — it has been guessed that her husband may have been the Tutankhamen of recent memory — and a Hittite king. The widowed Egyptian queen wrote:

My husband is dead, and I have no son. They say you have many sons. If you would give me one of them, he shall be my husband.

The Hittite king sent an embassy to Egypt to discover whether it was a hoax or a real connubial invitation. More correspondence ensued in which the queen takes the Hittite king somewhat testily to task about his suspicions. The *dénouement* throws a lurid light upon the stage of international relations at the time. A Hittite prince was despatched to Egypt both to satisfy the queen and to cement political friendship, but the match was evidently unpopular, because the Egyptian officials at court despatched the Hittite prince, not to assume the throne of Egypt, but to "that realm from whose bourne no traveler returns."

On the authority of W. H. Buckler of Baltimore, there are more than 800 ancient city sites in Asia Minor (now Anatolia) which have not been touched. About twenty sites, such as Ephesus, Pergamum, Miletus, Priene, Magnesia, Antioch in Pisidia, Sardis, and Laodicea, have been partially excavated. That country is an eastern Eldorado indeed. No wonder the aged Professor Sayce, the Hittite Moses, if we may say so, declared to the author that he absolutely *refused* to die until he had excavated a Hittite site! At Sizma, near Konia, Robinson of Johns Hopkins excavated a prehistoric site (about 2500 B.C.) of miners who mined cinnebar, or rouge, for ladies.

An expedition of the short-lived American Palestine Exploration Society in 1873 took casts of the five Hittite inscriptions at Hamath in Syria; this may be said to be the beginning of Hittite archaeological study.

The first silver Hittite seal ever found was bought by Hogarth at Bor for $2.00. The Ashmolean Museum got it in 1890. To Leslie Shear of Princeton must go the credit for one of the most exciting finds of coins in Asia Minor. While working with the American Expedition at Sardis he found in April, 1922, in a ruined tomb a pot in which were thirty gold staters of Croesus, the Rockefeller of antiquity.

The Biblical words "Great is Diana of the Ephesians!" call up a picture to which the spade has now given a real background. Wood discovered the ancient temple (the Artemisium) in 1874, but abandoned it. D. G. Hogarth in 1904 worked for two months clearing the temple platform, but found nothing. Finally he laid bare the remains of a small oblong structure covered with marble facing. As the second layer of slabs was being removed, Hogarth noticed some bright specks, which upon examination proved to be flakes of gold leaf. Then he found a gold plate, then earrings, beads, brooches, hair pins, etc. The objects were clearly a foundation deposit, a sort of corner stone-laying gift. Suddenly he visualized the find! Instead of the structure being an altar as Wood had thought, Hogarth recognized it as the pedestal on which had stood the famous statue of Diana of the Ephesians. Suddenly a terrific storm blew up and a torrential rain filled up the dig with débris and water. It was months before anything could be done. A steam pump had to be procured. Soon hundreds of jewels began to glitter as the sand danced through the sieves. Statuettes of ivory, bronze, and terra-cotta; gold and silver electrum plate engraved on both faces with old Ionic inscriptions recording contributions toward rebuilding Diana's shrine; crystal, amber, everything; over 3,000 objects in all. With every find both the pockets of the workmen and the eyes of Hogarth opened wider. A workman was just concealing a little jar when Hogarth interrupted him. It held nineteen electrum coins of the earliest mintage of Lydia, one of the most historically important of all our numismatic discoveries.

Laodicea was not entirely "lukewarm"; at least it had, as we have known since 1898, a system of waterworks that brought into the city two streams of clear cold water from the mountains. From the springs the water came several miles in a covered channel through a range of hills to a filtering basin. Thence, after crossing a valley, the water ran through a double conduit of two rows of perforated square stone blocks, which at one point is 126 feet below the hill-top, into a distributing tower at the edge of the city. Solomon was right. There is nothing new under the sun!

Two thousand years ago Antioch in Syria was the most famous of the towns of that name, called so after Antiochus, one of the generals who fell heir to the empire of Alexander the Great. But the most famous Antioch now is the one near Pisidia, in Asia Minor. It has lately been excavated by Kelsey of Michigan and Robinson of Johns Hopkins, director of the University of Michigan Near East Expedition to Asia Minor.

*Courtesy of D. M. Robinson*

A SHATTERED BEAUTY

The excavations at Antioch in Pisidia of the University of Michigan Near East Expedition to Asia Minor under the directorship of David M. Robinson found many pieces of ancient sculpture, of which this Victory (or *Nike*), is one of the finest.

Robinson uncovered a paved public square which had been built by the emperor Tiberius. Above it was a broad flight of stairs leading up through a triple propylaea to another one which Augustus had built, and above it, in a semicircle cut out of the native rock, was the great temple. The discovery of many blocks of the architrave and of the temple frieze, beautifully sculptured with life-like bulls' heads, of an arabesque border of scrolls (no longer now to be credited as a Renaissance design), of parts of the cornice, of columns, etc., has made possible a reconstruction of the building in a completeness which to a novice would be nothing short of marvelous.   The pieces found have made possible a restoration of this magnificent Propylaea through which St. Paul must have walked up to the temple.

Even more important was the discovery of many fragments of the famous inscription the original of which was dictated

*Reconstruction by F. J. Woodbridge, Jr.*                    *Courtesy of D. M. Robinson*

### THE ANTIOCH PROPYLAEA

Enough broken pieces of the triple arched gate of Pisidian Antioch were found during the excavations to make it possible to reconstruct this magnificent entrance way to the temple precinct.

by the emperor Augustus as his autobiography, and which was then carved on a part of his mausoleum in Rome.   This inscription was copied in Latin and also in Greek translation on many temples dedicated to Rome and Augustus.   The original disappeared.   The others were unknown.

When the gem collectors of Louis XIV of France first opened the Near East to archaeological enterprise, a Frenchman saw and copied a few lines of an inscription at Angora (the new Turkish capital).   Islam shut down its gates, however, and it was years before it was possible to copy it completely.   When it finally was copied, it was found to be a fairly complete copy of Augustus' autobiography, both in Greek and Latin. Now Robinson recovers more important fragments of a second Latin copy at Antioch.

A more important inscription discovered is the earliest known warning to food profiteers. It was put up by order of the emperor Domitian in 93 A.D., during the time of a famine in those parts. Here Robinson also found one of the earliest Christian basilicas. The name of Bishop Optimus is in the floor mosaic (370 A.D.). It was at Pisidian Antioch that Paul turned from the Jews to the Gentiles, and from his converts grew a Christian community which in the Fourth Century was large enough to have a diocese with its own bishop and cathedral. In such wise has Antioch of Pisidia stepped into the limelight.

The newly found Hittite civilization antedates by 1,000 years and more the Hellenistic and Greek towns of Asia Minor. While the merest start has been made on the Hittites, enough is already known to establish them as the fourth of the great early civilizations of the Near East, alongside Crete, Egypt, and Mesopotamia.

The word Mesopotamia means "the land between the rivers," — i.e., the Euphrates and the Tigris. The Tower of Babel, the Hanging Gardens of Babylon, Ur of the Chaldees, the "Assyrian came down like a wolf on the fold," are enough to make one visualize that part of the world.

Harpocration in 335 A.D. measured what was called the tower of Babel. An inscription of the sixth century B.C., set up by Nebuchadnezzar when he had restored the temple, says also that it had been built forty-two generations before his time. The foundation of this structure when measured was about 565 feet square and 80 feet high. On this foundation there was said to have been a tower of six steps, each twenty-eight feet high. On top was a sanctuary reached by 365 stairs, 305 of them being of silver and 60 of gold. We shall see below that the 200 × 135 foot tower at Ur, excavated by Woolley, is a tower of Babel.

*From a painting by Brueghel*

### THE TOWER OF BABEL

Excavations in Mesopotamia of several *ziggurats*, or tower mounds, have authenticated the form of a Biblical Tower of Babel. The imaginative tower of Babel painted by Brueghel lends its charm to a comparison with the Babel tower of Ur of the Chaldees.

Mesopotamia is threatening Egypt in the race for the greatest antiquity. Woolley has found in a temple at Tell el-Obeid, four miles from the *ziggurat* of Ur, a tablet which says that King Aannipadda of the first Ur dynasty dedicated the temple to the goddess Nin-Khursag. In this inscription we have the earliest written document yet discovered. It begins to look as if the world owes the art of writing to the early peoples in Mesopotamia.

The joint Expedition of the British Museum and the Museum of the University of Pennsylvania to Mesopotamia under the directorship of C. Leonard Woolley has occupied the attention of the world these past two or three years because objects have been found that have rivalled, if not out-rivalled, the marvels that came from the tomb of Tutankhamen. But

Babylonian records thus far discovered had contained no hint that human sacrifice had ever been practised in Mesopotamia. Now we have the definite proof of such sacrifice at a royal burial.

As one goes down the slope of the entrance to the tomb, one comes upon the dead proof of an almost unbelievable sham-

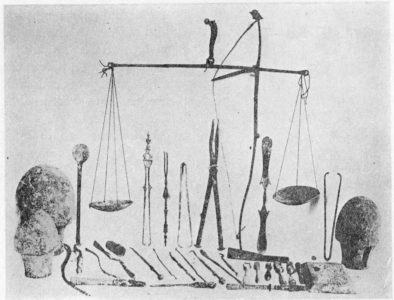

*Courtesy of The Johns Hopkins Archæological Museum*

ROMAN SURGICAL INSTRUMENTS OF THE FIRST CENTURY A.D.

bles of a ritual human sacrifice.   At the farther end of the tomb chamber against the side wall of the King's tomb were nine maid-servants opposite four men-servants.   Against the end of the tomb chamber stood nine court ladies who wore head dresses of stone beads and gold, and whose hair was confined by hair nets of gold ribbon.   Facing the entrance were two four-wheeled wooden wagons, to each of which three oxen were harnessed.   Two grooms were in front of the oxen; a driver was in one wagon, the other was on the floor beside his wagon. Collars of silver were on the oxen, and silver rings were in their noses.

The tomb was looted in ancient times, but the robbers overlooked in their haste a number of important objects, among which perhaps the most important is a model in silver of a boat, two feet in length, which is very like those found in Tutankhamen's tomb, although nearly two thousand years earlier in date. Important also were two ceremonial bulls of wood. The head of one was copper, that of the other was gold and lapis lazuli. Both decorated the frames of harps.

Confirmation of this sort of human sacrifice was made also at Kish, where the Field Museum of Chicago-Oxford University Joint Expedition under the Director S. H. Langdon concluded in 1928 their dig of the previous six years. Kish seems to have been the earliest great capital of Asia. To have uncovered seven stages of human history at Kish, dating from 4200 to 600 B.C., shows the limitless possibilities of work in Mesopotamia. Hundreds of priceless relics of Babylonian and Sumerian civilization will make the Field Museum and Oxford rich indeed. It is wonderful to have added to the objects of antiquity which are opening to us the history of times almost unbelievably long ago such things as two of the wheels and a copper rein ring of the oldest vehicle in the world, a cast copper candlestick of the finest artistic

*Courtesy of the Museum of the University of Pennsylvania*

A BANG–UP BLUEBEARD

This gold head of a bull, with bangs and beard of lapis lazuli, probably decorated a harp that was made about 3500 B.C. One of the great finds at Ur of the Chaldees by the Joint Expedition of the British Museum and the Museum of the University of Pennsylvania to Mesopotamia.

quality, mud dishes finger-printed by the child who made them, and contemporaneous sculpture of kings and commoners showing how Sumerians looked and dressed more than 6,000 years ago.

Out in Mesopotamia, B.C. is nothing. In the upper level of the Ur cemetery which dated only such a short time ago as 2600 B.C. many cylindrical seals were found on which were the names of various members of the household of the princess daughter of King Sargon of Accad. The graves in the next lower level of this cemetery dated between 3200 and 3100 B.C. The dead for the most part had been buried in coffins of basketry; in fact, some remains had been put into holes in which the lining of matting is still in good preservation. In this level was discovered a cylinder seal of lapis lazuli which bore in cuneiform the name of the wife of the king who founded the first dynasty of Ur.

In a still lower level, approximating 3500 B.C., many clay tablets were found that bore semi-pictographic scripts and seals of the names of kings of whom history knows nothing at all. Eighteen feet below the working level was found a hoard of tools of copper, mostly chisels, and of weapons of copper such as ax-heads, lance points, and spear heads. One spear head, however, is of solid gold. Many beads of beautifully wrought lapis and gold and of carnelian were also found. Perhaps the finest piece was a dagger, the hilt a solid piece of gold-studded lapis lazuli, the blade and sheath of solid gold, and on the front of the sheath a filigree design of almost incomparable workmanship.

Mr. Woolley's work at Ur has been helped very much in one way by the photographs taken from the air by the British Royal Air Force of Iraq. Badè got his lie of the buried walls of an ancient Canaanitish town north of Jerusalem from an air photograph. Just so do the photographs of the Royal Air Force give outlines of the *ziggurat* of Ur which workers on the ground cannot see at all. The complex of buildings around the tower from its top look like a lot of pits; but from the air, the palace of Ekharsag, the temple of Nin-gal, and the other buildings show in well-defined lines.   There are on the northeast face of the *ziggurat* three fine flights of stairs.   In fact, one looks at a structure which is in nearly every respect another "Tower of Babel."

Royal tombs are now in order in Ur.   The sensational finds in 1927 of tombs of King Mes-kalam-dug and Queen Shub-ad with their evidences of the ritual of human sacrifice

*Courtesy of the Museum of the University of Pennsylvania*

ANCIENT STEPS TO MODERN KNOWLEDGE

Workmen on the steps of the Ziggurat tower at Ur of the Chaldees cleared by the Joint Expedition of the British Museum and the Museum of the University of Pennsylvania to Mesopotamia, under the direction of C. Leonard Woolley.

broke down all remnants of incredibility.   Both tombs had been robbed in antiquity of what to the robbers of ancient as well as modern times was really valuable, namely, the gold and gems; but one wonders why they overlooked in the queen's tomb the bull's head made of a sheet of solid gold, and with beard, hair, and horn tips of lapis lazuli, or the wig — or ceremonial headdress — of fine gold in the tomb of the king.   The most marvelous object found was the headdress of the queen, of gold and gems.   It had fallen into pieces, however, and was more easily overlooked.

In another pit the headdresses of thirty-four court ladies were found.   Their hair ribbons were of gold, they wore wreaths of gold leaves, silver combs, and necklaces of gold and lapis. Three harps, the head piece of one being the gold head of a bull, were only surpassed by the statues of two rams with heads and legs of gold, horns of lapis, fleeces of white shell, and bellies of silver.

In the grave of a baby girl found in January, 1929, there lay beside her body her set of miniature silver dishes. Mr. Woolley himself should tell of one of his latest and most important finds. "Another most interesting discovery was that of a harp. The woodwork of the instrument had decayed and disappeared, but luckily a workman noticed the holes which it had left in the soil, and by filling these with plaster of Paris we obtained a complete cast of the harp's body, to which was attached the bull's head of copper inlaid with lapis lazuli. The most astonishing thing was the fact that when the earth was carefully cut away to expose the cast there were found surviving as lines of white fibrous powder the ten catgut strings of the harp."

A small shell cylinder seal was recently acquired by the

*Courtesy of the Museum of the*
*University of Pennsylvania*

AN ANCIENT ZOO

A plaque of engraved shell set in bitumen; used probably as the decoration of the sounding box of a harp. Found in a royal tomb at Ur of the Chaldees by the Joint Expedition of the British Museum and the Museum of the University of Pennsylvania to Mesopotamia. About 3500 B.C.

British Museum.  On it were two rows of six men each, all walking, with folded hands, toward the left.  Each man wears a Sumerian fluted skirt and a headdress with a knot (*chignon*) at the back.  One might have guessed, perhaps, what it was for.  But from the figure of Eannatum on the stele of the Vul-

*Courtesy of the Museum of the University of Pennsylvania*

### A KING'S PERMANENT WAVE

The gold helmet of King Mes-kalam-dug found in his tomb at Ur of the Chaldees by the Joint Expedition of the British Museum and the Museum of the University of Pennsylvania to Mesopotamia.  Its date is about 3500 B.C. Note the bun at the back built for the King's hair.

tures, and now from the golden helmet or headress of Mes-kalam-dug of Ur, it is clear that the long hair of the men was their pride, and that their helmets had to be made with a hollow protuberance, inside which the knot of hair could be protected.

While Egypt and Mesopotamia have been regressing in turn, each a bit farther back toward the starting point of civilization, a third competitor has entered the race and is drawing closer to the pace-setters.  This third entrant is India.

There has been little doubt that the earliest civilizations ought to be found in the valleys of the great rivers in the semi-tropics. There is therefore no *prima facie* reason why the Nile, Tigris, and Euphrates shall not be rivalled by the Indus, Ganges, Brahmaputra, Hoang Ho, and Yangtse-Kiang. For a number of years Sir John Marshall, the Director-General of Archaeology in India, has been steadily pursuing researches that have led him farther and farther back into the mists of antiquity until he is now able to describe the prehistoric civilization of the Indus as "a new chapter in archaeology."

Two great culture sites are being explored, Mohenjo-daro and Harappa in the Sind. Thirteen acres of the former site are now laid bare, and the remains of the three latest cities that occupied the site can be distinguished   All the structures are of burnt brick laid in mud or gypsum. Near the northwest corner of the city is an eminence on which is a Buddhist *stupa*. It is believed that the chief temple of the ancient city is beneath it, because it is well known that a later religion usually covers an earlier sacred place with a structure of its own. Among the structures surrounding the stupa is an ancient bath or reservoir 39 × 23 feet, which is coated with bitumen an inch thick. It has an out-drain six feet high and with a corbelled vaulted roof. Thus far the remains that have been uncovered are of private dwellings, but the interesting feature is that they show the citizen of Mohenjo-daro living in better circumstances and possessing more of the amenities of life than his contemporary either in Egypt or Mesopotamia.

At Harappa, 450 miles from Mohenjo-daro, antiquities of still earlier date have already been found, copper weapons and implements in particular. The earliest stratum uncovered yielded more than 150 seals. On one are depicted seven marching warriors who wear kilts and helmets, another shows a hunter in a tree, shooting an arrow at a tiger on the ground. The best find, however, was a copper model of a two-wheeled cart with a gabled cover and a driver. It disputes priority of age with the wheeled vehicles lately found in Mesopotamia. At all events, it is older than the stone fragment, with a chariot pictured on it, discovered at Ur, and the one in Chaldea is 1,000 years earlier than the oldest example in Egypt.

The vertical and horizontal drain pipes, the dust bins with vertical chutes from above, in addition to the great covered drain from the reservoir, all at Mohenjo-daro, and dating earlier than 3300 B.C., have already created considerable consternation in the camp of the proponents of Egyptian, Meso-

Courtesy of the Field Museum of Natural History, Chicago

NEBUCHADNEZZAR'S TEMPLE AT KISH

The late temple at Kish, as reconstructed by Nebuchadnezzar, is in the background. In the deep trench at the right, the Field Museum-Oxford University Joint Expedition discovered a four-wheeled chariot.

potamian, or Cretan earliest antiquity. The evidences of scientific sanitation with bath floors, latrines, and drains; the good stairways and windows, and the excellent construction, have all created the liveliest interest in Sir John's researches.

It had been presumed that because of the likeness to the Sumerian civilization there was an identity of culture. Research, however, has made it possible to discard that idea and with it the former name "Indo-Sumerian," and to substitute for it the cultural designation "Indus." That there was intimate commercial intercourse is clear. Datable seals in Mesopotamia of a date prior to 2700 B.C., which are to be associated with the seals in the three uppermost layers of Mohenjo-daro, make it possible to date the Indian cities between 3500 and 2500 B.C.

The spindle whorls found showed that the early inhabit-

*Courtesy of Sir John Marshall*

MOHENJO–DARO IN INDIA

A partial view of the excavations near the north-west corner of the ancient city at Mohenjo-daro in upper India. The immense thickness of the walls indicate high superstructures. Objects found here and at Harappa authenticate Indian civilization in the fourth millennium B.C.

ants of these Indian towns understood how to spin and work in wool. Statues and intaglios at Mohenjo-daro showed that the men wore a short garment like an apron with a strap over the left shoulder; at Harappa, 450 miles south, the men were nude. At both places the men wore side-whiskers and beard, but no moustaches. They had oxen, buffaloes, sheep, pigs, dogs, and horses; they raised wheat; they knew gold, silver, copper, tin, and lead. Of the greatest interest is the fact that they could write, because numerous inscribed seals were found.

Thus the race back toward or beyond Adam goes merrily on.

APOLLO'S CORNER AT CORINTH

When the American School at Athens began to dig at Corinth in Greece, there was little above ground except some massive corner columns of the ancient temple of Apollo, of the VI century B.C.

CHAPTER FIVE

# THE GLORIOUS PAST OF HELLAS

THOUSANDS of books have tried to explain why tiny little Greece is a giant among nations. Greece can be adored or resented, but not explained.

In the fifth century B.C. Greece stopped Persia and saved Europe from Eastern invasion, perhaps domination. For that we owe it thanks. Democratic government originated in Athens and since that time Athens has meant Greece (or Hellas). After the defeat of the Armada, England burst into the splendid flower of Elizabethan literature. After the defeat of Persia, Athens burst into a radiant bouquet and its flowers were not only literature, but also sculpture, architecture, painting, philosophy, and ceramic and numismatic art. The delectable aroma of its flowering has permeated civilization for 2,500 years.

In the fifteenth century A.D. Greek scholars fled westward into Europe before the oncoming tide of Islam. The Renaissance was the result. A century ago Greece won the admiration, the sympathy, and the help of the Western world by its almost superhuman struggle for political independence. Its free dower of humanistic glories enriches the world today.

Great museums take rank according to their possession of objects of Greek and Greco-Roman art. Classical architecture, for the most part, is in shattered ruins, but the lintel, column, frieze, and gable style of Greek architecture has spread throughout the world, and still satisfies it with a quiet beauty and dignified grandeur. In the paintings on Greek vases, real life vies with mythological fancy; the one portraying contemporaneously the people whose imagination conceived the other.

The museum side of archaeology struck Greece when victorious Roman generals and emperors carried off statues and other things *en masse* to enrich themselves, thus setting an example for Napoleon. It was, however, the Roman copies of these Greek spoils that inspired the medieval sculptors and artists. Medieval and modern pieces of sculpture are practically all of white marble. Cultured laymen have admired and

*Photograph by C. R. Ballance, Mentone on the Riviera*

GROUNDED GRECIAN GLORIES

The ruins of the temple at Selinunte, the ancient Selinus, in Sicily, with their scattered fragments, entrance every visitor.

bought these marbles, but for some unperceived reason, while praising their severe beauty, they at the same time resented their stark whiteness. These laymen are entitled to "have the laugh" on the artists.

There were as many ancient statues of bronze as there were of marble. The value of the metal easily accounts for the disappearance of the larger bronzes. Medieval and modern sculptors were unaware of this fact and clung to the use of marble. But their greatest mistake was in clinging to white. We now know, from recent archaeological discoveries, that all the backgrounds in metopes and gables were painted in brilliant blues, and that nearly all the ancient statues, both in marble and terracotta, were painted wholly or in part. But the color had worn or been washed off by rain from the pieces that survived. It should be remembered also that the majority of ancient statues were not nudes, but were clothed in armor or panoply, tunics and togas, and that these coverings had to be painted after

*From an old engraving by Purser and Floyd*

THE TEMPLE AT CORINTH

the style of the day or in accordance with the taste of the real or imaginary model. In passing, it might be said that our own sculptors have the best opportunity the world has ever had to enrich a type in a natural color. The nude Indian comes nearer being a model for a bronze type of statuary than any model a previous school of sculpture has ever had.

The archaeological spade works continuously on a historical antithesis. The deeper the spade and pick go, the more recent the work but the more ancient the find. Crete is not Greece at all, but Crete is the "Forerunner of Greece." That long island, forming a breakwater at the southern end of the Aegean Sea, the "half-way house between three continents, linked by smaller island stepping stones to the Peloponnesus and the mainland of Anatolia," is probably the Atlantis of Plato.

Now and then a man becomes so identified with a place or an event that mention of either one brings the other to mind. Arthur Evans and Cretan Cnossus are such complementary names. But although Sir Arthur easily dominates the front of the Cretan stage, in the near background are other archaeologists from various lands, among whom our own Edith Hall Dohan and Harriet Boyd Hawes and the late Richard Seager occupy prominent places.

For thirty years Arthur Evans has been excavating in the island of Crete. His own special dig has been at Cnossus, or as the Greek has it, Knossos. Here Evans laid bare an ancient palace, overlord of Crete and mistress of the eastern Mediterranean, in which were found the proofs of a civilization as high as that of Egypt and Mesopotamia, and almost as old. The scientific examination of the strata, and the vases, seals, gold ornamentation, magnificent frescoes, and thousands of articles of everyday life found in the different layers of the growth of the palace made it possible for Evans to set down a chronological scheme to which he gave the name Minoan, running from about 3000 to 1200 B.C. Since the discoveries by Schliemann at Troy in Asia Minor and at Mycenae and Tiryns in Southern Greece, there had been no such startling development in early Aegean history, but Evans and Cnossus made history take a sudden, and to many scholars a disconcerting, backward leap of more than fifteen hundred years.

The site of Cnossus is fairly high up the west slope of a valley down which one looks northward four miles to the blue gleam of the Mediterranean. Each year Cnossus grows larger; in 1926 by the excavation of the so-called "Little Palace"; in 1927 by the extension of lower buildings of the great palace and of the waterworks system. Work is also well along on reconstruction. It may be said in passing that reconstruction of any sort has been looked upon usually with grave apprehension by the majority of artists and archaeologists ever since their horrified appreciation of the creative restoration done by Thorwaldsen many years ago of mutilated statues in European museums. But Evans has restored little for which he lacks scientific evidence, although there are many of the best archaeologists who think his restorations a little fanciful here and there. The restored portions of the buildings, however, are in a concrete both of color and texture which can not be confused with the ancient stone or gypsum. The reconstruction adds greatly to a comprehension of the grandeur of the palace, and gives a reality of its size and levels which can not be attained by the general run of people untrained to build up in their imaginations the beautiful constructions which are implicit in the flat plans and elevations of an architect's drawing.

Imagination can run riot, however, in the museum at Candia, where the finds of Cnossus are displayed. Imagination will not fail to fill that ancient palace with persons whose features and dress are known from the many frescoes, or fail to house them properly, whether in reception hall, living room, or kitchen, or even to live with them in those good old days 4,000 years ago when smart clothes, backgammon, circus performances, Cnossian china, and other refinements of palatial luxury were as much the rage as ever they were, or are.

The early fresco of the Little Boy Blue, recently ruined by an earthquake, deserves his title better than does the picture by Gainsborough. The thirteen and one-half inch high snake goddess with her purplish-brown tiara, dressed in an embroidered jacket with a laced bodice, and a skirt with a short double pannier, is only one of the ancient Cretan ladies who elicited from a French savant, much to his own consternation, the famous phrase, "Mais, ces sont des Parisiennes!"

One walks in the palace and realizes he is in what would be a veritable maze were the walls at their original height, for if one could not see what direction to go to get out, he would find himself wandering about and probably landing finally where he started. No wonder the architects of the place, Daedalus and Icarus, anticipated the Wrights and made themselves airplanes. The story of Theseus and the Minotaur, in the presence of the painted frescoes of the charging bulls, now takes on real meaning.

Cnossus is not the only city that authenticated the great forgotten sea power of King Minos, 2,000 years before the time we think of as Greek history. Even Homer, that near-divine troubadour and bard of the ninth century B.C., collected enough from tradition to chant of Crete, the island of ninety cities.

*Courtesy of the Boston Museum of Fine Arts*

A GRECIAN SNAKE GODDESS

An ivory and gold statuette of the XVI century B.C. Note the proud pose. The trimmings applied to the Minoan dress are of gold.

To reach the palace at Phaestus in southern Crete, one goes up a flight of stone steps forty-five feet wide, the broadest state entrance staircase any royal palace ever had. Here there came to light a circular clay disk (6.67 inches in diameter) inscribed on both sides with 241 signs in 61 sign groups. But its writing is still in the same sphinx-like class with Hittite and Etruscan. It will not give up its secret to the philologists. An archaeologist will probably have to dig up a bi-lingual inscription or a tri-lingual like that on the Behistun rock or the Rosetta stone. At the ancient town of Hagia Triada — true also at Cnossus — the drainage system works as perfectly as it did more than 4,000 years ago. At Gournià, the Cretan Pompeii, a complete set of carpenter's tools was found in one house; a set of loom weights in another. At Gortyna, on a stone mill-dam from which the water was temporarily diverted, there came to light the longest and one of the most important codes of early Greek laws.

What a tremendous addition to historical truths came from a half dozen Cretan sites! Cretan and Egyptian art are now seen to be contemporaneous and directly interrelated. Given Crete and Egypt — minus archaeology — and one would have said that if they had relations with one another it must have been by way of Cyprus. But excavation in Cyprus shows no Minoan influence; therefore Cretan objects in Egypt, and vice versa, show a direct connection. We can say now from comparative ceramics that the best silica-base coating of pottery was in Egypt, but on the other hand it is clear that the Cretan faïence was the better, and that the Cretans were first in polychrome decoration. The discovery of Kamáres ware, so named from the cave in which J. L. Myres found it, gave the world a type of pottery that is practically egg-shell china as to thinness of its wall. We can now trace the Philistines as the last organized remnant of Minoan sea power, and name Goliath a Cretan. Spiral decoration is indigenous in Crete; the lily and the crocus are the flowers most used in painted decoration, but almost as common are the octopus, nautilus, coral, and algae: naturalistic designs, that is to say, from the fauna and flora of forgotten Atlantis.

*Photograph by Harriot Curtis*

INTERIOR DECORATION

A beautifully decorated jar, or *pithos*, found in excavations at Phaestus in Crete.

It was only a little more than a century ago that Lord Elgin began to collect the Parthenon marbles which were undoubtedly saved from destruction by being sent to England. There they now are, and rightly the most prized possession of the British Museum. The discovery of the frieze of the Greek temple at Bassae; the acquisition of the sculptures from the temple on the island of Aegina by Ludwig of Bavaria for his museum in Munich; the discovery in 1820 of the Venus di Milo; the uncovering in 1857 of the Mausoléum at Halicarnassus, which

*Museum, Crete*          *Courtesy of the Museum of the University of Pennsylvania*

### AN OCTOPUS VASE

Found at Gournià, Crete, broken in eighty-six pieces. The vase is pinkish-yellow clay; its black painted decoration is two writhing octopods covered with a lustrous buff slip. Height 19.5 centimetres.

Queen Artemisia had erected to her husband Mausõlus; the discovery in 1863 of the Victory of Samothrace: these were only the statuesque or architectural harbingers of marvels yet to come.

Heinrich Schliemann as a boy had been so thrilled by Homer's epics that he then and there decided to find the sites of the cities mentioned in the story of the Trojan war. Everyone laughed at him, much as did Noah's neighbors on another prophetic occasion. Schliemann had to work almost a lifetime before he earned money enough — part of it gained in business in Indianapolis — to put his faith to the test. He visited in 1868 what were believed to be Homeric sites. Then between 1871 and 1890 he found and partially excavated Troy, below the entrance to the Dardanelles, and Mycenae, Tiryns, and Orchomenus in Greece.

A number of scholars had spent their lives writing and declaiming against the reality of the Trojan war, pooh-poohing all ideas different from their own that the Homeric cycle of Trojan and Greek adventures were but fleeting figments and illusory pigments of the vivid Greek imagination. After the identification of these Homeric sites, it is said that several of the scholars mentioned above committed suicide in mortification.

Schliemann, then, is not the least of Homer's triumphs. Down through the hill of Hissarlik he dug, and one city after another came to light; nine altogether. Schliemann was an enthusiastic, not a scientific archaeologist. But it made very little difference that he thought the second city — that is, from the bottom — was ancient Troy, instead of the sixth, as Doerpfeld later showed. He had uncovered Troy, and also started real archaeological work on Hellenic soil. Calvert, American consul at the Dardanelles, has the credit of having shown Schliemann the site of Troy.

Even more important from the artistic point of view were Schliemann's discoveries and excavations of Golden Mycenae, the home of Agamemnon, of Tiryns, one of the earliest of Argolid fortress cities, and of Orchomenus in Boeotia. The tombs were full of palace utensils and objects of personal adornment of gold and other precious metal fashioned with an artistic skill almost beyond belief.

In the Argolid, on a mountain spur 912 feet high, Schliemann in 1876 first found a double ring (87 feet in diameter) of stone slabs. Twenty-three feet below the surface he came upon the first of five graves. In it and the others (a sixth grave was discovered later) were found face masks of solid gold, bracelets, rings, daggers (sixty swords and daggers in one tomb), ivory, amber, silver, bronze, alabaster, diadems, pendants, grasshoppers of gold with chains of gold wherewith the royal ladies attached them as ornaments on their dresses or in their hair; more than seven hundred ornaments in all.   Nothing to equal this had ever been found before.   Small wonder, is it not, that the world got into training for an archaeological race?

The British took Mycenae over later and A. J. B. Wace put the finishing touches on the earlier work.   How vividly the writer remembers that day, after Wace had walked fifteen miles over from where he was helping Blegen of the American School at Athens excavate Zygouries, how as we of the American School at Rome stood on the edge of the grave circle, Wace pointed down the slope to a copsed spot where he said he intended soon to start a dig.   It was golden, not black, magic. Under that very spot he came upon another domed tomb rich in treasure.   He later found several more bee-hive tombs, and in excavating the palace he found in one room a red bath tub, perhaps the very one in which Agamemnon was murdered.

Wace and Blegen are pottery specialists.   By its study they have set a definite Helladic chronology.   At Mycenae, by the pottery, Wace has put Mycenae into certain history:

| First Settlement | Early Helladic, | 2500–2000 B.C. |
| Flourishing City | Middle Helladic | 2000–1600 B.C. |
| Rich and powerful | Late Helladic I, | 1600–1400 B.C. |
| Cyclopean wall, lions' gate | Late Helladic II, | 1400–1100 B.C. |

The Greek historian Pausanias, recalling his visit to Olympia, mentioned the statue of Hermes which Praxiteles had sculptured.   Students of art writing in the eighteenth and early nineteenth centuries had no certain canon by which to distinguish Greek originals from Greco-Roman copies or Roman originals.   Therefore when in 1877 a marble Hermes was found lying only a few feet from where Pausanias in the second century A.D. said the Hermes of Praxiteles had stood, there was no question but that this was that very statue; and the greatest single statuary find it still is today.

The French began in 1877 to excavate on the island of Delos, the ancient center of the Ionian confederacy, and one of the two — Delphi being the other — greatest sites where the cult worship of Apollo was localized.   Architects and economists alike rejoice over the find in 1918 of an inscription in the ruins of Delos that records the payment for 153 cubical blocks (1 × 1 × 1 ft.) contracted for the theatre in Delos.   The excavated ruins of Delos today lie in terraced beauty up toward the steps cut in the rock that lead to the top of Mt. Cynthus, from where one gets an unparalleled view of the island Cyclades that surround the holy isle of Apollo.

It was not until 1893 that the French began to dig thoroughly at Delphi.   There, not so long ago, a certain American professor sat reading the *Ion* of Euripides to a rapt group of American students sitting on the floor of Apollo's shrine.   As he reached the passage in the prologue in which Ion chides the birds of Zeus for attempting to steal the sacrifice from off Apollo's altar, suddenly from the top of snowy Parnassus soared some of the Olympian's eagles over the heads of these American devotees of one of Athens' great writers of Tragedy.   Archaeology is bound to thrive in such an atmosphere.

It may not be too much to claim for Delphi that it was the greatest museum of combined art and treasure the world has ever known.   The Athenian Acropolis and Olympia, in Greece, the temple of Fortune at Praeneste (Palestrina), the temple of Apollo on the Palatine and the Forum and Temple of Peace of Vespasian in Rome would be, however, very close rivals. The ancient world gave to the priests at Delphi dedicatory and gratitudinarian gifts of unexampled beauty and value. There remain ruins of the so-called Treasuries in which they were deposited or the bases on which statues or tripods stood.

The bronze charioteer, however, is the best piece of sculpture thus far found at Delphi.   We know that he was the driver of a chariot with four horses.   The entire piece was dedicated by Polyzelus, the brother of Kings Gelo and Hiero of Syracuse in Sicily, sometime between 478 and 472 B.C., for his victory at the Pythian games; although others say it was Arcesilaus of Cyrene. The statue is doubtless that of the actual driver; his master was probably in the chariot or just mounting into it.

Any ancient Greek site that yields a Hermes by Praxiteles and a Victory by Paeonius has done its full share. Olympia was where the great quadrennial games were held from at least 776 B.C., when Coroebus won the 100-yard dash, to 394 A.D., when Theodosius abolished the games. Phidias made for Olympia his masterpiece, the seated Zeus of gold and ivory. There were made and dedicated there (through a thousand years) thousands of statues of athletes. The Germans, who laid bare the site with the most praiseworthy scientific care, have reason to be content to have been the first to lay the correct foundations for the science of archaeological excavation, and with getting as a Christmas gift their first year, in 1875, the marvelous Victory inscribed on the base with the name of its sculptor Paeonius, and with finding in 1877 the Hermes of Praxiteles.

The British have conducted many important excavations in Greece. They traced the walls of Athens' great rival, Sparta, largely by the aid of stamped tiles. In 1925 they found the head and armless body of a helmeted warrior made in Parian marble between 480 and 470 B.C. It represents probably either Leonidas of Thermopylae fame or Pausanias, the victorious general at Plataea.

The sites at Eleusis of the early initiation ceremonies into the great Greek Mysteries, and that of the sanctuary at Epidaurus of Asclepius, the god of healing, have been excavated by the Greeks. In laying bare the theatre at Epidaurus, the first one discovered with a full circle orchestra, a statement of Pausanias was verified. That ancient traveler and historian wrote that the theatre at Megalopolis (where the British worked in 1890–1891) was the largest, that the Roman theatres excelled in decorations, but that the theatre at Epidaurus surpassed them all in harmony and beauty.

The part played by Americans in the archaeological resurrection of ancient Greece is one in which this country may properly take great pride. Many of the scholars and fellows annually appointed to the School of the Archaeological Institute of America at Athens, working with its various directors, especially with Richardson at Eretria, with Waldstein at the Argive Heraeum, and with Bert Hodge Hill at Corinth, have made great contributions to history, art, and science. At the Heraeum, Blegen discovered the first Neolithic pottery in the Argolid, dating it by an Egyptian scarab found in the dig. At Zygouries, near Nemea, in a potter's shop were found in 1921 more than 1,300 vases, the first early Helladic things found on the Greek mainland. At Nemea, Blegen found the earliest skeletal remains thus far discovered in the Peloponnesus. At Eutresis in Boeotia, Hetty Goldman in 1924–1925 proved its occupation from early Helladic to Byzantine times. J. P. Harland at Aegina, on archaeological evidence, overthrew the contention of Furtwaengler as to a Minoan settlement on that island. Robinson of Johns Hopkins in 1928 laid bare the citadel and town of Olynthus on the Chalcidian peninsula, filling for the

*Courtesy of the Metropolitan Museum of Art*

A GRECIAN TOMB STONE

The grave stele of Me [gakles?], an Athenian, dating 550–540 B.C. It is the largest and perhaps the most important extant gravestone of this period. It bears the representation of the deceased youth and a little girl.

historians a greatly deplored gap in the period just before the time of Alexander the Great.   Of archaeological importance are the mosaic house floors slanting to a corner drain, bathrooms with terra-cotta tubs resembling the Victorian hip bathtubs, sling slugs inscribed with the name of Philip of Macedon, many coins and important terra-cottas and vases.   He found the barracks, the civic center, a terra-cotta factory with many

*Courtesy of D. M. Robinson*

OLYNTHUS

A view looking northeast over the excavations by Professor D. M. Robinson, Director of The Johns Hopkins University and Baltimore Museum of Art Joint Expedition to Olynthus.   Trenches 1, 2, and 3 in the fortress at the southern end of the site.

molds, a unique pair of bronze epaulettes, but especially, the first important houses to be excavated that date from the fifth and fourth centuries B.C.   Robinson's excavation is important not only for locating the site of Olynthus, but also for giving us a new chronology for Greek vases and terra-cottas.   Many types hitherto supposed to be Hellenistic are now dateable before 348 B.C.   George E. Mylonas has just published (1929) a book showing that the Neolithic settlement at Olynthus is earlier than the earliest city at Troy.

The strategic position of ancient Corinth marked it for the early arbiter of Greek destinies, and from the turmoil of the amalgamation of the invading northern Hellenes with the older settlers, Corinth rose into prominence as a colonizing and commercial city-state.   The chest of Cypselus (dedicated at Olympia), the wooden skidway for ships across the isthmus, the widespread circulation of Corinthian "colts" (*i.e.*, coins with a winged Pegasus on one side), Corinthian vases and bronze statues, gave this site of the Isthmian games not only fame and wealth but also pride.   After it became virtual head of the

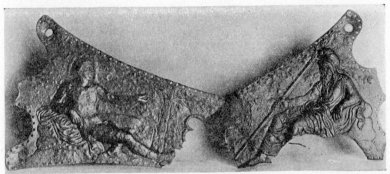

*Courtesy of D. M. Robinson*

OLYNTHIAN EPAULETTES

A fine pair of bronze epaulettes of the fifth century B.C.   The reliefs probably represent Apollo and some Thracian or Phrygian deity with a sceptre (or possibly they represent Achilles and Priam).

Achaean League it ran foul of Roman expansion.   The historian Polybius saw the Roman consul Mummius capture and utterly destroy Corinth in 146 B.C.   He saw thousands of priceless and inimitable works of art destroyed, and other thousands loaded upon Roman ships.   They later furnished to Rome the greatest auction sale of Greek art that ever was or ever will be.

When the School of the Archaeological Institute of America at Athens began in 1896 to excavate ancient Corinth, the only relic of former glory to be seen was part of a Doric temple. Excavation has continued intermittently from 1896 until now. American excavators took as many leads as possible from Pausanias, who had revisited Corinth about 165 A.D. and then written a description of the Roman city.   They began with the Agora, or municipal center, and worked out from it.   There now lie uncovered the two fountains so famous in ancient history, Pirene and Glauce, with their complicated systems of receiving and distributing the city's water supply, as well as the "Old Fountain," an Odeum and a theatre, and enough of the ancient temple to ascertain its plan and to guarantee its ascription to the god Apollo.

PEGASI

The obverses and reverses of three silver Corinthian staters.  The heads are of Athena wearing a Corinthian helmet.  Under each winged Pegasus is the letter *Koppa*, which was dropped out of the Greek alphabet and used as a brand for high-bred horses.

The reports of the work by and under the four Directors up to 1927, Richardson, Heermance, Hill, and Blegen, and by T. Leslie Shear in 1925, 1926, and 1928 have appeared in the *American Journal of Archaeology*, and a final and complete publication of the entire excavation is under way at the present time.

The importance of good water to a town is obvious.  The reservoirs cut into the living rock, and the dispensing basins, all lined with waterproof cement, tell their own story of the fountain of Glauce, the source of which was at the base of Acrocorinth.  According to Pausanias it got its name from Glauce, the second wife of Jason, the hero of the Argonaut story. The jealous Medea had sent her a beautiful robe as a wedding present. The new bride found her robe transformed into a garment that stuck to her and burned her with a poisonous flame. Glauce threw herself headlong into the fountain to quench the flames and thus ease the pain.

The excavation of the theatre, partly explored by trenches many years ago, has been carried forward by Leslie Shear with great success. It was necessary to dig out, and transport a half-mile away for dumping, thousands of tons of earth which covered the site at some places to the depth of forty feet. Among the many interesting objects found, perhaps the most valuable artistically, are a beautiful female head and a headless Artemis (1929). Important also, particularly for the evidence thus gained on Greco-Roman painting, are the once vividly colored gladiatorial scenes painted — faded out since their excavation — on the wall which divided the orchestra from the dancing space on the ground (*cavea*).

Perhaps the most interesting piece of excavation done at Corinth thus far was that of the "oracular" shrine, the details of which, as told to him on the spot by former Director Bert Hill, remain most vivid in the memory of the writer.

Near the Propylaea, as one goes toward the temple of Apollo, and at the edge of the Agora, there is a low wall, decorated with a band of triglyphs. As can be seen from two bronze spouts still *in situ* the style is demonstrably early fifth century B.C. For some reason the ground level was raised and an old spring house became a subpetrine chamber. The unworn condition of the steps during the fourth century B.C. showed that the public was not admitted to the fountain. Its water had become "holy water," and only the servants belonging to the nearby shrine were permitted access to the spring chamber. An ancient inscription in the old Corinthian alphabet, discovered by the Americans, says, "let no one go down here. Fine, seven drachmas!" The spring ran dry, but holy water was still desired at the spot. Therefore, a cement-lined conduit of stone was built and water brought from a long distance to a discharge basin, which was built seven feet higher and almost exactly over the earlier fountain reservoir.

Nearby, and always in communication with the old spring, is a sanctuary with a small round altar in the center of its apse. Very near it, on the east, is the opening for the off-run of water. Alongside it is a tunnel through which a man could crawl. The same roof covers both water-channel and tunnel, and both come to the terrace at the level of the triglyph frieze. The metope in front of the entrance to the tunnel is really a door, and the other metopes were made to match it so the genuine opening would not look different from the rest. Further, at the upper end of the tunnel, inside the shrine, there is a small megaphone-shaped hole. The evidence seems clear that Hill found an ancient priestly contrivance for operating oracular responses to the inquiries of the credulous. *Sic transit gloria.*

In 1928 Shear found thirty-three unrifled graves dating in the late sixth and early fifth centuries B.C. containing many vases, strigils (the ancient bath towel), lamps, and broken or perforated egg shells, the last being probably symbolic dedications of food for the dead.

In the Odeum, Broneer has laid bare the curtain channel of the orchestra and found a splendid archaic statue of Athena Archegetis holding an owl; and also a fragment of a statue wearing a cuirass with medallions on the lappets, on two of which heads of Zeus Ammon and Medusa are particularly noteworthy. The latest report for the week of April 6, 1929, is the discovery of 433 coins, three pieces of sculptured frieze, theatre seats, vases, and lamps.

Christians long for heaven, Mohammedans look forward to Mecca, certain American devotees dream of college football or professional baseball games; but Greek archaeologists sigh for Athens and the Acropolis, its holy hill.

Many of Athens' ancient monuments have never disappeared. The Hephaestaeum (still incorrectly called the Theseum) still stands as the best preserved Greek temple; some of the columns of the gigantic temple to Olympian Zeus, and the choragic monument of Lysicrates have withstood the shock of time and the hand of man. Other monuments which for one reason or another had disappeared, began to come to light in 1859 when the *stoa* of Attalus was excavated. Then in 1886 Doerpfeld began to excavate the theatre of Dionysus; Kastriotis located the Odeum of Pericles on the southeast base of the Acropolis in 1922. In 1026 part of the so-called Wall

*Restoration by Thiersch*

THE ACROPOLIS OF ATHENS

| Erechtheum | Parthenon |
| Statue of | Propylaea |
| Athena | Temple of |
| Promachos | Wingless Victory |

A fairly accurate restoration of the Acropolis of the time of Pericles.

of Hadrian was discovered, and both inside and outside of it, many tombs dating from the end of the sixth century B.C. to Roman times.

Brueckner of the German Institute in 1927, with funds contributed by Mr. Gustav Oberlaender of Reading, Pennsylvania, made a startling discovery. He was clearing an area inside the wall in the region of the Ceramicus (which region because of its fine clay for vases made Athens rich and famous, and gave to English the word *ceramics*), and below a layer of the geometric period came upon a sub-Mycenean necropolis. In the graves with the skeletons were ear and finger rings, *fibulae* (safety pins), and many vases of different shapes. This is one of the most important of the many early finds in Greece which will soon throw light on the inhabitants earlier than the Hellenes.

Nature left in the Attic plain the last spur but one of a chain of hills that ran from Pentelicon (whence the famous Pentelic marble) to the south coast. This spur is a hill 330 feet above the plain, with an area of 830 by 420 feet. As the Hill of Zion is the most eminent pinnacle of religion, so is this Acropolis hill of Athens the most eminent pinnacle of art.

Precipitous on all sides but the northwest, and steep even there, the Acropolis, or High City, was an ideal fortress for an ancient town. It soon had its early shrines, but it did not become the Holy Hill of Athens in all its glory until after it rose like the fabled Phoenix from its Persian-made ashes, at a period concomitant with the Golden Age of Pericles. It was no accident, it was the outburst of Attic genius that erected the magnificent Propylaea, or gateway, which admitted to the top of the hill, that area well-nigh covered with architectural and sculptural sublimity. Above one to the right stood the gem of Ionic structures, the perfect little temple of Wingless Victory (Nike Apteros). After passing the Propylaea portals, there towered before one the bronze Athena holding a spear the gold tipped point of which, gleaming in the sun, fascinated the homing gaze of Athenian sailors as they sailed up the Saronic gulf from Sunium.

To one's left the noble Caryatides supported in maidenly dignity the west porch of the Erechtheum — that close Ionic-style competitor of the Nike temple — with its marvelous door, its blue Eleusinian marble frieze, and its inimitable column capitals. But to one's right rose the architectural wonder of the world, a Doric temple, admittedly from then till now the most perfect building ever conceived by the mind and built by the hand of man — the Parthenon.

There stood for nearly 2,500 years that shrine to Athena, the patron goddess of Athens, *intacta*, as was the goddess herself whose gold and ivory statue by Phidias filled with her glory that splendid fane. On September 26, 1687, a shell, either from one of the Venetian Morosini's guns on the Pnyx or mortars on the Areopagus, where St. Paul once stood and made a famous address, fell into the temple and exploded a Turkish magazine of combustibles. The central portion of the temple was blown out, and the whole structure was terribly, almost irreparably shaken. It was an inspiration of Dr. John H. Finley's in 1926 that six fallen columns on the north side should again rise, and six American gentlemen have sponsored that restoration.

We all know the Parthenon from photographs, from its replica at Nashville, from the model in the Metropolitan Museum, but it needs repetition to keep in mind its standard-setting values. The mythological compositions in the east and west gables (or pediments) were sculptured in the round. It is fragments from these pieces that constitute the Elgin marbles in the British Museum, the finest group in the world. On the frieze that ran round outside the temple, in each of the ninety-two metopes, were two or three figures in fairly high relief (fifteen of which are in the Elgin collection). Thirdly, there was a continuous band, 524 feet in length (of which the British Museum has 249 feet), of figures in low relief representing a procession of the citizens of Athens, which ran entirely round the temple building proper, inside the free-standing columns. Some of these sculptural figures were done by Phidias himself — which ones we do not know — and the rest were done by his students, perhaps touched up here and there by the master of all sculptors.

But as inimitable as the sculpture of the Parthenon is, its architecture is perhaps more remarkable. It is quite proper to say that the Parthenon, built nearly 2,500 years ago, has the absolute perfection of proportion, the niceties of columnar and stylobate centre swell, of columnar lilt and considered intercolumniation, all proportionately out of level or plumb just enough to correct the eye; and that it has offered and still offers problems in exact symmetry, in purposeful asymmetry and bewildering simplicity of line, of ratio, and of effect; and that the Parthenon still offers an unaccountable combination of genius, technique, and art.

There have been many excavations on Greek soil. It is hoped that another will begin soon. Arrangements are under way with the Greek government by Professor Capps of the General Education Board, under which America, through the

THE ATHENIAN ACROPOLIS

At the crest of the Acropolis, at the left, are the Propylaea and the Temple of Wingless Victory; in the central background is the Erechtheum; in the right central foreground the shattered Parthenon stands in irreproachable majesty.

American School of Classical Studies at Athens, will have the privilege of laying bare the market place (or Agora) of ancient Athens. The area to be uncovered is a large one, extending from near the base of the Acropolis on the north side nearly as far toward the northwest as the temple of Hephaestus ("Theseum"). There are more than 500 modern houses standing on the ancient site of the Agora. These will be purchased as rapidly as necessary. It is anticipated that to do this excavation will take fifty years. Like all other digs, the number, the value, and the diversity of the finds is problematical, but its extreme importance is certain.

In Athens, therefore, for the next fifty years there may be for American students a magnificent outdoor archaeological laboratory.  What a tremendous scientific obligation and what a marvelous opportunity will be ours, if the present diplomatic difficulties are overcome!

## THE GLAMOR OF ROME'S PAST

The artist has brought together here a number of unrelated architectural and
artistic pieces which make a charming picture of "the grandeur that was Rome."

CALIGULA SELLS HIS GLADIATORS

The paintings of the lately deceased Signor Forti are practically perfect in archaeological detail. Note the mosaic floor of the palace room on the Palatine, the painted walls, the marble table, the bronze brazier, the praetorian standards, and the costumes.

CHAPTER SIX

## THE RESURRECTION OF HESPERIA

ARCHAEOLOGY is not a territorial word. Etruscan archaeology, for example, finds its field in Italy. Archaeology shows that during Etruria's independence its engineering and its art influenced the growing Rome. The things made by the Etruscans and their descendants after they were Romanized come, however, under the head of Roman archaeology. Spain and its territorial Morocco, France and Tunisia, Italy's Tripolitania and Cyrenaica, are full of Roman archaeology. Russia is rightly proud of the splendid Greek tombs that have been found north of the Black Sea where the Greeks were early colonists. Austria and all the Balkan States contain many fine old Roman sites. South Germany was Roman for hundreds of years. Scores of German towns maintain their old Roman walls. Cologne boasts a museum full of Roman antiquities. The Saalburg, near Frankfort-am-Main, has been restored.

It was one of the many Roman camps that protected the frontier wall with which Domitian tied the Rhine to the Danube. Carlsbad, Bad Ems, Nauheim, Wiesbaden, and scores of other modern spas were favorite Roman watering places. Not a year for more than a century but that an excavation has gone on in each of all the European countries, and their local museums

Photograph by R. V. D. Magoffin

PORTA NIGRA AT TRIER

The Black Gate at Augusta Treverorum (modern Trier or Trêves) is one of the
gates in the ancient wall of the Roman Army headquarters town in Germany.

are full of articles that both prove and explain Roman occupation during the first three or four centuries of the Christian era.

There are literally thousands upon thousands of articles and books dealing with archaeological finds of Roman things in European countries. Such constructions as the Roman wall and tower at Mainz, and the Black Gate, the Baths, and the amphitheatre at Trier in Germany; the Adamklissi monument in the Dobrudja in the Balkans; the Roman theatre and amphitheatre at Arles, the Roman arch at Orange, the Maison Carrée at Nîmes; Agrippa's aqueduct bridge over the Gard river near Nîmes in French Provence (= *provincia*); the splendid bridge at Alcantara, and the Roman camp and temple to Venus Marina at Almenara in Spain; the scores of recently resurrected Roman cities in North Africa; these, and hundreds of others like them, make the Roman Empire live again in reflected glory.

Buried antiquity is Italy's gold field, and the Apennine peninsula, although it has yielded so much archaeological treasure, has not yet been much more than scratched. But new treasures have been found lately in other Italian territory. The sands of North Africa are proving to be the most interesting cemetery in the world; all the more valuable, too, because the blowing sand sepulchred its victims fortuitously and gratuitously, but not irrecoverably. For a hundred years the sands of Egypt have been yielding treasures of artistic, literary, and economic value. For twenty years the sands of coastal northern Africa, westward from the Nile to the southern pillar of Hercules across the strait from Gibraltar, have been returning to the pick and spade of the archaeologist the remnants of ruined houses with their mosaic floors, the foundations and shattered walls of basilicas, temples, and theatres, and therewith in shattered masonry the topography and history of many an ancient town.

Perhaps of all provincial sites of Roman power the one about which more inquiries are made than any other is Carthage. It was not a Roman site until, having been utterly destroyed by the Romans in 146 A.D., it was restored, about a century later, to the standing of a colony. But it never amounted to very much. Its glory had departed, and its commercial importance had been taken over by other cities. Kelsey of the University of Michigan did some good work there recently, especially in finding the sanctuary of Tanit. But not much of real importance has been unearthed. Carthage remains a monument to the lasting force of literary phrase and sentiment.

Carthage has ever held a striking place, however, in men's regard, whether as the greatest of the Phoenician colonies, or as the capital of the state that produced the mighty Hannibal, or as the occasion of vengeful Cato's constant phrase, *Carthago delenda est*, or as a memory of the terrific salt-sown vengeance of Rome in 146 B.C., or as the home of Dido, that great heroine of poetic tragedy. Vergil, in the *Aeneid*, the second greatest of the world's epics, has given Carthage an intangible but unbreakable hold on the sympathy and heart of the world. It is therefore small wonder that the excavations at Carthage, although small and unimportant as yet, have excited so much interest.

The Cyrenaica is the northward jutting hump of Africa, almost directly south of the island of Crete. The town of Cyrene was on the upper of two terraces of tableland at a height of 1,800 feet above the sea. It commanded a magnificent view over the eight miles of low-lying land to the blue Mediterranean. The chief natural production of the district was a plant called *silphium*, which was used in food for cattle just before they were sent to market. It was also an aperient, and from its juice an antiseptic was obtained which sold in Rome for its weight in silver.

Soon after the Archaeological Institute of America founded its second School of Classical Studies in Rome, a permit was obtained from the government of Turkey to excavate in the Cyrenaica at the site of the ancient Greek colony of Cyrene. The American School began its work, Richard Norton, then Director of the School, and Herbert De Cou being for the most part in charge of the dig. Then came the war between Turkey and Italy, which the latter won. Part of its indemnity was the Cyrenaica.

Soon after the war Italy announced a governmental policy of excluding foreigners from the privilege of excavating in Italian territory. When the Italians began to excavate at Cyrene, they began where we left off, and almost at once recovered the Venus of Cyrene. She, like the Venus di Milo, with whom some have fallen in love, and for whom others have acquired a passion, as Gautier has said, is the kind of marble that Pygmalion is said to have carved and fallen in love with to such a heavenly extent that the gods granted his prayer and let the firm cold marble turn under his loving fingers into soft warm flesh. And all this, notwithstanding the fact that several writers of late have found fault with her ankles, and one has even said she is a Roman copy. The heaviness of her feet and ankles would be expected, if she were to have stood, as the writer believes, behind an altar, and ten or twelve feet above the floor.

Courtesy of Comm. R. Paribeni, Rome

### EXCAVATIONS AT CYRENE

Italian excavations at Cyrene on the coast of north Africa. The fountain and sanctuary of Apollo are in the middle background, the Greek theatre is this side of it, and the steps belong to the temple of Apollo. In the foreground is a Byzantine Bath. The famous Venus, now the pride of the National Museum in Rome, was discovered at Cyrene.

The latest excavations have laid bare the most important of the terraces on which the ancient city of Cyrene was built. A complex of buildings has been found and partly excavated. Most of the work, however, has been directed to uncovering the sanctuary of Apollo, which includes a number of structures not all as yet identified. The temple and altar of Apollo, around which the rest of the buildings of the sanctuary cluster, have proven to be very important. It is clear that the temple in its original form was built of brick laid up between wooden beams.   As this is exactly the way the Minoan palaces in Crete were constructed, this discovery takes a high place in the material for study of the growth of early building methods.   The altar was 70 feet long, and in the fourth century A.D. it had been covered with marble.   Soon afterwards the spread of the power of Christianity reached Cyrene, and the worship of Apollo ceased.   The marble slabs that had decorated Apollo's altar were taken and put down as paving stones in a Byzantine bath.   But, by Byzantine oversight, and consequent archaeological good luck, one — and one only — marble block was left in its original place, *in situ*, as it is called.   With this piece as a starting point, many other blocks have been brought back, put in their original places, and thus, little by little, the ancient altar has been reconstructed.

*Courtesy of Comm. R. Paribeni, Rome*

JUPITER

IUPPITER OPTIMUS MAXIMUS

This magnificent head was found by the Italian archaeologists at Sabratha, the ancient Roman city now being excavated in Tripolitania on the coast of north Africa.  A pick accidentally struck the face, and the missing part of the nose could not be found.

Italian Tripolitania has tripped after Cyrene into the limelight.   With rapidity, but no faster than archaeological science allows, the Italians have dredged out of an ocean of Sahara sand two more outposts of ancient Roman dominion. About fifty miles west of Tripoli (the ancient *Oea*, where for many years an arch of Marcus Aurelius has been known) a city which had been ruined by the Arabs in 643 A.D. disclosed itself to the excavators as the Roman town of Sabratha.   Excavations have brought to light enough of the local amphitheatre so that its measurements make it second in Africa only to the amphitheatre of El-Djem, and only one-third smaller than the Colosseum at Rome. But even Sabratha must yield to Lepcis Magna. Out from under forty feet of protecting sand has come the imperial city in which the Roman emperor Septimius Severus was born. The wharves have lately come to light and their measurement gives Lepcis Magna the largest harbor along the north African coast. A basilica, the great public baths, another Severus arch, and numerous pieces of excellent relief sculpture are part of this great new Italian find. A number of statues have also been found, although none ranks with the Cyrene Venus. A rather good Apollo Musagetes, *i.e.*, as leader of the Muses, was discovered at the bottom of a flight of steps, one leg broken off at the ankle, the other at the knee, lying with lyre unbroken in his left arm and his face buried in the débris.

It should occasion even less wonder that the discovery of Lepcis the Great has created such a tremendous stir, for suddenly there has leaped, as it were, from out of the ground a fullgrown ancient city, the best preserved of all Roman colonial foundations thus far discovered, although not so extensive and not so impressive as either Timgad or Djemila (Cuicul).

Lepcis Magna has come back to life. It was on the Mediterranean coast less than 100 miles eastward from the modern Tripoli, and only a mile or so east of the present town of Homs. Along the left bank of the Wady Lebdah, which meanders northeastward through the rocks and sand until close to the Mediterranean shore, have been uncovered thus far a fine arch of Septimius Severus, the great city *Terme*, or Baths, and behind them a complex of perfectly preserved private dwelling houses. Northeastward of the Baths lies the Imperial Forum, across the seaward end of which stretched a splendid basilica. Between it and the coast lies the great Forum, as yet undug, and also a complex of Byzantine walls, a Christian basilica, and the exedra of Severus. On the right of Wady Lebdah is the as yet unexcavated harbor part of the town, although two small Baths on the seashore have been partly uncovered. More than a mile eastward is the great Circus, one long wall of which parallels the present coast line. Back of the Circus is the amphitheatre.

In 146 A.D. there was born at Lepcis the person fated to be its most illustrious citizen, although born of an equestrian family, Lucius Septimius Severus, later the emperor of Rome. It would appear that Severus visited his old home town in the year 203 A.D., and that he memorialized the occasion by bestowing upon Lepcis, as he did also upon Carthage and Utica, Italic rights (*ius Italicum*).

A PORTAL TO THE BATHS

The Italians are digging the ancient Roman provincial city of Lepcis Magna in north Africa free from the sand that has covered it for centuries. Two of the statues that decorated the great City Baths (*Thermae*) stand exactly as they were found.

Lepcis retained its importance until the westward drive of Amr. ibn el-Asi destroyed everything in his path. Now, thanks to the Italian government and its excellent scientific excavators, Pietro Romanelli and Renato Bartoccini, Lepcis Magna has risen from the ashes of the Arabs through the protecting sands of the Sahara into the light of modern archaeological day.

The tragic fate of Pompeii has a great deal to do with the fame enjoyed by that still partly buried city. Bulwer Lytton, with his widely read novel, added sentiment to its tragedy. Its vicinity to the Italian port of Naples, where the majority of tourists begin their Italian journey, has made Pompeii perhaps the most visited of all the sites of the ancient world. No one ever forgets the visit there or minimizes the effect the death-like city produces. About ten years ago the popularity of Pompeii was challenged by Ostia, once the seaport of Rome, which, under a vigorous excavating administration, began to rise out of the complex into which it settled after business deserted it for the new seaport at the Mediterranean end of the Tiber canal. Ostia used to be called the Roman Pompeii. Pompeii may become known as the Vesuvian Ostia.

Pompeii and Herculaneum were not buried in a flow of lava from Vesuvius. Somebody wrote that years ago, and many books have broadcast the statement. Ancient Italic towns were built on isolated hills or on the tips of ridges. When lava burst out of some volcanic mountain, it flowed around the hills and down the valleys. Of course, villages that dared the mountain side, then and now, were and are occasionally overwhelmed by a lava stream. Excavation, however, shows that it was volcanic mud and ashes that fell on Pompeii and Herculaneum. That mass settled in rain and by weight into a blanket of *scoriae* which is very hard and stony; but it is not lava.

Pompeii has been so much visited, so widely published, and so profusely illustrated, that it were supererogation to tell the long story of its slow excavation. But work has begun again in recent years and is now going forward with speed and success. The discovery of a new street which has been named the "Street of Abundance" has restored Pompeii to immediate importance. This street led through the hitherto unknown commercial quarter of the city, where rows of taverns, shops, and factories are now coming to light. Beautiful wall paintings with colors as fresh as the day they were laid on are showing new designs, and wall and panel creations portraying unique scenes of religious, mythological, and historical importance are being discovered nearly every week. Outside balconies, painted advertisements, curtain rods between the columns of peristyles, furniture of marble, oil presses, bake shops: such are a few of the new things lately found. In 1926 the find of the bronze statue made into a candelabrum (described on pages 17–18) was the most startling discovery of the year. In 1927 a bronze statuette of Apollo and a beautifully chiselled silver cup were the best of the art finds. More important historically, however, was the set of wall paintings in the house of Cornelius Tages, portraying Nilotic landscapes.   These are as good as the Barberini mosaic found years ago at Palestrina which pictures in colored stone the Nile and life along its banks.   Three fine new mythological scenes are also among the wall paintings in Tages' house: Hercules in the Garden of the Hesperides, the rescue of Andromeda, and the flight of Daedalus and Icarus.

Thirty years ago the world was on edge for the beginning of the excavation of Herculaneum.   It was noised about that the permission had been given by the Italian government to America, the work to be done under the direction of the School of Classical Studies at Rome, one of the foreign schools founded by the Archaeological Institute of America.   But something went wrong with the negotiations, and the plan fell through.

A month to the day after Titus had succeeded his father Vespasian on the Roman throne, Vesuvius broke forth on a hot August day in the year 79 A.D. and overwhelmed with its volcanic discharge the towns that lay below its southwestern slopes. Pompeii was covered with a shower of redhot ashes to a depth of about twenty feet.   Herculaneum was several miles nearer Vesuvius than was Pompeii, and over it there ran also streams of volcanic mud in which was some lava and considerable ashes. Six eruptions since then have sent more volcanic material over the site until Herculaneum is now buried to a depth of from 60 to 100 feet.

An Austrian governor, Prince d'Elboeu, digging a well in his villa at Portici in 1719, discovered the ruins of Herculaneum. But for a hundred years no scientific work was attempted. Occasionally some small dig was made and the pieces found were taken into the Naples Museum.   Part of the theatre was discovered; so was the fine horse in bronze which has been so often compared to the bronze horses of St. Mark's in Venice. In 1753 some 3,000 rolls of blackened and decayed papyri were found, and it was good luck that they were not thrown aside as charcoal.   Some were finally unrolled and deciphered.   The works were nearly all on Epicurean philosophy, many being by Philodemus, a writer mentioned by Cicero.

It was in 1828 when the discovery was made of a house on the walls of which were frescoes better preserved and with more brilliant colors than those found on the walls of the houses at Pompeii.   The painting known as "Argus and Io" is perhaps the most famous.   It gave to the house the designation "House of Argus," which we still see in the books.   The famous statues of the two wrestlers, so well known to art, were discovered in the garden of the Villa of the Papyri.

Work progressed fast under Spinazzola and Maiuri, who was put in charge in 1927.   During the early part of 1928, while workmen were removing thousands of cubic yards of earth over what seemed to be an important public building of the ancient city, many rooms were cleared near the House of the Skeleton.   In the painted atrium was found a bronze-footed marble table of unusual design.   A pink marble statuette of Paris and a bronze Lar are the best sculptural pieces found thus far.

Guido Calza is making a great success in excavating Ostia. His finds of the oak piles that were the substructure of the Via Ostiensis of the second century B.C., of many fine statues, his clearance of the great Baths and huge storage granaries, have verged on the sensational.   The history of Ostia must be re-written in the light of Calza's archaeological work.

The sun begins to blink as he notices each day that his glory is reflected in the ever diminishing Mirror of Diana.   Lake Nemi, in the Alban Hills near Rome, was called in ancient times the Mirror of Diana because that goddess had a temple high up on the rim above the gleaming surface of that circular lake.   It is now being lowered by means of a powerful electric pump which has discharged enough of the water, through the ancient tunnelled outlet, so that one of the two ancient court barges which have lain sunken there for nearly two thousand years is now entirely out of the water.   During the past fifty years divers have recovered various bronze decorations and mooring rings from the rotting hulks.   Mussolini is the power behind this novel sort of excavation.

The recent discovery of tombs near Canosa, the ancient Canusium, in south Italy, is of absorbing interest, because they have not been pillaged. Earrings, a foliated wreath, a necklace with pendants, and another in the form of serpent scales, a ring, and other jewelry, all of gold and gems, have been found with the skeleton of a woman. Other clinging remains show that she was buried in garments woven of thread of gold. These tombs are the first found in a cemetery which may prove to be a real gold mine.

A NOBLE ETRUSCAN LADY

A wall painting from an Etruscan tomb at Tarquinii. Note the almost Grecian profile, and her ivory beret.

The Etruscans are still the mystery of Italy. No one as yet has been able to read their language, despite the fact that all its letters are Greek and Latin. About 8,500 of their inscriptions are extant, although they are for the most part short epitaphs. In fact, only nine inscriptions are of any length. One of the longer ones, containing 150 words, was found written on the linen bands around an Egyptian mummy.

The paintings on the walls of Etruscan tombs are really moving pictures of the life of that great people. In many tombs, also, on the walls and supporting pillars are carved in relief weapons, armor, dogs and other animals, dishes, and implements of various kinds. On the tops of hundreds of small urns, in which the ashes of the dead were deposited, one can see, carved in miniature, the very people who had been cremated.

Although the Etruscans are as silent as sphinxes, archaeology is able to speak for them. We know they came by sea from Asia Minor to their future home in Italy because the earliest of their towns are on or near the sea coast. They brought with them skill in working metals, and many of their earliest pieces in bronze, gold, and silver show the influence of

Egyptian, and even more of Mesopotamian, handiwork. They came to upper western Italy because of the copper there, and because of the iron ore in the island of Elba, just off the coast. They came in small successive groups, much as came the Northmen to Scotland, as the peaceful penetration of the country proves. The superior technique of the newcomers impressed

*Courtesy of The Metropolitan Museum of Art*

**AN ETRUSCAN CHARIOT OF BRONZE**

A chariot of the VI century B.C. from Monteleone. It is of wood (now restored) with bronze sheathing worked in repoussé reliefs representing warlike scenes.

the earlier Villanovans; and the Etruscans, settling on the high hills, easily established lordship over the ancient settlers, as did the Normans in England over the Saxons.

It is clear that before the Etruscans came, the native coppersmiths had no technique of artistic decoration. They were still in what is archaeologically called the geometric stage of art. It is wholly unhistoric to claim any appreciable Greek influence on Etruscan work before the middle of the 7th century B.C. The marvelous silver gilt bowls and dishes from the Regolini-Galassi tomb at Caere, and from the Bernardini and Barberini tombs at Praeneste, are not Greek at all. They may have been made in Asia Minor and brought along to Etruria by colonizing artists. At all events they were original models for the artists in Etruria for nearly 200 years.

The Etruscans began to portray Greek mythological scenes, intermingled with their own, about 700 B.C. MacIver thinks it was an emancipation from formalism and that the Etruscan artists of the succeeding century were working along the same lines as the later school of Giotto. It is not hard to recognize Greek influence when it begins in Etruscan art. The stylisms of Corinth came into prominence from 650 to 600 B.C., followed by the new methods and technique of Attica. It is partly by means of these vases that Etruscologists prove the northward colonization of Etruria. Toward the end of the sixth century B.C. they sent, among other colonies, one to Felsina (Bologna). There we have the clearest archaeological evidence in the world. The early inhabitants (who are called Villanovans from the modern Italian town of Villanova, five miles from Bologna) came from the northeast, from the Danube country, in the eleventh century B.C. Their earliest tombs are just outside the old city wall, and interments were made farther and farther out, as dateable grave contents prove. The Etruscan colony founded nearby fixed its cemetery at another spot separated from that of the earlier Villanovans by a clear space of fifty-six meters and a boundary ditch. Further, in the Etruscan cemetery have been found many Greek vases and *stelae*, but nothing earlier than 500 B.C.

Archaeology has shown that Italy was inhabited from prehistoric times by people of the Mediterranean race. From 3000 to 2000 B.C., approximately, a people who were akin to the lake dwellers of Switzerland infiltrated northern Italy, only to be overrun by successive groups of barbarians from the Danube region, who knew the use of copper. These people, called Villanovans, were as far south as Bologna by 1100 B.C., but by 850 B.C. were no farther south than central Italy. About 950 or 900 B.C. the Etruscans, sailing from Asia Minor, began to land on the upper western coast of Italy, because of the copper and iron ore in Tuscany and Elba. After gaining control of that territory by virtue of their superior culture, they began to extend their power, north into the valley of the Po, and south into Latium and Campania. By 500 B.C. they were the lords of most of Italy. Perhaps at that time they began to grow overconfident, perhaps it was because of a sort of Hellenic or Polish inability to "get together" at a crisis; at all events, when the Gauls from the north, the Romans from the south, and the Greeks from the sea, all began to attack them, the Etruscan ship of State shivered, shook, subsided, and sank.

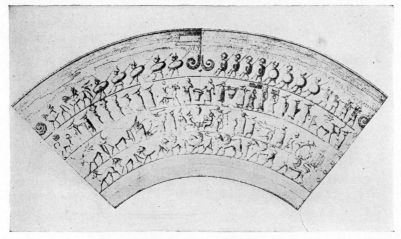

HISTORY ON A BUCKET

The funeral procession of an Etruscan nobleman portrayed on a bronze bucket, the famed Certosa *situla*.

Etruscology is a great archaeological subject in itself. From the thousands of wonderful Etruscan objects that have been found we shall describe the best one discovered in recent years. It is a pictorial bronze bucket.

This Certosa bucket (*situla*) dates from about 500 B.C. On it are figures in relief that portray the funeral procession of an Etruscan being buried with military honors. The procession is headed by two men on spirited horses. Behind them come representatives of four different infantry divisions. Five spearmen wearing strangely knobbed helmets and carrying shields of oval shape follow directly behind the horsemen. Then come eight warriors with crested helmets, four carrying quadrangular and four carrying circular shields. These thirteen spearmen, detailed from three infantry detachments, all carry their spears points down, much as modern infantry under like circumstances carry rifles at reverse. Next come four warriors wearing conical helmets and carrying over their shoulders a single bitted axe with a wide blade, exactly like those which have been found in the tombs.

This military part of the funeral procession is separated from the sacrificial and family section by a big dog, probably the master's pet, who with his tail curled over his back, brings up the rear. Preceding the dog are a man with a bronze jug on his back and a bronze jar in his hand; three servant women carrying bronze water jars on their heads; three men enveloped in long cloaks; a man servant leading a ram; two men servants carrying by its handle a large bronze bucket; two men carrying a *situla*, exactly like the one on which the designs being described are embossed, by means of a pole on their shoulders, which has been passed through the bronze ring handles of the *situla*; three servant women, one carrying a bundle of faggots, one a bronze vessel coopered with two heavy bands, and the third a basket; and, finally, a splendid bull for the sacrifice. The women wear long cloaks hooded over their heads, leaving only the faces uncovered. The men, who must be relatives, wear, in addition to mantles that cover them to their ankles, large hats with upturned brims. Such is the funeral procession.

The relief also shows the life on the master's estate. His farmer, plow on shoulder and whip in hand, drives to the field two sturdy oxen. Facing the other way, the master, behind whom comes a servant dragging a freshly killed pig, steps forward toward a great bronze couch on which two of his family, or friends, are performing a duet, one blowing the syrinx, the other thrumming a harp. The ends of the couch are lions' heads from the gaping jaws of which hang the upper half of partly eaten boys. On each lion's head stands a small bronze statue. Beyond this musical scene a servant with a ball-headed stick drives a rabbit into a net. Behind him two servants carry on a pole a deer freshly slung from the hunt. Beneath

the deer walks the same dog seen above in the funeral procession. The men have come to a stop while the master takes a
dipper and puts it into a bronze wine jar to get the wherewithal to slake his thirst. This bucket gives a wonderful picture with such a multitude of multifarious details of Etruscan
life and art of 500 B.C., such a wealth of inferential facts, such

*From an engraving by Piranesi*

A TIBER WHARF

Visitors to Rome gasped in amazement when they landed from the Tiber boats
to see the capital of the ancient world.

a plethora of circumstantial evidence, that this sketchy word
picture could be enlarged many times and there would still
remain plenty to see and to be explained.

But despite the scores of sites now being excavated in Italy
and the Italian colonial possessions, Rome continues to be the
focal spot of archaeological interest. Archaeologists have
recently traced the trek of peoples from north central Africa
across Gibraltar and around the Spanish and French coast
into Italy. By finds of pottery and houseware, by discoveries
of cremation burials, by bronze implements and weapons, ar

chaeologists have traced later invaders into Italy from the northeast; by settlements chronologically fixed by the relics of their past, the Etruscans are shown to have arrived in Italy by sea from the east. Archaeology has dug up facts in artifacts that compel historians to rewrite entirely the history of pre-Roman Italy. By virtue of conquest and then of attraction, Rome was the greatest magnet of antiquity. It still remains the magnetic spot of Roman archaeology.

Livy and Tacitus, and all other Romans, believed that their city had been founded by Romulus in 754 B.C. They did not know as much about themselves as we do, due to the discoveries of our archaeologists. The cemetery found by Boni alongside the Sacred Way in the Forum contained objects much older than any dated things from early Rome. Some years later a cemetery containing objects of the same sort was found near the Alban Hills under a lava stream, which geologists dated as earlier than 900 B.C. Both cemeteries, therefore, because of their distance from their city gates, were probably earlier than 1000 B.C. The history of Rome took a backward leap of two hundred and fifty years.

Rome might not have left much for archaeologists to find if the Roman legions had not overrun the world. Fabulous wealth in booty and in adulatory gifts poured into the city on the Tiber. No other city of the ancient world ever dressed itself so magnificently to play a lordly part. Julius Caesar was a great builder, but Augustus was the first real architect of Rome. It was said that he had found Rome brick and left it marble. After each successive fire, and they were many, Rome rose more glorious from its ashes. The hundreds of temples, baths, circuses, and stadia, the miles of porticoes, the scores of arches, private gardens, public buildings, and palaces made Rome a marvel of structural grandeur. Niches, columns, arches, temples, fora, held or supported thousands of the most beautiful statues of bronze and marble bought or taken from the conquered world. Fourteen obelisks of granite transported from Egypt stood in as many stadia on the *spinae* round which the chariots raced. But after five hundred years of overweening pride of possession came the deluges of barbarians, the reign of turmoil, the drear desolation of medievalism. Some monuments were too big to be overthrown; but most of them fell or were thrown down in stratified ruin. The débris of ages buried them ever deeper until modern archaeologists came to their rescue.

Courtesy of the University of Michigan Expedition          Photograph by G. R. Swain

UPPER PART OF THE ROME FORUM

Looking across the Forum over the House of the Vestal Virgins to the imperial palace substructures on the northwest corner of the Palatine hill. Under the sloping roof near the lower righthand corner of the picture is the spot where the body of Julius Caesar was burnt in 44 B.C.

The clearance of the Circus Maximus has begun. Unsightly medieval structures are being pulled away from many of the ancient buildings in the Campus Martius. Nineteen courses of the substructure of the temple of Jupiter found on the Capitoline Hill under the Caffarelli palace go back to the original temple built by the Etruscan Tarquins when they ruled Rome. The paintings in an underground room in the Viale Manzoni done in the time of Septimius Severus and camouflaged as gnostic revelations have turned out to represent the Sermon on the Mount. The hidden cross was found by Wilpert. Among the figures of the Apostles is the earliest representation in painting of St. Peter.  The underground basilica beyond the Porta Maggiore becomes more interesting with each new interpretation of its decorations and ancient use.  The House of Livia on the Palatine is now found to be the older mansion of the Hortensii which was purchased by Augustus.  The late excavations by Bartoli in the palace of Domitian on the Palatine, and the researches of Lugli, are bringing to light more evidences of the architectural magnificences of that emperor.  Ashby, for many years director of the British School of Archaeology in Rome, has fixed the lava-topped radiating roads of Roman dominion fast to the gates of the Servian wall that surrounded the ancient Seven Hills.

The programme for archaeology in Rome is a long one.  Much work has already been done on Nero's Golden House, from some of the lower vaults of which medieval artists, lowered through holes in the ceilings, got many designs both for their painting and stucco work.  The Altar of Peace of Augustus (*Ara Pacis*) is to be restored.  It is believed that some of the original pieces now in foreign museums will be returned to Rome, an archaeological gesture of great international import.  The great Baths of Diocletian are to be entirely cleared and will house the National Museum, formerly known as the *Terme*.  The so-called Court Church now occupies one of the former great halls of the Roman Baths.  The work of Comm. Roberto Paribeni in the National Museum is no small part of Rome's archaeological programme.

One cannot mention Roman archaeology apart from the great names of Lanciani, Huelsen, Boni, Ashby, Mrs. Strong, Paribeni, and Rostovtzeff.  But it is matter for pride that the foremost Roman archaeologist is an American woman, Dr. Esther B. Van Deman, Carnegie Research Professor in the University of Michigan.  Her early work on the House of the Vestals set those canons of concrete and brick-faced construction on which all Roman archaeologists rely in dating structures of the imperial age.  Her work on the Rostra and on Caligula's palace put them in the category of solved problems.  Her work on the Neronian Sacra Via is perhaps the neatest piece of scientific archaeology ever done in Rome. She has brought the seemingly unrelated and wildly confused mass of ruins extending from the Atrium Vestae and the Regia up to the Arch of Titus out of an inexplicable limbo into two sets of arcades flanking an avenue one hundred feet wide which led straight up from the Forum to the vestibule of the Golden House of Nero.

*Photograph by R. V. D. Magoffin*

A FORUM COMPLEX

The ruins in front of the Arch of Titus cover one of the two porticoes that flanked the Sacred Way as reconstructed by Nero to make a monumental approach to his Golden House. This discovery was made by Professor Esther B. Van Deman.

In the pocket below three of the hills which later made famous the "City of the Seven Hills" there was in early times a lake. The Roman youths who drove their cows down from the Palatine hill to water the milk naturally looked both with earnestness and eagerness upon the daughters of the Sabines who drove down the family herds for the same purpose from the Quirinal hill. Such was probably the homely and pastoral but sentimental beginning of what Roman and later history canonized under the caption "The Rape of the Sabines." At all events, when the Romans and Sabines became reconciled to each other because of the *cherchez la femme* bond that drew them together, they drained the lake into the Tiber river. In its stead there was soon a market place. This gave way to successive building "booms" until the place became the great Roman Forum, *Forum Romanum* or *Forum Magnum*.

Rome had outgrown its Forum by the time of Julius Caesar, who opened a new forum adjoining the old one, which he called after himself, Forum Julium. His successor, Augustus, added a second one, the Forum Augusti, with its Hall of Fame. By the time of the accession of the Flavian emperors, some fifty years later, a third forum was necessary. It was called the Forum of Vespasian or the Forum of Peace, and inside its walls the emperor built not only the Temple of Peace but also filled the Forum with such objects of art that it became the greatest museum of the day. Vespasian's son Domitian began a fourth Forum between those of his father and Augustus, but did not live to see it completed. It was finished by his successor, the emperor Nerva. A little later Trajan then built the fifth and last ancient Roman Forum, to which Hadrian made additions.

*Courtesy of Boston Museum of Fine Arts*

A REAL ROMAN

A head in terra cotta of a typical Roman of the governing class.

The Romans were immensely proud of those Fora, for in them the traditions of the past were enshrined by the art and in the architecture of the progressive present. But Rome fell upon hard times after Constantine moved the political and religious administration to Byzantium on the Bosphorus. Little by little fire and flood, neglect and decay, defaced and undermined the monuments of former greatness and the heavy hand of medieval barbarian well-nigh completed the destruction of ancient Rome. The columns of Trajan and Antoninus Pius topped with Christian saints, two or three triumphal arches, a few temple columns here and there, protruded from the ground and stood forlorn in neglected isolation.

When Goethe visited Rome 150 years ago, the former site of Rome's ancient Forum was so forgotten that the German poet walked around in the Campo Vaccino (cow pasture) and

J. V. Falke

A restoration

THE ROMAN FORUM

Looking toward the Capitoline. The later Fora are back of the buildings at the right.

mused over fallen Rome, not knowing at all that the Forum Romanum was twenty feet or so beneath his feet. It was not until after 1870 that any real work was done on the excavation of that old municipal center. But now the Roman Forum is the pride of modern Rome and the first and greatest sight it has to show to the traveler and tourist. And of the myriads who tread the spot where for a thousand years trod the mighty men of Rome, none comes away unmoved.

It has been the dream of modern Rome to see these imperial Fora excavated, and for years work looking toward the realization of that dream has been going forward steadily and carefully under the best archaeological direction.  Mussolini has been an ardent supporter of the archaeologists in this project.  The work of clearing away the houses on the area of the Fora is now done, and the municipal centre of ancient Rome has again come into its own.  One may walk down from the Arch of Titus on the Sacred Way past the vast "giant porches" of Constantine's basilica, past the spot where the body of Julius Caesar was burned, and, turning in front of the Rostra from which Cicero spoke, go past the senate house into and through the newly opened areas of the Fora graced by the temples of Minerva and Mars the Avenger on to the column toward the far end of the Forum of Trajan.  Then it is only a step to modern archaeology.  Against the Capitoline hill rises the gigantic Altar of Modern Italy, the magnificent architectural background for the equestrian statue of King Victor Emmanuel II whose gaze looks straight ahead along the ancient Roman Broad Street (*via Lata*), the modern Corso, where thousands of years ago Roman armies marched through strewn and pelting flowers toward Rome's holy hill.

## A ROMAN PORTRAIT IN BRONZE

The John Huntington Collection in the Cleveland Museum possesses in this realistic portrait of the first century A.D., done perhaps by a Greek artist in Rome, one of the finest of extant bronzes. The eyes were originally of glass or semi-precious stones, and of course were stolen. The surface of the bronze was much corroded when found, but was restored by **Dr. Colin Fink** of Columbia University with his electro-chemical process.

148

## CHAPTER SEVEN

## ADVENTURES IN ANTIQUITY

INCIDENTALS of archaeology we shall class roughly as unique and unrelated finds, as objects which throw unexpected light on later history, and as hoaxes or forgeries. Such incidentals are interesting, but they do not lend themselves to easy inclusion in a running narrative; their importance, however, would seem to justify their story, even at the risk of making a somewhat disconnected chapter.

Out in Afghanistan at Hadda, at the end of the Kabul valley, the French have excavated thirteen of fifty known ancient sites, and have found thousands of statues and statuettes. They have cleared out more than five hundred funerary Buddhist sanctuaries (*stupas*) and have found them strangely indebted to Hellenistic influences. Sometimes they are adorned with Buddhas, many of which wear Greek draperies, but crouching classical Atlantes and Cupids are also found. The art also is independent of Hindu influence; Greek artists must have gone there in the wake of Alexander the Great. The costumes and coiffures are important, because they picture many new types of Scythians and other barbarians.

In the British Museum there is a fragment of a clay tablet, found at Kish in Mesopotamia in 1924, which completes the astronomical series of the risings and settings of the planet Venus during the twenty-one years of the reign of Ammizaduga, the tenth king of the first Babylonian dynasty. To be compared with this astronomical inscription is the chart of the heavens represented on the ceiling of the tomb of Senmut, the architect of Queen Hatshepsut. Orion and Sothis are shown in their position in relation to the stars in the southern skies. An ancient terrestrial map of the third century A.D. was found lately near Damascus. It is on a fragment of a shield of skin that had belonged to a Palmyrene archer. The sea and rivers are painted on it in blue, the land in red. The itinerary written on it in Greek shows that the archer had combined business with biography and statistics. He had listed carefully the stages he marched, with the intervening mileage.

Courtesy of the Metropolitan Museum of Art

SENMUT'S STAR CEILING

A photograph of part of the ceiling of the tomb of Senmut, the architect of Queen Hatshepsut of Egypt. Orion and Sothis are shown in their relative position to the stars in the southern skies.

An announcement was made not long ago by a foreign firm of world-famed makers of glass that they had *discovered* the method of making perfectly clear yellow-white glass. Only a few weeks later their glass idol was rudely shattered. In the stratum of the second century B.C. of an ancient city in the Fayum in Egypt, excavators discovered a complete unbroken dinner set of clear yellow-white glass of more than one hundred fifty pieces. The danger in announcing a discovery is illustrated nicely in this case. The glass firm ought to have felt more chagrined even over their discovery than did the writer after he paid a rather tidy sum for a rare Greek coin and then saw the bottom drop out of its value when a few weeks later a pot full of the same issue of money was dug up in Egypt.

Egypt has yielded lately a succession of unique treasures. Papyri have commanded perhaps the greatest interest. Among them are a letter in hieratic (hieroglyphic shorthand) dating about 2000 B.C., with official epistolary formulae; part of a model letter to be used by scribes when writing to officials; and a lot of business contracts. Some interesting pieces of faïence ware which came to light were a checker or gaming counter in the form of an Arab petting a gazelle, a caricature of a monkey riding a horse, and a relief with part of a procession of blindfolded men, perhaps a representation of an initiation into some hieroglyphic letter fraternity. A figure with the head of a dog playing on a harp, an ape-headed man drinking out of a bottle, and a man playing on a double flute or pipe are three other unique faïence toys.

The mysterious and deadly bug that is said to bite the foreign archaeologists who find scarabs, sacred bulls and crocodiles, mastabas, and Tutankhamens belongs to the hoaxes of Egypt. Nothing is said of the hundreds of archaeologists who come safely away from Egypt; much is said of a Carnarvon who dies. The fetid closeness of those Pharaonic tomb shafts, and the rays of Ra, the Egyptian sun god, constituted the Nemesis that overtook the fatigued, overwrought, and naturally frail Lord Carnarvon.

The English Captain Alexander Hardcastle, who has lived for many years at Girgenti in Sicily, has contributed royally at various times to archaeological excavations, and has himself engaged in several digs. In 1928 he measured the distance between certain ancient wheel tracks of the fourth century B.C. The inside tread between the iron tires was exactly 4 feet 8½ inches. Other wheel tracks near Viterbo in Italy had been found also with the same inside tread. In Malta the prehistoric cart tracks are also of the same width. Railroad engineers ought to be able to connect themselves to a long ancestry.  That ancient tread is the same width as the standard modern railway gauge.

History tells us that Mesopotamia and Egypt fought each other for centuries for the domination of the Near East world. Archaeology tells us that they carried on a battle royal also to see whether the cuneiform writing of Mesopotamia with its clay tablet and stylus or the hieroglyphic writing of Egypt with its roll of papyrus and reed pen and ink were to win the "battle of the books."  The Tel el-Amarna letters of about 1400 B.C. on tablets of clay written to the Egyptian Pharaoh were in the Mesopotamian style of writing.  Thousands of square yards of wall both in Mesopotamia and Egypt are covered with engraved cuneiform and hieroglyphic.  There is a famous joke penned by Macaulay, who said, "It is recorded that Pharonezzar, the Assyrian Pindar, published a bridge and four walls in praise of King Gomer Chephoraod."

Perhaps the pertinacity of the Egyptians in holding on to their system of writing is to be explained by one of their somewhat widely spread beliefs.  It was thought that one could obtain learning if he would wash the writing off sheets or rolls of papyrus with beer, and then drink it.  Prince Naneperkaptah took just such a drink after he had washed the magic book of Thoth.  Some people will probably think he ought to have known better; others that he ought to have known more.

Archaeological objects do not lie.  Even "faked" antiquities do not lie.  They may deceive for a time, but the truth of their falsity is there for the seeing eye, and sooner or later they are all seen through.  Forgeries are legion and even the experts are occasionally fooled.  The forging of ancient documents and inscriptions to prove some contested or desired point is a well-authenticated matter of modern history, just as the forging of modern letters and signatures is a well-known matter of the present-day law courts.

The recent report that the tomb of the great Genghis Khan had been found, imposed upon several papers abroad, much to their later natural chagrin.  Every now and then the report of the discovery in Canada or the United States of a tablet inscribed with the ancient runic characters of Scandinavia is carried in the press.  Thus far they have been shown by scientific examination to be either forgeries or tracings some of which resembled accidentally runic characters.  A generation ago a traveling showman in the South made considerable money by imposing upon many persons a petrified giant until such time as it was discovered to be a figure of concrete which he had molded, buried for a time, and then discovered.

The finds in France a few years ago at Glozel imposed upon several scholars of note, and the proof that they were planted modern forgeries is still a very sore point in some quarters. The forgeries of Dossena, whose statues fooled the experts in several of our greatest museums, is a matter of very recent memory.  The Metropolitan Museum has a room devoted to forgeries.  On the other hand some objects, over the authenticity of which a great discussion arose, were quite absolved of doubt as to their genuineness.

The sculptured slabs in the Boston Museum of Fine Arts, known as the Ludovisi throne, were attacked at first quite savagely as forgeries.  L. D. Caskey of that Museum and Miss Richter of the Metropolitan Museum gave the reliefs searching analyses from the points of view of material, technique, style, and spirit.  They exploded the theory of forgery in masterly fashion to the satisfaction of all connoisseurs.

Tradition and sentiment together are a combination which can be opened by a turn of fact or by a turn of fancy.  Both sentiment and tradition were tremendously moved some years ago when it was announced that the inner vessel of a chalice said to have been found at Antioch was probably the very cup used by Christ at the Last Supper.  Small wonder indeed that vast interest was aroused!  Nor should there be any wonder that the question of authenticity became paramount at once. To have such a chalice as this one turn out to be a hoax would be to bring discredit upon something which to many people is almost sacred in character.  The most noticeable point in regard to this chalice, however, is that as soon as its discovery was announced it changed almost immediately from a possible object of religious veneration to an object the genuineness of which had first to be guaranteed by scientific archaeological investigation.

The "Great Chalice," on a low base of solid silver, is an ovoid bowl of crude unfinished silver with a shell of soldered ornamentation over it. This ornamentation is an intricate design of grape vines so trained and looped as to provide space for twelve seated figures. A band of rosettes, of which one was interpreted as a star, runs round the top of the chalice. The two central figures on opposite sides of the cup were interpreted as Christ. One has a lamb at his right. It was soon noted that the figures called Christ did not wear Jewish dress or the Greek *pallium*, but the toga of a Roman citizen. In fact, everything about the chalice has been given analyses that are searching and critical. Perhaps no single piece claimed as an antique has had more careful consideration; certainly no find has better demonstrated the need and value of comparative scholarship. The oxide of silver encrustation seems to have satisfied all who have examined the chalice that it is a real antique. A few first-rate scholars attribute it to the late first century A.D.; one or two would put it as late as the sixth century. The weight of authority at present puts it in the third century A.D. But much water will yet run under the mill before an agreement is reached as to the interpretation of the figures and as to the use of the cup.

Inscriptions are archaeological objects of the utmost historical value. The photographic copying of the Egyptian hieroglyphic inscriptions by Breasted and the members of the Oriental Institute of the University of Chicago will fix for good and all thousands of square yards of historical and religious texts the misreading of which would be deplorable and the loss of which would be irreparable.

In the higher Assyrian and Babylonian levels of the Mesopotamian valley, near Nineveh, there were found in 1928 some fragments of a new edition of Ashurbanipal's annals, engraved in prism cylinders. On one fragment is an account of the first war carried on by that king, and it gives new facts that allow some legitimate changes in the dating of the affairs of the reign.

The laws of Hammurabi (the Amraphel of Scripture), the Greek dialects, the tribute lists of the Delian League, the dates and names of the Athenian magistrates called archons, the Roman calendar, the stations of Roman legions and separate troop details, the locations of scores of monuments and build-

*Courtesy of David M. Robinson*

GRECIAN COSTUMES

Tanagra figurines of terra cotta authenticate hundreds of ancient Greek costumes with their varied and stately styles of drapery.

ings, to mention only a few cases, are all guaranteed and authenticated to historical research by inscriptions, sometimes by a mere fragment of one.

The discovery of a gold safety pin in Italy at Palestrina, the famous *fibula Praenestina*, with the four words, *manios med fhefhaked numasioi*, engraved in the bar, gave occasion for hundreds of pages of comment on the forms of the Latin of the sixth century B.C. The knowledge gleaned from other inscriptions in bronze letters, as to how many nails were used and where, in order to attach the metal letters, made it possible to restore the deleted lines of an inscription on the arch of Septimius Severus in the Roman Forum simply by the empty nail holes which a Roman emperor, in removing every trace of his brother's name from public record, did not realize could be read by some future archaeologist.

College students of Latin usually read a poem written by the poet laureate Horace for the centennial celebration of the secular games at Rome. There is in the National Museum in Rome a piece of inscribed marble that was put up soon after the games as a memorial tablet. One line reads Q. HORATIUS CARMEN CONPOSUIT, i.e., *Quintus Horatius composed the ode.*

Persons of consequence who came to Delphi to consult the oracle of the god Apollo usually left a present of some kind. After a time, many of the Greek city-states built beautiful little treasure houses on the terraced slope of Delphi to contain the valuable gifts which were deposited as offerings to the god. A fragment of a Greek inscription found at Delphi as long ago as 1907 has just been published with a scholarly discussion. In the first place, the form of the letters dates the inscription at about 350 B.C. There remains only part of the letters in thirteen lines and no more than nine letters in any line. The seven letters in line 6 (to latinize the Greek) are *alyakto*, which gives a known form of the name of Alyattes, a king of Lydia. With this as a clue, the French savant Reinach shows that this line and the next refer to the weight of a silver bowl dedicated by that king. The next two lines give enough to certify to some object of gold that had been dedicated by the Lacedaemonians; the next line gives the last part of a word that means *bronze* and the first part of a word that names the *Magnetes*, a people living in a town on the Meander river in Asia Minor. Out of these very fragmentary words Reinach shows that the entire inscription was an inventory of the objects dedicated at Delphi which had been confiscated by the Phocians in the Second Sacred War (354–346 B.C.). But such is the stuff that epigraphical archaeology is made of.

The first piece of Greek marble was brought to England by the Earl of Arundel and Charles I (through his admiral, Sir Kenelm Digby). Now the British Museum is full of such marbles. In Samothrace in 1863 the French vice-consul discovered some two hundred fragments of marble and sent them to Paris.   Six years later, near the end of the colonnade where the earlier fragments had been found, there came to light more of the same sort of broken pieces, with a block of the base on which a statue had stood. When the pieces were put together they made the prow of a marble war-ship.   This and the statue matched the figure stamped on one side of coins which Demetrius Poliorcetes had had struck to commemorate his naval battle off Salamis in Cyprus in the year 306 A.D.   Such are the archaeological reasons why the beautiful Victory of Samothrace in the Louvre at Paris is correctly restored.

Earlier in this book it was stated that ancient statuary was painted.   The thousands of terra-cotta Tanagra figurines without color could be repainted on the basis of the hundreds more recently found which are painted.   Within the past decade many pieces of marble statuary have also come out of the ground that have not only painted garments but also many traces of paint inside the ears, and in the undercutting of the hair.

*Louvre, Paris*

THE VICTORY OF SAMOTHRACE

One side of the coin, below, proves the original base of this famous statue, and shows also that she was represented as blowing a trumpet.

In 1928 a fragmentary head of a Zeus of Phidian type of the best Greek period was found at Cyrene in north Africa.   Many traces of gilding are left on the hair and beard.

There has never been any doubt about the correctness of the attribution to the sculptor Praxiteles of the statue of the Hermes found at Olympia in 1877.  To that certain attribution must now be added the head of a bearded Zeus, four times life size, which was discovered recently in the temple of Aegira in Achaea.  It is incontestably the very head of the statue seen and mentioned by Pausanias, and attributed by him to the Attic sculptor Euclides.

In the fourth century A.D., even after repeated robberies and lootings, there were still in Rome thousands of statues of bronze and marble.  In the fifteenth century there were visible and known in Rome only *five* marble statues, and *one* equestrian statue in bronze.  In the early middle ages bronze statuary was utilized for altar screens and such like, and marble statuary made a good lime mortar; which is sufficient comment on the artistic appreciation of those sorry times.  The bronze Chimaera at Florence, with its lion's head, its goat's body, and its snake tail, was discovered in the twelfth or thirteenth century.  Its appearance aroused a superstitious terror, however, that outweighed its metal value, and it was reburied.  It was discovered again at Arezzo in 1553 A.D., and hailed as a treasure of ancient art, for by that date civilization had again awakened in the Italian *Rinascimento* (a better word than the French word *Renaissance*).

In 1927 fishermen off Marathon caught a beautiful bronze statue of an athlete.  It is now one of the treasures of the Museum in Athens.  In 1928 a bronze hand came up in the net of some fishermen off the northern point of the Greek island of Euboea.  Fish were forgotten.  Soon the men were rewarded by the discovery and recovery from the bottom of the sea of a bearded bronze statue, eight feet in height.  The head was encrusted with seashells.  After they were removed the statue was recognized as a magnificent example of the best work of the middle of the fifth century B.C.  It represents Zeus, or in Latin, Jupiter.  It has already assumed its place among the ancient sculptured elect.  Later, there were also recovered from the same place the fore part of a bronze horse, his foreleg, neck, and

### AN EQUINE MASTERPIECE

Bronze statuette of a horse, Greek, of about 480–470 B.C.  Perhaps the most important piece (from an artistic point of view), in the Metropolitan's Classical collection.  It has the combination of realism and stylization that give to Greek sculpture of the first half of the fifth century B.C. its distinctive character.

head thrust forward as if straining in a race.   This idea was substantiated by the recovery also of the bronze statue of a boy holding the handle of a whip in his left hand.   The spreading posture of his legs would seem rather to show that he was riding a race than that he was driving a chariot.   For that reason he has been called "The Jockey."   These pieces are of the Hellenistic age, a century and a half at least later than the Zeus, which lends color to the belief that the pieces were part of the cargo of a ship that foundered at or near the Euboean cape.

At Ur in Mesopotamia there has just been found a miniature lady of white marble, about nine inches high, which is
undoubtedly a portrait statue.    She is a delightful personage,
with a dress that came to her knees, with hair bunched over
her ears as was the style a few
years ago, and with a most en-
gaging smile upon her face.

It is believed that there are
many unknown objects of antiquity reposing in the basements of the Vatican.    That
this belief is well founded is
shown by the discovery there
not long ago, by Amelung (recently deceased) of the German
school, of a head from one of
the metopes of the Parthenon,
a replica of the head of Harmodius, a replica of a head of
Athena from Myron's group
with Marsyas, and a Praxitelean head of Aphrodite.    At
the present rate of discovery,
the archaeologists will soon
have repeopled the museums
of the world with ancient
statues.

*Frankfort-on-Main*

ATHENA

It is believed that this is the head of the
Athena from the group of Athena and
Marsyas made by the Greek sculptor
Myron.

In clearing away the old wall on the Acropolis hill at Athens,
which Themistocles about 500 years B.C. had to build very
hurriedly with anything that came to hand, there was found
in the débris two marble bases with sculptured reliefs on them.
One of them shows a fine fight between a dog and a cat.    But
the other portrays the start of a real struggle.    In the center
stand two young men, hockey sticks in hand, the ball on the
ground between the sticks, and the referee about to give the
signal for the game to begin.

Our boys whip tops at the regular top season.    We thought,

until a few years ago, that the boys in ancient times did not
know that sport.   In the Johns Hopkins museum in Baltimore there is now an ancient Greek cup, or cylix, that was
painted and fired some 2,500 years ago.   In the center of its
bowl is a picture of two persons, a man and a boy, with some
sort of object on the ground between them.   The man holds

*Courtesy of The Johns Hopkins Archaeological Museum*

A SPINNING TOP

A man holding a stick to which three strips of leather are attached (not visible
in the photograph) is whipping a big wooden top.   The young man makes
either a gesture of surprise or is directing the man how to whip it.

a short stick, from which hang three little black painted strips.
They represent leather.   The object on the ground is a big
wooden top.   The man is whipping it, and it spins there as
nicely as any top of the most modern make.

But the ancient Greek or Roman boy did not know the luxury of that greatest juvenile necessity, a pocket knife?   Didn't
he, though!   There have come to many of our museums in
the last few years, from the recent excavations, scores of ancient pocket knives, a good many with the blades of bronze still
in them.   Even if our knife blades are a bit better than those of
two or three thousand years ago, the handles of bone and ivory

on the ancient knives are more beautiful than ours.   A handle
of ivory on one is carved to represent the figure of an Atlas,
another represents a full-armed gladiator, another is like a fish,
and so on for scores of different handles of beautiful shapes.   Ancient footrules have been found in France, Italy, and Switzerland.   An ivory rule found recently at Brugg is divided on one
side into twelve inches, and on the other side into four marked
spaces of three inches each.   A beautiful set of surgical instruments of bronze of the first century A.D. was found some years

HOCKEY 2,600 YEARS AGO

A sculptured slab; companion piece to the Dog and Cat match.   It seems strange
to find that Greek boys of 600 B.C. played our supposedly modern games.

ago at Colophon.   They are now at Johns Hopkins University.
There are several other sets also in European museums.

A half century ago a fortune was made by the invention of
the safety pin.   Some ancient person will rise from the dead
one of these times and sue for accumulated royalties.   The
safety pins in bronze, in silver, and in gold, with pin, bow, catch,
and all — except that all the thousand varieties are artistic
in shape without losing safety value — are now by the hundreds in every good museum, and many of them go back in
date a thousand years more B.C. than we are since.

But of course we beat those ancients in the pride of our
civilization, waterworks and sewers?   If digging them up and
keeping them in public view is the criterion, we certainly do,

The excavations of Sir Arthur Evans at Cnossus in Crete laid
bare a sewerage system of some 2,500 years or so B.C. about as
good as ours of today.   The lead water pipes in Pompeii and
Ostia are only 2,000 years old.   Yet in one of the houses in the
Street of Abundance at Pompeii which was excavated only last
summer, you can turn on the ancient faucet, just like ours,

*Vatican Museum, Rome*

SEVEN COME ELEVEN

A painting on an ancient Greek vase signed by Execias shows Achilles (left)
and Ajax (right) casting dice.   Achilles calls out "Four!" and Ajax "Three!"
as the letters in front of their mouths show.

and the fountains will play for you from the same openings
through which the water sprayed or shot, two millennia ago.

It begins to look as if we do nothing that those ancients
also did not know how to do.   Painted Greek vases show that
they "shot craps," that they played checkers and parchesi,
that they had perfect form in leg action in the sprints and the
distance races, that they threw the discus, that they used knucks
instead of gloves in boxing, that they wore clothes as short, as
brilliantly colored, and as diaphanous as any that show off the
dancer, the actress, or the debutante of today.   Icarus had no

A DOG AND CAT FIGHT

Relief sculpture on a stone slab found below the Acropolis hill at Athens. The archaic date of the work is shown by the stiffness of line in the hair and garments of the men. The dog and cat are as modern as if the relief had been cut yesterday.

*The Art Institute of Chicago*                                        *Gift of Martin A. Ryerson*

ARTEMIS WITH A TORCH

A Greek bowl called a *cylix* painted by Douris of Athens, V century B.C.

harder luck than many an aviator of today; Tantalus was just as thirsty as any modern American. Many a winning charioteer drove as many races as any modern jockey ever rode and made as much money; the ancient gladiator had even more lady devotees than the modern prize fighter. Sir Arthur Evans has lately found at Cnossus a caravanserai with stables and guest rooms, and even a cafeteria, the walls of which are painted with life-like partridges, evidently a specialty of this Minoan restaurant. No wonder Solomon is esteemed as the wisest of men.

## CHAPTER EIGHT

## ARCHAEOLOGY IN THE BRITISH ISLES

WHEN Caesar moored his ships at the southern chalk cliffs of Britain in 54 B.C., he was met by excited natives whose bodies were stained blue with woad, and who knew nothing of the refinements of the world from which the Roman conquerors came. Those Britons, shown to us through the eyes of the powerful Romans, seemed negligible. They were merely some of the barbarians who stood in the way of Roman expansion.

But when archaeologists gave the Britons a chance to speak for themselves, they proved to be people well advanced along the road to civilization. They tilled the fields and raised sheep and oxen. Their villages and hill forts were governed by local princes. Druid priests directed the religious affairs and conserved the wisdom of the tribes. And before the Celtic Britons there had been earlier inhabitants on the island — colonists, traders, and invaders, coming and going. Gradually the cold trails left by those early wanderers are being picked up and it begins to be possible to sort out the lives led by the Gauls, the Picts, the Britons, and the rest.

The accurate assembling of Britain's buried prehistory started with John Frere, in 1797. While this careful observer was watching workmen in Sussex one day, he saw some pieces of pointed flint tossed up by their spades. He examined the pieces, noted the deep soil from which they came and the symmetrical way in which the flint was hacked, unlike nature's work. At the next gathering of the Society of Antiquaries, Frere read a paper which contained the daring statement that these flints belonged to "a very remote period and to a people who had no use of metals." Decades were to elapse before such a notion could gain serious attention; but the voice of John

Frere was that of a prophet in the wilderness with a message of truth.

Long before Frere, to be sure, strange-looking stones had been found in British soil. But the usual fashion was to set down any such unfamiliar thing as an object specially created or else belonging to the Roman invasion. Scotsmen who picked up rough stone axe-heads unlike anything in a civilized man's tool kit called the stones "purgatory hammers." Some foresighted men, they concluded, had heavy stone hammers buried with them, so that they might knock with force on the great doors of Paradise.

The oldest inhabitant of Britain known today has been assigned to an antiquity that would have taken the breath of John Frere. When fragments of skull were dug out of a gravel pit at Piltdown, in Sussex, in 1912, the heavy-jawed human represented by the skull was pronounced a "dawn man," some 200,000 years old.

Another early inhabitant, a woman, was discovered in 1925, while workmen were excavating in London. Part of her broken skull lay under forty feet of earth, and nearby was the leg bone of a woolly rhinoceros. Scientists, who have no feeling of reticence about ages, feminine or otherwise, proclaimed this "oldest Londoner" to be 20,000 years old, more or less. Her flat head gave rise to uncomplimentary conclusions as to brain development, and there was disagreement as to whether she belonged to a vanished race or to the proud line of *Homo sapiens* to which the modern human stock belongs.

Having met these ancient inhabitants, about whose lives we know nothing, we can skip over 10,000 years, and travel west to the Welsh border to a site known as King Arthur's Cave. From recent excavations at this one site we can get glimpses of life in Britain from 10,000 B.C. to about 1800 B.C.

This cave must have been a desirable apartment, for one prehistoric group after another took it as a home, without improvements. The carefree housekeeping of the cave man and woman was to toss the bones from the daily meal on the ground in front of the cave, and to leave there any trash such as broken or cast-off axes or worn-out skin garments. Perishable materials vanished into dust. Dinner bones and flint tools remained fairly well preserved as the earth accumulated over them, forming a new floor for the next housekeepers.

Taylor, who has been working at King Arthur's Cave, has removed tons of material, and in the cartloads of earth has found clues to six successive types of residents. The oldest, most deeply buried objects that he has unearthed are flint weapons, standard equipment of the primitive hunter. The flints are accompanied by teeth of animals unknown to modern zoos or forests — the cave bear, woolly rhinoceros, and mammoth — creatures that lived when the glaciers were retreating to their Polar headquarters and Britain was still shivering from the receding, melting ice sheet. A hard, dreary life those human contemporaries of the woolly beasts must have led !

Slowly, the climate grew milder, and the cave men made progress. Successive layers of earth built up at the cave entrance hold traces of improvements in stone tools. In the second layer from the top comes evidence of something important and new. Heretofore in Britain men looked upon animals as potential food and clothing or else as dangerous enemies. But here are bones of domestic animals, along with flint weapons and bones of large deer, all dating about 3500 B.C. About this time the custom of heaping earth in mounds over the dead was imported. The mounds, usually of long shape, are known as long barrows. Skeletons buried in some of these mounds are of such type as to suggest that the original home of the makers of the long barrows was the Mediterranean region, and that they wandered north until they crossed the land bridge where the British Channel now flows, and entered England.

Returning to King Arthur's Cave, we find in the top layer the cast-offs of the last tenants. They left earthenware cups of beaker shape and flint arrowpoints. The beakers identify these tenants as some of the tall immigrants who began to arrive along the east coast of Britain about two thousand years before the Christian era. Beakers were so characteristic a feature of their equipment that they have been termed Beaker Folk. They came, it is supposed, from Germany, and finding Britain satisfactory here they stayed. By their time, the biggest and fiercest animals of the Old Stone Age were losing out in the struggle for existence, and human beings could come more safely out of caves and build houses in the open.

Settlements of the Beaker Folk are marked by the circular mounds, or barrows, which they raised. When excavated, some of these round barrows yield articles placed with the dead, such as incense cups and bowls, amber beads, and jet buttons. What happened to the older inhabitants when the Beaker Folk came? Apparently the newcomers did not always fight to exterminate the earlier possessors of the land, for in some of the round barrows are found both the small, long skulls of the older inhabitants and the very different looking skulls of the Beaker men. Since the barrows are round, it follows that the Beaker manners had become dominant. Arrangement of some of the graves suggests that many of the long-headed people became subordinates or slaves. The finding of an adult and a young child lying together in a Beaker grave is sufficiently common to raise a question as to a sinister significance. Sir Arthur Keith, in a recent address, pointed to two possible explanations: The Beaker folk might have sacrificed children to give youth to their dead; or, they might have sacrificed an adult to furnish a guardian for a child in the future world.

In late round barrows archaeologists have unearthed spearheads, daggers, and knives made of bronze, which are signs of new advances in culture. A workman or fighter could now equip himself with keen metal. The Beaker Folk are not generally credited with discovering how to smelt copper and tin to make bronze. It is likely that they learned the process from newcomers arriving from the continent, or from traders who came from as far away as the Mediterranean, seeking pearls, jet, and other wares.

Mounds of the Beaker Folk have yielded only small articles of bronze, possibly because the art was new, possibly because the people were loath to commit the valued metal to the earth. Archaeologists were greatly interested, therefore, when the home of a Beaker family was discovered in Heathery Burn Cave in Durham, and the durable equipment of the family was recovered complete and still well preserved after more than three thousand years. The family that had taken refuge in the cave apparently were drowned by a flood, and the things they tried to save remained hidden. The bronze objects from this cave rank with the finest pieces of prehistoric art in Britain. There is a bronze sword turned green with age, leaf-shaped spearheads, a bronze bucket, and bracelets. There are gold and jet ornaments, bone spindle-whorls showing that the art of spinning thread was known, bone skewers, parts of bridle-bits, and some fragments of undecorated pottery.

Like prehistoric men elsewhere, the early inhabitants of Britain attempted — successfully — to move great stone blocks and to convert them into monuments. The tribes progressed from the construction of simple rock pillars and tables made of several standing stones with a flat boulder on top to more ambitious plans. There is Avebury, where one hundred huge stones were set in a circle more than 1,100 feet in diameter. Most impressive of all is Stonehenge, the greatest mystery that the prehistoric inhabitants have bequeathed to modern Britons.

Not so broad as Avebury, Stonehenge was far more pretentious. It might have stood complete until today, battered only by time and weather; but farmers and builders have used the place as a quarry, and tourists at one period were supplied with a hammer and encouraged to break off souvenirs. Evelyn, seventeenth-century diarist, visited Stonehenge and recorded that the stone was "so exceeding hard, that all my strength with a hammer could not breake a fragment." Others who tried were more successful. There remain about eighty stones, some fallen, some still towering in their places. The complete monument seems to have consisted of a circle of stones sixteen feet tall, with spaces between them. Flat slabs were laid on top to make a continuous series of arches. Inside were smaller rings and semicircles of stone.

It was long supposed that Druid priests built Stonehenge as a setting for weird rites by moonlight. But when archaeologists began to dig cautiously around the monoliths, the Druid tradition was damaged, if not ruined. Excavations

GIANT BOULDERS OF STONEHENGE

A section of the great circle, topped with flat stones, and part of a smaller, inner circle made of stones as tall as a man.

brought to light old beaker-shaped cups left where Stone Age stone-cutters worked. And this is taken to mean that the building of Stonehenge was a crowning project of the Stone Age in Britain, about 1800 B.C. One circle of the stones apparently was set up even earlier. That the Druids found this site suitable for moonlight incantations may well be true, but Stonehenge was old, centuries old, by the time the Druids came into power.

The theory that Stonehenge was an astronomical observatory was proposed by Lockyer. Wise men planned the circles, he argued, so that they could watch the sun rise over a stone known as the Friar's Heel, and by sighting from this they determined the summer solstice. Photographs taken from the air in 1921, however, proved that the orientation of the circles and avenues leading to them is not so exact as had been believed. If there were observations of sun and moon, they were incidental. The latest discoveries indicate that Stonehenge was built as a temple, and probably also as an assembly place where priests and military nobles made laws and dispensed justice. Perhaps it was an honor to be buried here, for the land round about is thick with the barrows that mark Bronze Age graves.

While tribes of southern Britain progressed from the Old Stone Age to the New and into the finer Age of Bronze, more or less similar changes took place in Scotland and Ireland. Interest always attaches to the oldest inhabitants of a country. Proof that Scotland had her Old Stone Age inhabitants to match those of England was announced in 1927, and attracted wide notice. The discovery was made by Cree, who set out with a grant from the Royal Society of London to dig in four caves of northern Scotland. Here he unearthed two human skeletons and with them the bones of cave bears and Arctic foxes. From a deeper layer of earth his spade brought up tools of reindeer horn, antlers that had been cut and scratched by human agency, and bits of charcoal which showed that the cave dwellers had burned fires to keep warm or to scare off wild beasts. What appears to be conclusive evidence that Ireland, too, had cave men and women at the end of the bleak Ice Age was obtained at Kilgreany Cave in 1928. Archaeologists from the Royal Irish Academy and the University of Bristol found five strata containing objects at the entrance to this cave. A skeleton deeply buried in the cave floor was pronounced contemporary with the wild boar, Irish great deer, brown bear, Arctic lemming, and other animals whose bones also lay in deep soil at the cave entrance.

How the oldest immigrants came into Scotland is unknown. The easiest route in later prehistoric times was around by way of Ireland; for when the northern climate became favorable, a thick forest grew up across Britain and formed a barrier, preventing southern tribes from entering the north country.

The Picts who found their way into the isolated north country have been especially mysterious. In 1928, V. Gordon Childe of the University of Edinburgh succeeded in excavating a Pict fishing village in the Orkney Islands, north of

*Photograph copyrighted by V. G. Childe*

STONE AGE HOUSEKEEPERS USED STONE CUPBOARDS

Interior of a prehistoric Pict house in the Orkney Islands, showing the wall
cupboard, the fireplace in the center of the room, and the stone seat.

Scotland. The stone huts cleared of sand are large, with ceilings as high as ten feet, but the doors are low, so that even a short man must stoop to enter. Inside a typical house were found stone tables, stone cupboard shelves, a fireplace, and scattered household articles of a seaside home of the Stone Age — bone ladles, drinking cups of whalebone, simple earthenware dishes, and polished stone axe-heads. In addition there were beads and amulets of walrus ivory, which the fishermen and their dark-haired wives wore to set off their costumes of animal skins or to ward off evil. An unexpected discovery was that the huts were connected by a network of indoor streets made of roofed-over stone passages. The untidy villagers cast kitchen refuse on the roofs of these indoor streets, and at times even built campfires there and cooked their meals.

In the corner of one cottage the archaeologist discovered a mysterious grave containing two skeletons. These appear to be not the remains of inhabitants of the stone house but victims entombed by some gruesome rite when the house was built. Barbarians elsewhere have been known to sacrifice a victim at the foundation of a new building in order to confer a magic stability upon its walls. The meaning of the burials is carved in plain view on a slab in front of the grave; but the marks have defied modern scholarship. They are like, and yet unlike, runic letters. "Provisionally, we may call it a new alphabet," Professor Childe declared. Now, to find writing in a Stone Age village is a puzzling combination. From the absence of metal and from the crude pottery, the islanders belong to the Stone Age of about, say, 3000 B.C. But writing was practically unknown in the world at that time. The village seems to say that these Picts continued in old-fashioned customs even after the Christian era, but they did see the usefulness of signs for recording events or as an aid to magic. It may be that they learned the lesson from Norsemen who sailed to their coast, and learned it none too well. If so, their inscriptions — runic and yet not runic—may be like a child's early attempts at letter writing, destined never to be read.

Many excavations are revealing new facts about traders and attacking tribes who brought new blood and new ideas into prehistoric Britain. Great collections of rings, pins, knives, and all manner of bronze and iron objects are found in evidence of skilful industry and work of ingenious craftsmen, and these are proof, too, of a large population. The last to come before the Roman invasions were the Britons, a tribe of Celts that began to stream into the country from the south about 400 B.C. Knowledge of iron came with them or near this time.

It might seem that with the planting of Roman standards on British soil archaeology would have great help from fluent

Roman writers; but Caesar and other historians of the campaigns did not always give the information desired by modern investigators.

London, for example, was conspicuously neglected in Roman accounts. No one can say certainly whether it was even in existence before the Roman era. The latest conclusions, based on negative evidence, are that if London was on the map in earlier centuries, it was no more than a crossroads trading post. Its status as a town appears to date from about the time when the Emperor Claudius was fighting in southeastern Britain in 43 A.D. It grew rapidly to be the greatest city of the island. Yet today, that Roman London is established as a visible town by only thirteen fragments of wall and bastion and brick pier. Haverfield once said, "We do not know for sure the plan of a single house or the line of a single street." And that statement still holds true.

*Photograph from London Museum*

A ROMAN RIVER–GOD FOUND IN LONDON

What there is of Londinium lies buried eight to twenty-five feet beneath the streets of modern London, as a result of the piling up of wind-blown dirt, débris, and remains of fallen buildings during almost two thousand years. Construction gangs working on office buildings often dig through the Roman layer, and turn up pottery and other objects, but not yet have they struck the foundation plan or walls of a Roman villa. Excavations for a bank building in 1928 reached a mud layer twenty-five feet down, and in it appeared an object of hard stone. This proved to be part of a mill such as was used by bakers in Pompeii, but never before known in Britain. No doubt some Roman brought this useful article with him when he set out for the provinces.

Considering that probably ten emperors came to London in the course of four centuries, it is not strange that archaeologists have hoped persistently that some lucky spade would reveal an impressive villa or relics in the style of splendor befitting a conqueror. A bronze head of Hadrian which was fished up from the Thames in 1834 is the sort of art work that might be expected in a city frequented by royalty, but this bronze was a rare specimen in 1834 and it is rare today.

The busy centers of activity were constructed chiefly of wood and brick — all the barracks, legion headquarters, the markets, the temples where Roman and Celtic divinities were curiously blended. There is only one visible trace of such a catastrophe as the firing of London in 60 A.D. by the enraged British Queen, Boadicea, who revolted against the demands of Rome. This is a layer of red soil, apparently burnt, sandwiched into London's subsoil ten or twelve feet below the streets.

The facts about early London will have to be dug up if they are ever to be learned, for there is no mention of the city in written history for so long a time as 60 A.D. to 296 A.D., a period of 236 years.

Roman forts and towns in other parts of Britain have revealed more satisfactory information about the Roman period. Foundation walls of villas have been found, showing the hot-air heating flues in the walls, the drainage system, and the mosaic pavements, all indicating that in this island province life was made comfortable if not luxurious for important Romans. Public interest in these excavations is growing. Even schoolboys have taken an organized part in digging up the foundations of a villa in Staffordshire, and with small recompense to themselves except the glory of discovering the glass, pottery, and floors of a house in their own neighborhood, almost two thousand years old. Roman fortresses are being studied with special care in order to trace events of the Roman conquest. Every line of clay rampart and stone fortification is part of the story.

In the search for hidden vestiges of Roman forts aviators have unexpectedly lent aid. The first to set an airplane to work for the cause of archaeology in England was Crawford, former flying corps observer. His photographs taken over Wessex have revealed Roman forts and earthworks and also traces in the earth of great circles that may have marked arenas or sacred grove enclosures. The secret lies chiefly in the sensitiveness of plants to differences in soil and moisture. These differences occur where there have been earthworks or other disturbances of the soil. After the Romans left Britain, and their carefully built defenses fell into ruin, farmers who found the earthworks in their way simply plowed the ground and planted grain there. And anyone would have said that all trace of the Roman occupancy was wiped out. But where the buried trenches ran, the disturbed subsoil is apt to be moister than the rest of the field, and of different texture. Plant roots descending for nourishment are fed differently, and in early summer the crops trace the ditches and breastworks in lines of darker and more luxuriant green. An individual walking over the land may notice the difference but can never visualize the plan. One recent revelation made by the aviator's camera is the entire street plan of an unexcavated Romano-British town, including two temples and other buildings.

The battle of Colchester between the Romans and the soldiers of the golden-haired Boadicea left two rare military trophies in the soil of Britain. One is the iron field chair belonging to the Roman commander and the other is a complete bronze military standard, decorated with the face of Nero. The Roman military standard is the only complete specimen that has survived these eighteen hundred years and more. Even fragments of the metal banners have rarely been found, for the Romans worshipped their standards; and when Christianity spread, the pagan symbols were destroyed. The two historic objects, according to E. J. Seltman, who owns them, were probably carried in the rear of the fighting, with other property from the general's tent. When luck of the battle went with Boadicea's men, some of the elated Britons paused to look for booty. The soldier who carried off the beautiful chair and standard buried his plunder, expecting to recover it at a quiet time, but never returned.

Of all the remains of Roman Britain, Hadrian's Wall has proved the greatest attraction, both popular and scientific. This monumental wall stretched across the country, up hills and down valleys, for seventy-three miles, forming an effective barrier between north and south. The strength of it may be imagined from the fact that it stood fourteen feet high and was almost eight feet thick and at intervals of a mile there were castles for sentries and troops. Eventually it fell into ruin, parts were buried, and many a stone from the wall went into houses and fences of nearby farms. Year

Photograph by E. J. Sellman

A RARE RELIC OF ROMAN DAYS IN BRITAIN

This folding camp chair used by a Roman general is of iron overlaid with silver, and ornamented with a pattern of copper and gold.

after year there is excavation of segments of the ruin; new mile-castles are found, and there is much enthusiasm over each new discovery. Steps have been taken to locate about four hundred owners of the wall and to schedule the whole ruin from Carlisle to Newcastle-on-Tyne as an ancient monument.

The story of the wall at the present stage of knowledge is that in the second century A.D. a string of Roman forts was constructed at intervals across the country. About the same time, a broad earth ditch with sloping sides was dug parallel with the forts, south of them. The frontier forts were first linked by a turf wall, and later the turf was replaced by the massive stone barrier.

Only a few temple ruins of the Roman period have been found, though the Roman army took foreign soldiers into its ranks, and many a new cult and form of worship were introduced into England by these legionaries. One temple that has been known for more than a century was the scene of fresh excavations recently, and although the site had been studied with careful effort long ago, many new facts were disclosed. This temple in Gloucestershire was dedicated to a Celtic god named Nodens, a deity about whom very little is known. Nodens appears to have been a god of healing; numerous pilgrims came to his temple seeking a cure for diseases. Bronze representations of arms and other parts of the body indicate types of cures made at the shrine. Close by the temple runs a line of shops, apothecary shops they have been termed. It is supposed that apothecaries carried out the prescriptions ordered by the priests of Nodens. Or, if the healing of the shrine was wrought by faith alone, it may be surmised that the apothecaries were competitors of the temple, who established themselves as near to it as they could in the hope of selling drugs and potions to pilgrims who failed to benefit by visiting the temple. A house near the temple is considered to have been a sanatorium where the worshippers stayed. The fame and prosperity of the shrine are suggested by the fact that six thousand coins have been taken from the ruin at one time or another. Dates and portraits stamped on the coins indicate that the temple reached the height of its popularity in the fourth century A.D. The new excavations have shown that the plan of Nodens' temple included seven chapels, forming an architectural design strangely like an early Christian church, rather than like a pagan shrine. Yet the pagan character of the worship is evident at every hand. The dog was held sacred here, judging by little bronze figures that were brought as offerings.

An account of discoveries in British archaeology might well carry us forward into Saxon times and even farther toward the present. We have lingered over early periods, because it is the prehistoric times that are receiving the most attention from British archaeologists and those are the periods in which the most illuminating finds are being unearthed.

THE FAMOUS OSEBERG SHIP PARTIALLY EXCAVATED

In this beautifully carved pleasure yacht, a Viking queen of the ninth century
was buried with her luxurious possessions arranged around her.

## CHAPTER NINE

## BURIED TREASURE IN NORTHERN LANDS

ANTIQUITIES are a standard crop from the soil of Scandinavian countries. If Norway is not heralding the latest north European discovery, then it is Sweden, Denmark, or Greenland, Iceland, or the Island of Gotland. As the plentiful harvest of bronze swords, flint knives, coins, and medieval jewelry is stored up in the museums, the story of these north lands, from about 8000 B.C. down to the Middle Ages, is becoming familiar to the people of Scandinavia. Gradually the world in general is beginning to know the real Vikings of the centuries just prior to the Middle Ages, and also the prehistoric forerunners of those great sea rovers.

Norway and Sweden have no deeply buried past because the Ice Age held the land in its grip until very late. Finally, about 10000 B.C., the soil thawed and trees grew and beasts began to roam the country. Then Stone Age men followed the trail of the deer and the wolf and wild boar into the north. Where these men hunted and wherever their clans camped, they left bone and flint that they had chipped into pointed weapons. These old weapons and the shell-heaps that accumulated along the shore at fishing settlements are the proofs of the earliest semi-wandering tribes.

After several thousand years, new immigrants seem to have come to contest the use of the land, and the old pioneers were absorbed into the new groups or driven away. Cattle and sheep were brought into the country, and the hunters learned to raise rye, wheat, and millet. It began to seem worth while to build more substantial cottages than the old camp shelters.

Farming was a less time-consuming business than hunting had been. The men practised shaping tools and weapons until, in the course of generations, they attained a perfection seldom equaled by any race in the Stone Age state of development. Success in this art was aided by the unusually fine quality of flint that lay at their doors, where it had been left in the ground by the melting, retreating ice sheet.

To test the efficiency of such exceptional stone tools, a modern Danish archaeologist built a house, using the old flint celts, saws, and scrapers. With one keen celt he cut down

*Courtesy American-Swedish News Exchange*

INSIDE THE BURIAL MOUND OF A BRONZE AGE WARRIOR,
A FORERUNNER OF THE VIKINGS

Stones were set in the form of a ship to honor the young man, who appears to
have been a sea captain and a nobleman.

twenty-six pine trees in a single day; and his cottage was finished in about two months. A test of weapons of the same age could be another interesting experiment, because the stone-workers reached the height of their technique in the making of weapons. It was natural that they should give most attention to their daggers and arrow-points, considering that these were the equipment by which a man defended his land and his life.

If we could walk into a village of the Stone Age of about 2000 B.C., we might just happen to see one of these grim fighters taking the time and trouble to cut a miniature copy of one of his own tools as a plaything for his young son. A number of such objects, presumably toys, were unearthed recently in an old settlement near Stockholm. In the collection was a well-made stone axe less than an inch in length, which must have given some prehistoric youngster opportunities for endless experiments.

One of the grindstones used by the old tool-makers for sharpening the stone blades has had a strange career. Several thousand years after its practical usefulness was over, the grindstone turned up in a Lapland settlement, not far from the Arctic Circle. Here it became elevated to the status of an idol. A few years ago, it was discovered by scientists, and its next centuries, perhaps, will be spent in a museum case.

A Stone Age village on the Swedish Island of Gotland was excavated in 1928 by Dr. John Nihlen. The most striking observations that he made dealt with the inhabitants themselves rather than with their simple housekeeping and industries. The bones of these men who lived about 5,000 years ago show that ill-health was one of the worries which beset prehistoric families. We do not think of the Stone Age woman, especially of the race that produced the sturdy Vikings, as suffering from decayed teeth. We would scarcely picture her children as having feeble little legs, bent by rickets, or her husband hobbling about with rheumatic joints. But all these types of infirmity occurred to some extent, and their signs are preserved in bones unearthed at the village. Rheumatism of the joints has been attributed partly to the climate and partly, perhaps, to the exclusive diet of meat. That the people were forced to eat hard meat day in and day out is shown by deformations of the jaws from arduous chewing.

No one can ever learn how the European Stone Age doctor treated most of the diseases that plagued his community, but the surgical procedures can often be understood by marks on the bones of the patients. We find surgeons of the Island of Gotland making use of the favorite operation of prehistoric surgeons from Egypt to Peru — trepanation of the cranium. The operation consisted of scraping and sawing a round hole in the skull. The main purpose was to remove pain or pressure caused by a depressed fracture; but in some cases it was undoubtedly merely reasoned in a general way that a hole would let out the evil that was tormenting the patient.

The life of Stone Age men and women in northern Europe was lonely and isolated, but the Scandinavian flair for trading was groping for expression. The people had already found that their skill in making tools was of value to neighboring tribes. Tools of the fine Skane flint have been dug up six hundred miles away from the province of Skane. Amber and stone articles found in England and more distant countries suggest that traders were very early on the road with Scandinavian products. Some of the exports spread to lands as far away as Spain, Italy, and Egypt, and contact with that outer world brought bronze into the North about 1800 B.C.

Courtesy American-Swedish News Exchange

THE BRONZE DAGGER AND TOOLS OF THE SEA CAPTAIN

Introduction of bronze into Scandinavia created no revolutionary changes that can be detected in the lives of the people. The stone tools, as we have seen, were far from being the poor makeshifts that such articles are often regarded. At first, a bronze sword must have been a rarity that only a prince or a wealthy trader would aspire to own. The supply of materials for making bronze was limited to the size of the import trade, because neither copper nor tin was found in the north countries. In time, however, the descendants of the expert flint-workers were turning out splendid shields, knives, and swords of bronze.

Meanwhile, imported ideas other than the making of bronze brought more progress to the people in general. How far along the road to civilization the Bronze Age Northmen had come is revealed by numerous pictures carved in the flat surfaces of rocks about the countryside. The artists who thus depicted their contemporaries had a crude and childish way of out-lining men and animals. Yet the action of the figures is successfully conveyed. There is no mistaking the farmer plow-ing with his cattle, nor men riding horses and driving two-wheeled chariots. And here are the forerunners of the Viking ships. When the pictures were made, the Age of the Vikings and the great Viking ships were still some 2,000 years in the future. Yet one of these boats, with its tall prow and figure-head and its long line of oarsmen, might be a modern child's drawing of a Viking ship. But it has no mast. Sails were apparently still unknown to these seamen.

We should hardly expect to see and handle samples of cloth-ing worn by a warrior or business man of this Bronze Age. But the Danes adopted a custom of burying an important person in an oak log that had been cut in two and hollowed out. The tannic acid in the wood did not prevent the dead man from turn-ing into a skeleton, but in a coffin discovered in a Danish mound the acid had preserved the clothing. When archaeologists opened this coffin, they found a circular cloak, a knee-length woolen tunic, and a high cap. Remains of leather shoes could be seen, and a bronze sword and razor. A woman of the same period would have dressed in a bodice with elbow sleeves, a long skirt with a belt, and, as accessories to her costume, there were combs, hairnets, bracelets, and buckles.

The most remarkable article of prehistoric clothing from this region was found in a Swedish peat bog in 1926. This was a woolen mantle which had been carefully folded and laid on the ground and weighted down with stones. Moss grew over the cloak and formed a five-foot blanket of peat, yet the acid water of the bog continued to protect the old woolen fabric. Scientists who examined this garment reported that it was woven of wool and the hair of game animals, probably deer. Grains of pollen clung to it in muddy particles, and there were holes such as a dagger would tear. We can suppose that the wearer of the cloak was beset by a robber and killed and that his mantle was laid aside by the slayer as being possibly worth returning for. Had the fight been a fair one, the cloak would probably have been removed before the encounter, and the incriminating holes would not be in the cloth.

The grains of pollen were recognized as the clue that could tell the age of the garment. A scientist of Stockholm sorted out the grains and found that the trees represented were chiefly oak, linden, and elm, and pine, birch, and alder. He made exact counts of the grains to determine the proportion of the different kinds, and announced that oak, linden, and elm trees must have flourished in the forest to a greater extent than in modern Sweden. Hence, the climate was mild when the mantle was laid under the stones. According to geologists, there was just such a cycle of warmer seasons at the time when the Stone Age merged into the Age of Bronze. Thus the cloak is dated as being between 3,000–4,000 years old.

In the Bronze Age, men of the northern countries began to worship the sun. Sacrificial vessels ornamented with symbols of the sun are shown in rock carvings, and such vessels themselves have been found. Fear of evil spirits was rampant, judging by the elaborate precautions taken to avert trouble. In one grave in Denmark provisions for safety included an amber bead, claws of a bird, the jaw of a squirrel, pebbles, and a shell from the Mediterranean Sea.

Mounds that mark Bronze Age graves can be detected in many parts of Scandinavia, particularly in southern Sweden. In one province it is estimated that there are about a thousand such mounds. There is little digging at these interesting sites, because they are protected by the Swedish Academy of Antiquities. Usually it is only if a mound stands in the way of construction projects, or if it offers unusual prospects of importance, that a permit is given for excavation.

A large mound that was discovered in 1926 near the west coast of Sweden was probed to see what it might contain. It proved to be the grave of a young man who was a true pre-

Viking, a sea captain, fighter, and man of influence. Because of the position of the mound overlooking the sea, it has been suggested that there was a sea battle and that the leader slain in the encounter was brought ashore for burial. In planning the grave, his followers had set an outline of stones in the earth to represent the ship he had commanded. The young captain was then cremated, and his bones placed in an earthenware urn beside the stone ship. His bronze dagger was laid in the urn. A man of heavier build, possibly his servant, was buried nearby. To form the high monument that was to mark the important grave, the workers piled layers of stones, turf, and sand over the site. This mound has been hollowed out and lighted by electricity to enable visitors to inspect the ship grave.

Burials of the Iron Age unearthed in central Sweden show that eventually real boats were used as graves instead of the earlier symbolic figures of stones set in boat form. Beneath one of the Iron Age mounds of about 400 A.D., a Swedish government archaeologist found the remains of a boat, and in it a man and his wife and a horse and dog for each. Supplies of food and iron arrowheads for emergencies were part of the equipment for the long voyage into the future.

What the ship-grave custom ultimately came to be is revealed by the burial of a woman of rank who lived at the dawn of the Viking Age — 800 A.D. In casual conversation any Scandinavian of pre-Victorian existence is likely to be termed a Viking, but historically the Viking rule was limited to the years between 800 and 1050. The ship burial of the Viking woman, which has become a classic of archaeology, was found by chance, as are so many archaeological treasures. A Norwegian farmer of Oseburg was digging into a hill when his spade struck the wooden beam of a ship. He notified officials, and, later, professors from the University of Oslo came to his farm and investigated. As the contents of the mound were uncovered it became more and more evident that this must be the grave of a queen, and most likely that of Aasa, who ruled the Norwegian Vikings early in the ninth century.

Whoever the lady was, the opening of her earthen tomb recalls the discoveries of Tutankhamen, though the two rulers lived more than two thousand years apart, and in countries very different in ideas and customs.  The possessions placed in the two graves give the same impression of completeness and luxury.

Queen Aasa, for we may believe it was she, had as a last resting place the ship in which she had cruised the bays of

*Courtesy Norwegian Government Railways*

CARRIAGE FROM THE BURIAL SHIP OF A VIKING WOMAN

The carvings on this cart from the Oseberg grave show that Norse craftsmen
could do more delicate work than build a ship.

Norway.  It was brought up on shore, and no doubt the graceful bark looked queer and unhappy to the attendants who had seen it riding the waves with its bright colored silken sails bellying in the wind.  The queen and one other woman were laid in the ship.  The brief scene of tragedy through which the other woman came when she joined the queen at her grave can be fancied in a dozen ways.  Whether she was sacrificed by some formal rite is not known.  Around the queen were placed the articles she might need during the mysterious voyage presumed to be before her.  They brought into the ship her bed and soft quilts and down pillows, fine rugs, and kitchenware and supplies of grain, vegetables, and wine.  The sewing kit was brought from her boudoir, and chests of her clothing and jewelry. There was a loom at which the queen could work when she felt industrious, and a chessboard to amuse her if the voyage grew boresome. Everything was prepared for continuance of the journey on some other shore. A cart and four sleighs went into the ship, and fifteen horses, four dogs, and an ox were killed and added to the cargo.

The grave had suffered the fate of so many tombs of ancient royalty. It had been plundered hundreds of years ago. But what caught the attention of the bandits was probably, in the main, jewelry and dishes of silver and gold that would have been the glittering high lights of the royal outfit. What they left, as not worth carrying off, is sufficient to show that standards of living among the Vikings rose to a state of comfort, and that industry and art were as capably handled as in any European country of the time. The wooden ship, sleds, and carriage remained sufficiently intact to enable restoration to their original shape. The carving is ornate and masterly.

Some years before Queen Aasa's ship appeared, another, more strongly built ship had been found not far away, at Gokstad. It had been so completely plundered of its contents by medieval robbers that little remained except the ship itself and the skeleton of a man. In spite of the robbers, the Gokstad ship was another landmark in Scandinavian archaeology. When it had been removed to a museum and carefully restored, it gave the modern world for the first time a strong seafaring Viking ship. The suggestion was raised that at last the question of whether the Norsemen could have sailed their craft across the Atlantic could be settled. Eventually a duplicate of the ninth century ship was constructed, and two young men with no experience at handling a ship at sea sailed it successfully to America.

Until graves of the Vikings were systematically opened and the contents interpreted, the Norsemen were known necessarily through the sagas sung by minstrels. The Vikings became renowned across the world as rude and ruthless fighters and bandits extraordinary. It is now realized that in some respects the great sea-rovers were the victims of yellow journalism on the part of the singers who reported their deeds. In their homeland the Vikings are now coming to be thought of also as men who admired beautiful articles and had them in their homes, and as level-headed business men who sailed to foreign countries, not always to terrorize the inhabitants, but often to conduct peaceful trade.

The commerce that started in the Bronze Age, or earlier, had grown wider through the Age of Iron. Its international scope is revealed by coins of many countries, bearing the faces of many kings. These media of exchange have lain for centuries in Scandinavian ground. More than 20,000 Arabic coins from Near Eastern trade have been found in Sweden. Cautious people, no doubt, have always buried their savings when they did not know how to invest them, and many such old hoards have been struck in recent years by farmers and children digging in the soil. In 1926, a farmer on the island of Oeland, in the Baltic Sea, was plowing his field when he came upon a kettle filled with Roman coins of the fifth century. Another Swedish farmer struck a hoard of more than two thousand coins, most of them English, of the reign of Aethelred II in the tenth century. These were probably tribute money, exacted by Viking raiders from England. There were also Irish, German, and Arabic pieces in the lot. The finder turned over the treasure to the government, as required, and received the value of the silver in weight, or about eighty-six dollars, and in addition an extra eighth for the "antiquary value." The policy of the government in requiring that all finds be reported and of giving a fair bonus to the informant is a stimulus to public interest in antiquities. Lonnberg of the Swedish Historical Museum declared that in the six years leading up to 1927 there were delivered into the government's historical museum and royal coin collection no fewer than 122 finds of metals. These included rings and other small objects of silver and gold as well as coins.

Rome's far-flung influence touched the northern countries

during the Iron Age. A particularly interesting bit of evidence is a vase found 100 years ago in a remote province of Sweden. The vase is marked with the name of its maker, Lucius Ansius Epaphroditus, a Roman whose work has turned up in Herculaneum and Pompeii, and also in England, France, and Scotland.

One of the important commercial centers of the North was

*From a painting by C. G. Hellquist*

THE SACKING OF VISBY BY KING VALDEMAR OF THE DANES, JULY 27, 1361

Gotland, in the Baltic, where trade routes between the Orient and the West had a meeting point. During the Viking Age nearly every farmer of Gotland was a shipowner, and with his own boats made trade expeditions to foreign ports. In the Middle Ages, which followed the Viking Age, one city on the island gathered all the lines of Gotland's prosperous trade into its own hands and became a leader in one of the most important medieval commercial organizations, the Hanseatic League. Why this city named Visby should have become so distinguished was mysterious until it was accounted for in 1926. In the town were unearthed the remains of an extensive iron-works, and evidence to show that Visby was a center for the smelting and refining of iron and copper and that it carried on an important export trade in iron. The existence of such an industry here had never been suspected.

So strategic a city would inevitably make enemies, and one of the most virulent against Visby was the Danish king Valdemar Atterdag, who swore to destroy its power. The story as it has survived in tradition is that Valdemar came to Visby disguised as a merchant and made love to a goldsmith's daughter in order to gain knowledge of the island's defenses. He sailed away and returned with an army, July 27, 1361, and a terrific fight was waged outside the walls of Visby. Valdemar, triumphant, then set three beer vats in the city market place and ordered that they be filled with gold and silver before sunset lest the city be burned.

*Courtesy American-Swedish News Exchange*

A SKELETON IN ARMOR

Rare preservation of chain mail worn by a fighter who fell at the battle of Visby.

Excavations in the meadow outside the city walls demonstrate that the legends contain much truth. Many skeletons of fighters who fell and were buried here in huge common graves have been unearthed by Clason, a Swedish archaeologist. Broken bones and fearfully mutilated skulls testify to the fury of the fight. Women, children, cripples came out to aid the strong fighting men, and when they died they were hastily buried for fear of plague. All the evidence suggests that those who lie here were not members of the strong invading army of the Danes, but Gotlanders, and the tradition of their blood flowing in torrents until the Baltic Sea ran red is better understood from these graves. Some of the warriors are real skeletons in armor. This is of great interest, because chain mail is durable-looking material that has vanished almost completely since its day. Besides mail helmets and sleeves, there are traces of armored gloves, chest plates, and iron bands, all of which add to the knowledge of medieval military equipment.

One of the significant developments of the Viking Age and the Middle Ages was the spread of Christianity into the north countries. Before the year 800, Christianity was preached

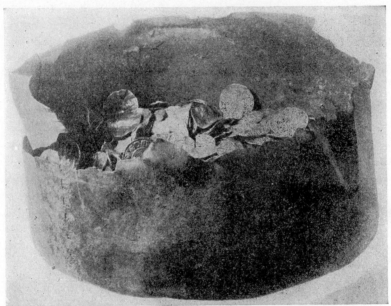

*Courtesy American-Swedish News Exchange*
A KETTLE FULL OF GOLD, DUG UP BY A PLOW
A farmer on the island of Oeland unearthed this hoard of fifth-century coins
in 1926.

in one of the islands off the coast of Sweden. As the Vikings who worshipped Thor and Odin forsook the old gods there appears to have been less uprooting of associations than usual when a new religion is introduced. Some of the old wooden churches standing in Norway display carved doorposts evidently taken from pagan temples. It must be so, for the carvings represent Norse Gods and Norse myths.

Even Greenland, an outpost of medieval civilization, had

its cathedral and its bishop. Excavations have revealed the little cathedral with its seven chapels and the bishop's palace; also the grave of a bishop who died in the isolated province and who was buried there with his carved crook and his ring on his right hand. The Norse settlement in Greenland, established in 1000 A.D. by that busy Viking Eric the Red, evidently became a more flourishing and important colony than was recognized. There were fifteen churches and three or four thousand settlers scattered about the coast on farms. The fate of the colony was tragic. After about five hundred years, Europe paid less attention to the isolated colonists. Skeletons show the degenerative effects of malnutrition and intermarriage.

The garments of rough wool were woven and made at home, but the Greenlanders knew precisely what was the approved fashion in the leading cities of Europe. So, we find these colonials wearing fitted waists, full gored skirts and snug, pointed hoods, all cut faithfully to medieval decrees of elegance. By studying the garments, Norlund of the National Museum at Copenhagen has even traced the gradual changes of fashion through several generations, thus demonstrating the close contact and interest which these most distant of European colonists tried to maintain with the centers of their civilization.

While medieval Scandinavians kept up with the march of fashion, they still clung to some customs reminiscent of ancient times. About the countryside, particularly in Sweden, may be seen today stones set in large circles, or in the outline of a great ship after the favorite Scandinavian pattern. How old are these stone rings and why the boulders were dragged into place originally are questions yet to be explained. It is variously speculated that the rings were established as impressive stage settings for worship or for rites of death or for the administration of justice. At any rate, it appears that in the middle ages the stone circles were used as Thing-steads, or assembly places, where justice was dispensed and civic affairs decided. The outdoor courts of justice were also held on summits of grave mounds and at other ancient monuments. Presumably, officers and principals of the ceremonies took their places conspicuously within the stone enclosures or atop the mounds, while the public gathered around to follow the proceedings.   In spite of the discomfort of attending court in winter in one of these spacious outdoor halls, many rural communities continued holding Things out of doors as late as the seventeenth century, and the custom is still said to be followed occasionally in country districts.

## THE OLDEST KNOWN OBJECT DATED BY PREHISTORIC AMERICANS

The famous Tuxtla statuette represents a Buddha-like man wearing a cloak made of penguin skin. The date in our calendar system would be May 16, 98 B.C.

## CHAPTER TEN

## DISCOVERERS OF AMERICA

WE Americans easily catch the feeling of our relationship to the buried cities of Europe and the Near East, for our civilization had its deepest roots in the soil of the Old World. We can see the origins of our possessions when we look at the house furnishings, the jewelry, and the architecture of those departed civilizations. We can recognize in our own customs the ways of those distant forefathers.

Our personal relationship to prehistoric America is less often recognized, and yet there is a valuable heritage of material knowledge from the Indian farmer who grew corn a thousand years before Christ, and from the South American Indian who first tamed the potato. Many Pilgrim customs that we think of as colonial would more accurately be known as Indian, for the settlers took lessons from the native men and women in cooking and farming. We still use corn-cribs, rubber balls, and many another Indian invention that white men borrowed. This heritage is just as direct as any that has come down from the Greek or the Gaul.

And then, the buried past of America strikes a responsive chord in a different way from overseas civilizations, because it is the prehistory of our home country. The more we learn of the prehistoric background, the more we realize that it is picturesque, dramatic, surprising.

Explorers fighting their way through modern jungles in Yucatan find ruins of great desolate cities with beautiful buildings of stone. The farmer in Ohio plows up the remains of Indians who were planting corn on his land and smoking tobacco in carved pipes many centuries before the white man heard of corn and tobacco. In Illinois can be seen a prehistoric man-made hill that was the center of a wigwam settlement as large as a good-sized modern town.

197

The population of this Indian world is not to be thought of as a scattering of small bands dotting the vast expanse of a continent.   In such regions as the Mississippi Valley, the California coast, the Southwest, Mexico, and Peru, Indians clustered in thick centers.   According to an estimate recently made by Spinden of Harvard, there were 50,000,000 or even 75,000,000 Indians in North and South America about the twelfth century.   It is surprising to realize that Indian farmers living in settlements were far more numerous than roaming Indians who depended on hunter's luck for their sole food supply.   But the villages being dug up by archaeological expeditions add to the evidence of how numerous such Indian "settlers" were.

If our concern with America does not start properly in 1492 where school histories traditionally pick up the story, where does it begin?   That is a puzzler.   We may eliminate the very ancient times — say several hundred thousand years ago — when men in the Old World were just beginning to deserve the name human.   No evidence of primitive, ape-like Americans 500,000 years old has appeared, at least as yet, to match the groping dawn-men of Asia and Europe.   Nor is there any trace in the Americas of the biological types that might be expected to foreshadow human beings in the process of evolution.

Scientists are fairly well agreed that the first American, the first human being to find this side of the globe, came over the short passage of Bering Strait into Alaska.   Others of his tribe must have come with him.   None of them had any romantic vision of discovering a continent.   When a group moves often in search of food, discovering new country becomes an everyday adventure.   Although there was no planting of flags, no claiming a new land in honor of royalty, no recording of the heroes' names and the date of the discovery, that event is the oldest landmark in our prehistory.   We are fond of setting up monuments.   Some day that unknown first American may have a statue to his memory on the Alaskan coast.

After the first band of immigrants, there were many others. Hrdlicka of the Smithsonian Institution has described the peopling of the New World as a steady and natural passing over of small groups lasting until recent times. Siberia, he points out, is an inhospitable region where famine and cold always threaten. The tribes which wandered or were forced by other tribes up into the northeast corner of Siberia could look eastward and see the signs of a shore freer of snow and ice. And it was only about fifty miles away. Islands broke the distance to be crossed, and it was easy in suitable weather for boats of skin to carry groups of these Asiatics safely across the northwest passage. They did not necessarily stop in Alaska, but most of them pushed on southward, looking for warmer and pleasanter places ahead. So during the course of centuries the continent was gradually populated.

How long ago did this migration take place? There the arguments begin. Dr. Hrdlicka, and some other scientists with him, would say that the oldest Americans probably came over Bering Strait not more than five or six thousand years ago; that no convincing proof of greater antiquity of man in this country has been established; and that if men had been here earlier, proof would in all likelihood have been forthcoming by this time.

Other scientists find it incredible that the varied types of Indian could have developed in a short time limit. They also point out that signs of ancient Americans, 20,000 years old or older, might easily be few and far between. As Cook of the Colorado Museum of Natural History once stated: "It is only in special and exceptional circumstances that searchers may hope to find such remains, save by accident. Considering the exceedingly small percentage of trained people who might uncover such finds, in proportion to the great population who are quite as apt to find them in any one of endless ways, and, considering that most of these would not know what they had found, nor would they save and report them — it is to be expected that much priceless evidence is thus hopelessly lost."

More than one hundred different discoveries suggesting that man lived in America in early antiquity have been reported since the search began. The finds are various: arrowpoints buried beside queer, prehistoric animals of types that long since vanished from this part of the world; bones of human beings in layers of earth so deep that it would seem that many thousands of years must have been required for the accumulation of such a soil blanket; crudely chipped stone arrows in glacial drift deposits, suggesting that men lived in the region of New Jersey in the Ice Age more than 20,000 years ago.

Florida has been the happy hunting ground chosen by a number of scientists bent on unearthing America's past. Sellards, a Florida geologist, Loomis of Amherst, Gidley of the Smithsonian, and others have dug into Florida soil and found arrowpoints and human bones buried in a layer of earth which contained the bones of mammoths and mastodons. These giants of the elephant family have been extinct since the Ice Age, it is generally believed. If men shot darts into these creatures, it implies that those men were living at least 20,000 years ago.

At Folsom, New Mexico, bones of thirty bison of an extinct type have been dug out of the earth lately, and with them fragments of sixteen flint arrow or javelin points, such as savages would use in hunting game.

Now the various specialists who have examined the exhibits said to represent ancient Americans, or who studied the scientific reports describing them, have never agreed as to what they mean. Every time a discovery has been made, a new argument has been launched at scientific gatherings and in learned journals. The "optimists" say, "Well, here is more evidence of the existence of ancient Americans." The "pessimists" counter by pointing to the possibility that the stone implements and the bones came together by accident; or that significant objects were buried intentionally by later Indians and so were placed in a deeper layer of earth than they were historically entitled to occupy. Meanwhile, the mysterious arrows and bones have usually been removed from the earth for examination, and so there can be no further visitation of specialists to observe the objects at the scene of the find and to render their opinions as to the age of the earth layer and the conditions that brought the objects into it.

But at the scene of the Folsom bison slaying, some of the spear points were left untouched, thus enabling a number of experts to examine closely the site and the evidence.   One of

Courtesy American Museum of Natural History

AN AMERICAN BISON HUNT 20,000 YEARS AGO

An artist's conception of what happened at Folsom, New Mexico, where bones of thirty prehistoric bison have been found together with flint javelin points.   Insert: A flint point found beneath one buffalo.

these stone points was lying close to the rib of a bison in such a way that observers declared it must have been in the animal at the time of its death.   An incidental point of interest about the weapons is that they were chipped into shape with remarkable skill, and down the center of each flint is a hollow groove. One visitor to Folsom pointed out that in the recent war the bayonets were grooved to cause greater bleeding, and it may be that the early Indian hunters had the same end in view when they added this finishing touch. Impressive as the Folsom site is, however, some scientists hold that the bison and flint weapons do not belong together in point of age.

The matter is one of importance. If men have been in America 20,000 years or longer and not merely 6000, then there are many more chapters to be dug up and fitted into the story of the continent, and the perspective of events will be very different. But whatever the stone points mean, they are archaeological evidence of value. If it should be demonstrated that they are only a thousand years old, and were buried by some freak of geology and weathering, then the understanding of how that happened will serve the purpose at least of preventing scientists from future confusion of the same sort. Unsettled problems of science like this one often seem to the layman to be none of his affair. But the oldest Americans can hardly be sidestepped by anyone who reads his daily newspaper. They will continue to bob up in the headlines with persistent frequency, because new evidence is being continually revealed. Each new find will be weighed in the balance; finally the scale will tip heavily and permanently on one side, and science will turn its attention to another uncertainty waiting to be clarified.

Whenever they came, the early wanderers who crossed Siberia and Alaska went through hard experiences that set a mark on the mental and emotional makeup of the race. This, at least, is the opinion of Ellsworth Huntington, who has given special attention to the effects of climate on human life. The strain of the frozen north would eliminate the more nervous and active types of mind, he concludes. These could not bear the cold, hunger, and the darkness of long winter nights: "Perhaps that is why the Indian, though brave, stoical, and hardy, does not possess the alert, nervous temperament which leads to invention and progress."

Survivors of the struggle gradually worked their way across the continent, even east to Labrador and south to Tierra del Fuego. They developed hundreds of languages. Pottery technique was discovered, and the art spread widely. Corn was domesticated, and the valuable seed was traded from one group to another until it became the property of many tribes. How long did it take for such changes to come? Do they not in themselves convey the impression of a panorama of many, many centuries? This question of dates is a difficult one that is being studied from various angles.

The only actual dates from pre-Columbian America that can be read today are the glyphs devised by the Mayan and Mexican tribes in middle America, and carved chiefly on stone monuments. The oldest object in America dated in the strange picture writing is not one of the tall monuments, however, but a little jadeite figurine known as the Tuxtla statuette, from the place in Mexico where it was found. The date carved on it in Mayan chronology is read as May 16, 98 B.C. Study of the Mayan calendar has convinced Spinden and Morley that the Mayan astronomers started their system of recording the years long before the Tuxtla statuette. To be precise, it is concluded that they reckoned time from August 6, 613 B.C. And the Mayan civilization had surely advanced through many undated centuries before that remarkable calendar was perfected.

The annual growth-rings of trees offer the most promising method of fastening dates on America's other pre-Columbian settlements, particularly in the Southwest. The astronomer Douglass of the University of Arizona is lending aid to archaeology by working out this calendar. He first studied tree rings in search of evidence as to the effect of recurrent sun spots on tree growth. His reports brought out the point that a tree not only records its life span as its annual rings form, but it also keeps account of the calendar year in a more or less distinctive manner. This is due to the fact that rings added in dry years are narrower and different in appearance from rings added in exceptionally rainy years. Indeed, any unusual climatic conditions in a year or series of years produce conspicuous types of rings, not in one tree, but in every tree in the region. Douglass' particular goal was to make the prehistoric ceiling beams at Pueblo Bonito, in New Mexico, reveal their ages. Since Pueblo Bonito is believed to have been abandoned and to have fallen into ruin about a thousand years ago, this was a hard test for the tree calendar. By studying older and older cross-sections of trees, and by overlapping certain conspicuous ring series, the astronomer has carried his wooden calendar back to 1260 A.D., making a perfect record for dating the past 600 years in the Southwest. Still, the old beams from Pueblo Bonito have not been reached. When that is achieved, archaeologists will have a marvelous tree ring yardstick, long enough to date practically any pueblo that has a readable bit of wood left about it. More remarkable still, there are hopes that some day the tree ring calendar can be carried back to pre-Pueblo days.

As you read of the prehistoric Americans referred to always as Indians, perhaps there loom in your mind rumors of Egyptians in Mexico, and stories of bones dug up in the Southwest so large as to invite speculation whether there were giants here, once upon a time. You have heard that the Mongols found their way to Peru. Every year sees one or another of these entertaining theories fought out in the daily press, and "a good time is had by all." But at scientific society meetings and in the journals where the experts report their theories and proofs, all the evidence leads away from such fanciful possibilities.

Tales of prehistoric Americans twelve feet tall may be dismissed at once. The giant's bone turns out to be the leg of a prosaic beast. Or else the first excited report proves to be exaggerated. The man was only a powerfully built Indian of football star proportions. A fact which explains some of the rumors is that a skeleton tends to fall apart or is disturbed by burrowing animals and is thus elongated. On discovery it appears to be of impressive proportions.

Every Indian design or bit of language that suggests any part of the Old World has been made the basis of a theory that the Americans came from that precise location. Tones resembling Chinese in the Mayan language have set off arguments as to whether Chinese boats brought visitors or immigrants across the Pacific to the American tropics. It has been suggested that prehistoric immigrants came to South America from mid-Pacific islands. Some of the island tribes made large, strong canoes that might be capable of such a trip, particularly if there happened to be stepping-stone islands to shorten the stretches of the voyage. Traces of island languages and customs have been noted among some South American tribes. But if trans-Pacific migrations took place they were probably rare and sporadic adventures.

The discovery in Honduras of carved figures suggesting elephants and belonging to about the fourth century A.D. has been good for ten years of discussion. Flapping ears and snout-like noses of these figures suggest elephants to some beholders, but only conventionalized macaws or grotesque masks to others. It is difficult to believe that an artist who had never seen an elephant could imagine the peculiar combination of features that go into that creature's face and head. But it is equally difficult to believe that people from a country where elephants were common, such as India, reached this country fifteen centuries ago. One other possibility would be that the mammoths survived in the south later than is supposed, late enough for the earliest men to have seen them and to have recorded the picture on some cave wall or rock. This would have given later artists a pattern for an elephant. But after all the ways of materializing an elephant in prehistoric America have been discussed, we come back to the realization that most matter-of-fact scientists have never been able to see any elephant in the designs at all.

Since people of the American tropics knew how to erect pyramids, it has been said that they learned this technique only by getting the plans from Egypt, though this seems unlikely. The tradition that the lost ten tribes of Israel helped build the civilizations of Central America has been especially persistent. Indeed, the Jewish origin of the American Indians was a favorite theory as early as the sixteenth century; and much later when serious efforts to trace the Indian family tree were instituted more than one investigator thought he found striking resemblance to Hebrew language and rites in the land of the Mayas.  Others, however, have never been able to see any similarities really significant.  The kingdom of the Israelite tribes fell about 700 B.C., and if any wanderers set out on the journey across Asia and America, they would not have arrived in the tropics for many, many centuries.

A British writer declared in 1827 that the Mongols conquered America in the thirteenth century, and brought elephants with them.  Before that, he said, America was in "the rudest condition."  Then, suddenly there were founded in America two empires and there was order and justice and pomp and ceremony, and architecture and the elegant art of the goldsmith.  By this theory, the founders of the royal line of the Incas in Peru and of the Aztec rulers in Mexico were Mongol nobility.

Still another theory as to people who influenced prehistoric America deals with the negroes.  A Harvard professor has published three volumes setting forth his view that African negroes reached America before Columbus and set their cultural stamp on Indian languages and customs.

There is one group of traditional discoverers of America that has a fast hold on both popular and scientific attention.  These are the Norsemen, whose overseas adventures read so plausibly in the sagas.  Archaeologists have long hunted along the eastern coast of America for evidence of these adventures, some Norse weapon or cup or some runic inscription that they could take as proof.  The sagas tell how Lief, son of Eric the Red, set out in 1000 A.D. to find a strange land that another Viking had sighted on a previous voyage.  Lief came first to a forbidding coast where mountains white with snow faced him.  He turned the ship and sailed on and found a coast of forests, and finally a pleasing shore that he named Vineland.  Here he spent the winter.  Several expeditions followed, the sagas declare.

Up and down the coast, archaeologists track each promising clue to those settlements.  A large flint spearhead found on the beach at Pemaquid, Maine, a few years ago, is one of the "possibly Norse" exhibits that serves to keep interest on edge. The spearhead is now in the possession of Walter B. Smith, who has made extensive studies of Indian remains in this section. His conservative opinion is that it may be of Indian manufacture, and yet, he says, it is not made of flint such as the Indians used, but seems to be identical with a rock called halleflinta which is well known in Scandinavia.

If the Vikings presented gifts and trade objects to the Indians, or if Viking weapons were occasional trophies of a battle, carried off by a surviving redskin, the European articles would most likely be found at an Indian village site. Any Norse articles of iron would be masses of rust by this time. But copper, bronze, lead, and silver, and fragments of Norse pottery and beads might have been preserved.

A place that held the name of being a Norse ruin, at Sculpin Island, off the Labrador Coast, was investigated in 1928 by an expedition from the Field Museum of Natural History. But Strong of the museum staff reported that the stone ruins bear no resemblance to authenticated Norse ruins in Greenland, and no typical Norse implements could be found. The site seems to have been occupied by Eskimos.

It is barely possible that the Vikings explored the northeast coast as thoroughly as tradition insists and yet no trace of their visits here might ever be found. The places where they settled may have been re-settled long since by permanent Americans, with the usual loss to archaeology. In less densely populated neighborhoods, rare Norse objects, battered and discolored by time and exposure, may be carted off nowadays as so much junk, unless the finders realize the possible importance and preserve them for identification. The Indians themselves may have helped to destroy the evidence. Some of the stories indicate that a Viking's natural inclination on seeing an Indian was to shoot him. In the circumstances, Indians surviving a Viking visit might be understood if they fiercely burned, hacked, or threw into the sea everything that would remind them of the invaders.

Pictures painted or etched on boulders in various parts of the country have often been reported to be runic writing, and therefore sure evidence that the Norsemen penetrated into the country, even to the far west. But these so-called writings have never suggested anything to the well-known experts in Indian life except the crude pictographs that the Indians often made.

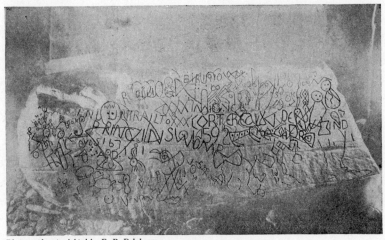

AN OLD AMERICAN PUZZLE — DIGHTON ROCK IN
MASSACHUSETTS

Can you find the name of Miguel Cortereal and the date 1511? These were discovered lately by means of flashlight photography. In this picture the figures cut and scratched on the rock have been filled in to make them clearer.

The most famous of all the picture rocks, Dighton Rock on the Taunton River, Massachusetts, has for two centuries not only been held up as an exhibit of Norse writing, but it has also impartially lent aid to practically every one of the picturesque theories of old American exploration. In 1690, Cotton Mather referred to Dighton Rock in his publication on the wonderful works of God. And even before that time, and certainly ever since, puzzled persons have strained their eyes over the inscriptions on the boulder. What they saw has often been magnified by their own interests and knowledge, so that it seemed sure proof of the strangest theories.

Different people who inspected Dighton Rock have seen traces of Phoenician writing, Druid signs, evidence of the lost tribes of Israel or the Chinese, clues to the inhabitants of the lost continent of Atlantis, and what not. Reading about all this we get the fanciful impression that Dighton Rock must have been the hotel register that innumerable strangers in the country rushed to sign to establish their arrival.

A psychologist of Brown University got at an unexpected secret of the rock after all the exhaustive examination of its weather-beaten surface. The professor, E. B. Delabarre, lives near the rock in summer and has studied it for many years at the hours when the tide permitted. He has achieved the new and none-too-easy task of making flashlight photographs of the surface. These put a new light on the rock in more ways than one. Beneath the pictures scratched in the boulder there appear traces of a name that could be filled out to spell Miguel Cortereal. The date 1511 is also revealed.

Now, Cortereal is the name of two brothers who sailed from Portugal to Labrador and Newfoundland. One set out in 1501 and failed to return home. The other, Miguel, sailed in 1502 to rescue him and was never heard of again. If the psychologist is correct, Dighton Rock stands as testimony that Miguel came to New England and survived among the Indians for some years, more than a century before the Pilgrims landed. The hidden name and 1511 also mean that the scratchings made later must be Indian, as unimaginative observers insisted.

Most of the theories that civilized men reached America before Columbus have been leveled straight against what was long regarded as the most fantastic theory of all: namely, that the careers of the Aztecs and other Indians developed without foreign intelligence and aid. But that once unbelievable theory now holds the field with little dispute. Some of the Asiatics may have hailed from China or southern islands. But it is pretty well accepted that the immigrants brought to the New World only such simple accomplishments as the craft of shaping tools out of stones and the art of hunting game. The rest of the Indians' culture was made in America.

*Drawing by Elizabeth Goodwin*

## A BASKET MAKER INDIAN HURLING HIS SPEAR WITH AN ATLATL, OR SPEAR-THROWER

This is the oldest type of Indian about which archaeologists can supply details at the present time.

## CHAPTER ELEVEN

# THE GREAT SOUTHWEST

## I. WHEN BASKETS WERE POTS AND PANS

THE earliest chapter in American prehistory now being assembled by archaeologists deals with the Indians of the Southwest. Thirty years ago, it would have seemed visionary to suggest that Indians lived in this country as contemporaries of the ancient Egyptians. Perhaps it seems incredible that human beings who had already passed the stage of wild savagery and had entered the tribal stage should have lived in this stimulating land for several thousand years without catching the American spirit, inventing an alphabet, taming some not-too-wild animals to serve as strong beasts of burden, inventing wheels to speed up transportation, finding out the possibilities of iron, and in general acquiring what we call a civilization. If the people of Egypt could advance from Stone Age culture to a complex civilization in a few thousand years, why not the Indians?

But evidence unearthed in the Southwest in recent years makes us believe in the existence of those Indian tribes of the B.C. era. At a number of American museums may be seen the possessions of Americans who lived in the days of Tutankhamen, and even many centuries before him. While the Pharaohs were erecting the royal pyramids and living in luxury as the rulers of a highly organized population, life in the Southwest was a simple tribal existence. In caves of Utah and Arizona, where the principal remains of this early period have been found, the household pots and pans were baskets. Hence, the name Basket Makers becomes a convenient label for these old Southwesterners. What they called themselves nobody knows. They had no writing. They left no record of their chieftains, their wars, famines, or trade relations.

The restoration of these Indians to their place in prehistory has been due largely to investigations of Kidder of Phillips Academy at Andover and Guernsey of the Peabody Museum. From the evidence accumulated by such expeditions, we can picture the Basket Makers as Indians who developed beyond the state of homeless savages who lived on wild plants and game. They had gardens and farms, and, since they must stay near the growing corn until harvest time, they built simple shelters in the open and slept in caves in cold weather. Having established homes, they collected household equipment. Their clothes were fur-cloth blankets and square-toed sandals.

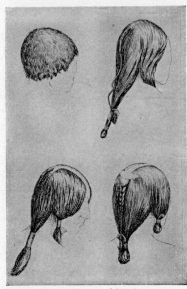

*Courtesy Peabody Museum of American Archaeology and Ethnology*

SHORT–HAIRED WOMEN AND LONG–HAIRED MEN

These dwelt in the Southwest several thousand years before Columbus' arrival in America.

The women wore bobbed hair, hacked off with stone blades, the only barber tools available in this Stone Age community. These women seem to have cut their locks for utility, not for fashion. Human hair was valuable for making string and a good deal of hair string has been found. Heavy thongs and handles contained as many as fifty strands of hair. The men do not appear to have sacrificed their hair to any such cause. Mummies found in old graves show that men wore their hair arranged in an elaborate system of partings, braids, and loops. The middle part was a wide barbered space and the side hair was looped up in long bob style, while the back hair grew to its natural length.

The bobbed-hair women kept house with baskets for cooking, baskets slung on their backs for gathering seeds and carrying loads, baskets even for water jars. The woven containers of yucca fiber, shredded roots, and wooden splints were made water-tight or as durable as necessary with a coating of mud and ashes or with piñon gum. Cookery was limited to the simple processes of roasting, and of heating food in baskets into which hot stones were dropped.

Ruins of homes inhabited by late generations of Basket Makers have only recently been discovered. The foundation of such a house was a round or square pit more than two feet deep, with slabs of stone lining the walls. Posts were set within the walls. The roof was made of slanting poles covered with brush and grass, and over that a layer of earth. In Chaco Canyon in New Mexico the whole side of one of these houses was found where it fell, thus setting an end to much speculation as to the houses built by early prehistoric Indians. For the greater part, settlements of that time have long since vanished. Even household effects left in an abandoned village soon disintegrated or were seized by other Indians.

The Basket Makers have come back from oblivion to take their place in the record of departed tribes chiefly because they followed the old custom of ceremonial burial — the careful laying away of the dead, accompanied by their possessions and special gifts. The graves remained long undiscovered because they were small pits or cists dug in caves. Archaeologists exploring cliff dwellings walked unsuspecting over hardened earth floor which covered the remains of the oldest tenants. When they did spade deeper into what appeared to be undisturbed soil, they found the holes that had been dug, sometimes as hiding places for food, but more often as burial places. And in the round pits were curled up the remains of men, women, and children who were at once recognized as different from the cliff dwellers in appearance and who were seen to be surrounded by different possessions. Many of the burials were not merely skeletons but shriveled "mummies," preserved naturally by favorable conditions. Overhanging cave roofs kept the soil dry; and the arid climate proved as favorable to material immortality as the climate of Egypt.

Seeds of squash and ears of corn have been found in the pits. Government experts who handled the corncobs assigned them to a type known as Tropical Flint and pronounced them a primitive form of corn not like any grown today. This corn is different even from the corn grown by the Pueblos, who developed into better farmers than the earlier Southwesterners. The presence of corn indicates contact between the Southwest and Mexico, for corn was grown first of all in tropical America, and found its way into the Southwest fifteen or twenty centuries before the Christian era. Abalone shells from the Pacific coast are further evidence that the early Southwestern tribes had contacts with distant places. The shells might mean that the Basket Makers migrated from the California region; the more likely explanation, however, is that the West Coast started advertising its native products toward the East even in that early age.

*Photograph from Peabody Museum of American Archaeology*

TWO OF THE OLDEST DOGS IN AMERICA

Mummies of a big yellow dog and a little black and white dog, taken from Basket Maker graves.

The clothing in which Basket Maker mummies are wrapped is mostly fur-string, a durable and ingeniously made cloth. Fur hide was first cut in strips and twisted around a yucca cord, so that the hair stood up in whirls. These heavy threads, resembling woolly bear caterpillars, were then woven. The probable method is that two stakes were set in the ground at a distance apart as great as the length desired for the blanket. Then the fur threads were wound flat and even around the two stakes, and the result was a flat blanket of fur standing up end-wise. The fur was held in place by twined threads of yucca cord, and the robe could be taken off the frame. By this procedure small animal skins could be converted into big blankets.

The Indians had no horses nor cattle until the Spaniards brought these animals, but there were dogs in America, even thousands of years ago. At Chaco Canyon were found the skeletons of two dogs carefully buried by Basket Maker Indians. With the dogs were placed two red painted deer bones; so that the dogs would have food for their journey into the next world. We are naturally curious to know what kind of dog followed these Indians. The smaller has been pronounced a spaniel, a rare type among prehistoric dogs. If brought from Mexico by traders, as it

*Photograph from Peabody Museum of American Archaeology*

A BASKET FOR CARRYING WATER

A lining of piñon gum made the weave watertight.

very likely was, it must have been held at a high price, and the owner's care of it to the last is readily understood. The other animal is less distinguished — a dog of the plains Indian type. But somebody thought enough of him several thousand years ago to give him a funeral. Mummies of two other Indian pets, from Arizona, a yellow collie, and a black-and-white lap dog of a breed found as far south as Peru, won distinction when they were exhibited at a dog show in Boston. They were awarded blue ribbons as the oldest dogs present, with no close competitors.

Baskets of the Basket Makers are found in considerable profusion. The containers are of varied shapes, suggesting use as trays, bowls, water jars, and panniers. Designs on them in black and red are mostly whirls, zigzags, and other simple patterns. No story or symbolism can be read into the designs. Any message recorded there is probably lost forever. Yet some new knowledge of the Basket Makers has been gained from these basket designs, not by interpreting them, but by comparing them with the oldest pottery in the San Juan area of New Mexico. It is found that the same designs appear on both pottery and baskets, and this suggests that the Basket Maker housewives became potters by some natural step of progress. Perhaps an absent-minded housekeeper set a basket with a durable clay lining too close to the fire and instead of its being ruined by carelessness, the clay hardened and entered into its rightful state of importance. Or, perhaps outsiders initiated the women of these tribes into the art of clay firing.

Expeditions to the Southwest have been looking particularly for missing links that would make clear the transition between the Basket Makers and the Pueblos. In 1928, Roberts of the Smithsonian came upon ruins of a village in southwestern Colorado that show the state of Indian culture in the transition period. This village had been swept by fire and the flames had left the ruins in a condition particularly favorable to preservation. The fire trapped some of the inhabitants of the village, and their charred skeletons lay in the ruins of their homes. The harvest had just been gathered when the tragedy occurred, for jars lying about were filled with corn, beans, and dried fruits.

This fire appears to answer the question: Were the early Southwestern Indians wiped out in ruthless warfare; or did they mix peacefully or hopelessly with incoming Pueblos and lose their identity? The answer of the village is that the Basket Maker type did not perish suddenly. All but three of the Indians whose bodies were found in the ruins were Pueblos. But there were three others living with them as neighbors or slaves who were Basket Makers. The two types are distinguished by head shape. The Basket Makers had long-shaped heads, like the cranium that the modern Nordics proudly possess. The Pueblos had round-shaped, bullet heads, and they were proud of that. In fact, they thought that nature had not gone far enough; so they exaggerated the broadness and

*D.S.W*

*Ref.*

flatness to the point of deformity by tying the babies' heads against stiff cradle-boards. The pliant little skulls soon acquired the fashionable shape, and, judging from the scarcity of unflattened skulls among the prehistoric Pueblos, an individual who grew up naturally was not merely unfashionable but was nearly a freak. Here, then, in this village, were both types, and also a blending of the customs typical of each. Bone needles and tools in the houses were comparatively primitive, representing the older culture, but the pottery showed progress into the art ideals of the Pueblos. And the houses showed how one group was learning from the other, for the architecture combined ideas from both the old and the new Southwesterners.

A 200–ROOM PREHISTORIC AMERICAN APARTMENT HOUSE

The Cliff Palace ruin in Mesa Verde National Park, Colorado.

*Photograph by Smithsonian Institution*

POTTERY FROM ELDEN PUEBLO

## THE GREAT SOUTHWEST

### II. THE PREHISTORIC APARTMENT DWELLERS

Banditry, insecurity, warfare — the Southwest has long had a reputation for this sort of drama. It became accentuated about the beginning of the Christian era, after the pueblo builders had established themselves in the region. In the centuries that followed, inhabitants of the Southwest increased rapidly. As wealth in corn and turquoise was amassed in Pueblo villages, wandering and aggressive tribes found it well worth while to harry the settlements. The Pueblo tribes held their own by being constantly on the alert. Cautious families took to the caves in the sides of inaccessible cliffs, or built square huts of rock or stucco on top of high mesas. Later, Indian farmers combined for protection. Then began the building of tall terraced pueblos, strong-walled community houses.

The preparations against emergencies were far from unnecessary measures, as traces of battle in the old ruins prove. Nomad tribes in a season of poor hunting would turn their thoughts eagerly to the Pueblo villages where there were jars filled with corn from the harvests. Raiding parties would creep up quietly, and if the watchmen posted at lookouts did

219

not warn the inhabitants in time, there was a holocaust and young women and children were captured. The bandits would depart with their captives and supplies, and, if they could carry more, with them would go the turquoise jewelry and other valuables of the unfortunate community. Feuds and rivalries may have caused some guerilla warfare, but the struggle for food in this magnificent but arid region was the dominant factor of life.

Driven always by the need for greater protection, and inspired by the great natural architectural ideas all about them in the rock formations, the Pueblos became the leading prehistoric architects north of the Rio Grande. Unknown designers of their remote period evolved a good many of the features of building construction that we look upon rightly as "American" but wrongly as "modern American."

Their community houses, occupied by hundreds of villagers, were as compact as our apartments that we jestingly call cliff dwellings. Pueblo architects built skyscrapers seven terraces tall. Not so high, you say, thinking of our latest steel frame construction. No; but those old, old skyscrapers seem taller when you recall that it was just about sixty years ago, 1869 to be exact, that New York achieved its first seven-story building, and that was looked upon by our own grandfathers as a sensational experiment.

Architects who step back the upper stories of skyscrapers in a terraced effect are acclaimed as developing a modernistic style for tall buildings. The origin of the device is the ancient pyramid, but it is worth remembering, too, that Pueblo architects worked out the same system for their buildings. The Pueblos did it, not for better lighting nor to improve the skyline, but in order to leave ledges on which ladders could rest and to provide space before each dwelling for conducting domestic work. Ladders stood at intervals around a typical pueblo, in twentieth century fire-escape fashion. They were not emergency exits, however, but emergency entrances. In time of attack the inhabitants hurried home, scrambled up the ladders, and pulled in the stairways after them.

Even town planning was known to these people, and that really is an impressive thought, when we know that such recent cities as Boston grew along lines of least resistance. Indian towns grew in haphazard fashion, too, very often. But a systematic program of construction is demonstrated at the pueblo at Aztec, New Mexico. Recent excavations have shown that this place was built and finished in a few years, so that 1,500 people could move in.

The Indians who had apartments in these pueblos were different in many ways from the old provincial Basket Makers. Progress in building construction has been described, and their eccentric fashion of beautifying the head has been mentioned. The flat-headed farmers and traders of a Pueblo metropolis wore cotton garments instead of the old yucca fiber cloth. Square-toed sandals would have been as conspicuous at a Pueblo gathering as a dust-trailing skirt among us today. Pueblo fashions called for sandals with pointed toes. Fur-cloth, too, was out. Feather-cloth was the thing, as a result of the Pueblo farmer's conquest of the wild turkey. That American bird had been domesticated, and the uses found for it rivaled the modern packer's success with the pig. The turkey to the Pueblo meant dinner, but, more important than that, it meant cloth, bone tools for weaving, sewing, and other fine work, and feathers for use in ceremonies.

And then there was the most significant development of all — Pueblo pottery. American ceramic art reached its highest development in the villages of the Southwest, where prehistoric women sat in the shadow of pueblo walls and shaped the clay with fingers instead of potters' wheels. Of course, some tribes outshone others at this craft. Bowls made in the Mimbres Valley of New Mexico arouse critics to enthusiastic comparisons with Greek vases. At the other extreme is some of the oldest pottery, which is childlike in its crude attempts at making beauty. But somehow the average Pueblo woman was never satisfied to turn out a bowl efficiently ugly. The clay in her hands took on smooth curves, and the blank finished surface generally cried out for a design. Each tribe had its

Photograph by U. S. National Museum

A SCIENTIFIC JIG-SAW PUZZLE

When time and weather jumble Pueblo pottery into chaotic fragments, the task
of re-assembling a jar is one that calls for an expert.

traditional shapes and customary use of color and decoration. Experts can tell at a glance what part of the Southwest produced this or that fragment of clay pot. But within those broad limits the Pueblo women displayed remarkable versatility, as thousands of pieces of their work testify.

Exploration parties eager to dig up ruins in the Southwest have been more numerous than parties to any other area of America. Every expedition returns at the end of the summer season with new facts to be fitted into the gaps in the Pueblo story. Each ruin unearthed reveals its personality. Only a few of the latest expeditions can be mentioned here, and only some highlights of these. The entire record of a single site as reported scientifically by expeditions returning from year to year often runs into a shelf-full of volumes.

One of the best known ruins is Pueblo Bonito, the "beautiful town," in Chaco Canyon, New Mexico. In 1896 this site was partially excavated, but after the custom of archaeologists then, the ruins were again covered with earth for protection. So, it was not until 1921 that an attempt was made to restore this pueblo to some of its former glory. For seven summers, expeditions sent out by the National Geographic Society and directed by Judd of the United States National Museum worked to unearth the story hidden here.

As the story began to unfold, fancy pictured this Indian settlement as the Athens of the Southwest. Just as the Athenians represented Greece at its best, so the Indians of Pueblo Bonito are good spokesmen for the Southwestern culture. Their eight-hundred room, four-story pueblo was a masterpiece of primitive engineering. It is at least as old as 500 A.D., and it was abandoned probably about 1100 A.D. In the course of those centuries it went through four periods of building activity, and, strange to say, two distinct groups of similar and yet unrelated people worked as neighbors on the construction projects.

Addressing the National Academy of Sciences in 1927, Judd explained: "Those of the first group dwelt for several generations in their moon-shaped pueblo before the second group arrived, presumably by invitation, and introduced superior architectural and cultural practices that quickly won for Pueblo Bonito preëminence among all contemporaneous villages north of Mexico. All archaeological evidence shows these two Indian peoples to have been entirely distinct and independent from each other. And yet they dwelt side by side and lived the same sort of life in the terraced town."

Photograph by O. C. Havens, Courtesy National Geographic Society

THE ATHENS OF THE SOUTHWEST
Showing the moon-shaped plan of Pueblo Bonito.

The first residents were conservatives and built small, low-ceiled rooms with rough sandstone slabs. Rooms were added in irregular fashion, as families increased. The second set of tenants made their additions and repairs in more orderly manner, and with the skill of master craftsmen. First, these better carpenters and masons built walls of hand-dressed stone, and filled the spaces between the stones with small chips. Later, they evolved more artistic masonry by setting large, dressed blocks in horizontal layers. And, at last they found that laminate sandstone with uniform, natural cleavage required less reshaping and yet made stronger walls than the softer, irregular blocks. While the late comers progressed in the study of masonry, the old inhabitants continued to build in the crude and hazardous manner of simply piling up stones as their ancestors had done.

Pueblo Bonito was both influential and prosperous. In the valley outside the walls, farmers raised maize, beans, and squash in fields watered by midsummer floods. Turquoise

Photograph by O. C. Havens, Courtesy National Geographic Society

PREHISTORIC ROBBERS AT PUEBLO BONITO LEFT THIS CONFUSION

They sought, apparently, the turquoise jewelry for which the pueblo was famed.

and lignite were obtained and made into beautiful ornaments. Pottery fashioned by the women was among the best of the time. Long-distance trade was lively, judging by foreign objects in the ruins, such as macaws from Mexico and shells from the Pacific coast.

Intelligent and cautious as the people must have been, they were at last overcome. Enemies? Drought? Nobody knows. But their stronghold was abandoned and fell into ruins.

Pueblo Bonito had its suburbs, and a strange discovery made at a suburban development consisted of the bones of

five youthful Indians so treated that the question of cannibalism is raised. The bones had been piled in a heap and
burned, and some were split and scraped of their marrow.
A similar find was made in 1927 in Colorado: bones of two
individuals lying in a pot in a fireplace. Such remains are rare
indeed in the Southwest, and the circumstances in which man-
eating was resorted to, if at all, are far from understood.
Among the Indians of the United States region this kind of
ceremony appears to have been limited to a few tribes.

Besides Pueblo Bonito, there were eleven other community structures in the shelter of Chaco Canyon. One of
these, Chettro Ketl, was partially excavated a few years ago
by the School of American Research. The skill of the Indian
builders, the unexpectedly large size of many of the rooms,
the carefully laid ceilings of logs covered with cedar slabs,
then with cedar bark, and finally with hard-packed earth, all
betoken the great interest the workmen took in their community.
As Hewett, who directed the excavations, pointed out, these
Indians were not like the slaves of Egypt, working under duress
to build fine palaces for a royal master. They were building
of their own volition better homes and stronger walls for the
protection and comfort of their own families.

The outstanding feature of Chettro Ketl was a bowl-like
structure about sixty-two feet in diameter. The builders had
dug a circular room in the earth and had surrounded it with a
stone wall three feet thick. This wall extended above the
ground and was originally roofed over, partially at least, with
wood and adobe. The use of the great bowl has not been definitely determined. There were many smaller structures of
the same general plan in Chettro Ketl, and these were the
kivas regularly found in pueblos. Apparently the people of
this particular settlement had great enthusiasm for religious
rites and conclaves, and the bowl was the community's most
impressive hall.

The pueblos of Chaco Canyon were all abandoned centuries before the white man's coming. The air of baffling silence
and mystery that surrounds the canyon is not felt so keenly

at a ruin such as Pecos, near Santa Fe. Pecos has different claims to distinction. It was inhabited until 1838, and we know how it looked in the sixteenth century when it entertained the Spaniards and impressed them mightily by its strong organization and its architecture.

The quaint narrative of Castañeda, chronicler of the Coronado expedition in 1540–42, tells of Pecos:

"It is square, situated on a rock, with a large court or yard in the middle, containing the estufas [kivas]. The houses are all alike, four stories high. One can go over the top of the whole village without there being a street to hinder. There are corridors [terraces] going all around it at the first two stories, by which one can go around the whole village. These are like outside balconies, and they are able to protect themselves under these. The houses do not have doors below, but they use ladders, which can be lifted up like a drawbridge, and so go up to the corridors which are on the inside of the village. As the doors of the houses open on the corridor of that story, the corridor serves as a street. . . . The village is enclosed by a low wall of stone. . . The people of this village boast that no one has been able to conquer them and that they conquer whatever villages they wish. The people and their customs are like those of the other villages. . . . The people came out from the village with signs of joy to welcome Hernando de Alvarado and their captain, and brought them into the town with drums and pipes something like flutes, of which they have a great many. They made many presents of cloth and turquoises, of which there are great quantities in that region."

The prehistory of Pecos stretches back about a thousand years. After Kidder had excavated here a few years, he reported the discovery of more than 2,000 skeletons. This pueblo, with its long succession of residents all buried at the site, is expected to aid scientists in tracing the changes in human beings from generation to generation. A thousand-year graveyard, too, should offer a rare opportunity to study the types that came into such a community and mingled with the population. The bones should show with exceptional completeness some of the diseases of America and the wounds from warfare. Bones of Pecos inhabitants are being studied. They have shown that tuberculosis was one of the diseases that plagued the Southwest.

One of the recent striking discoveries at Pecos was the burial of a prominent Indian physician. In his grave was placed the prehistoric equivalent of a modern doctor's little black bag. There were the medicine flutes on which he played to the sick, his stone pipe, a pouch containing medicine stones, and the paints which he needed in decorating himself appropriately for the ceremonies of healing. This old doctor's prominence is judged chiefly by one remarkable possession: a string of 5,700 shell beads. The beads were not hung around his neck, but were twined about the matted pigtail at the back of his head. The labor involved in completing such an ornament and the value of it may be imagined from the fact that each of the 5,700 beads was drilled by hand with a hard wooden drill, and each little disc of shell was polished. Doctors since then have received valuable gifts from grateful and important patients. It could have happened a thousand years ago in America.

When Coronado with his resplendent army reached the Southwest in 1540, the first pueblos visited by him were those which formed the "Seven Cities of Cibola," inhabited by the ancestors of the present Zuñis. These pueblos were abandoned by 1680, the Zuñis seeking refuge from the Spaniards, against whom all the Pueblo tribes had rebelled. In 1917 the ruins of Hawikuh, New Mexico, the principal Cibola town, were selected for excavation and the work continued during six seasons by the Hendricks-Hodge Expedition of the Museum of the American Indian. As the digging progressed, several stages of occupancy were revealed, as shown by the differences in the pottery at varying depths, in the evidence of fire that had destroyed large parts of the pueblo, and in the changes in the wall masonry. Spanish objects were found in the later houses and graves and their association with particular types of pottery helped to establish the sequence of manufacture and disclosed contact with other Indians as far away as southern Arizona. Information on ancient Zuñi custom and ceremony was obtained, such as the weaving of cotton into excellent fabrics, the domestication of the turkey, the manufacture of turquoise mosaics, the cult of the parrot, and the practice of three forms of burial, including cremation in "killed" vessels, that is, in jars which had a hole knocked in them.

From Hawikuh we can turn to Elden Pueblo, near Flagstaff, Arizona. Elden is one of the latest additions to the archaeologist's map of the Southwest. In 1926, a clearing in some pine trees not 200 yards from the National Trail Highway was pointed out to Fewkes of the Smithsonian as a possible settlement. He dug here and found crudely built walls of large stones and rubble. The pottery from this pueblo is generally coarse and its decoration frequently evidences the fumbling efforts of human beings when they take to art with clumsy fingers. Obviously, Elden was prehistoric but, unlike Pueblo Bonito with its career of progress, Elden did not "make the grade." Perhaps the inhabitants showed their progress by moving to a better site.

Out of this old pueblo came pottery that illustrates how the same ideas have occurred to different types of humanity separated by thousands of miles and living in totally different ways. At Elden, the excavators picked out of the earth toy-sized copies of pots and bowls that had been buried with the dead Indians — the same sort of device that the ancient Egyptians often used, reasoning that there was no need to bury good furniture and possessions with the dead. The spirits of miniature imitations would be just as serviceable in the spirit world.

Elden is an important discovery chiefly because it lies in the center of a large area which from an archaeological point of view is as yet unexplored territory. The farthest borders to which Pueblo culture spread are still undetermined. In the same year that Elden came to light, M. R. Harrington for the Museum of the American Indian discovered a few dried-up corncobs and fragments of gray and black pottery in a cave in Nevada. A few years earlier this would have seemed an unprofitable place in which to search for Pueblo clues. But Harrington's find of old corn and pottery made it clear that the Pueblos had touches of the wanderlust, and that some pioneers tried raising corn much farther north than anybody had previously imagined. Harrington has found fragments of Pueblo pottery as far west as California, showing that further clues should be sought there before modern progress destroys all the evidence.

Another Southwestern settlement that may be taken as a sample is the White House ruin in Canyon de Chelly in Arizona. This holds the distinction that a stream was turned aside to rescue it. The reader will recall the story of the discovery of the Greek inscription at Gortyna, in Crete, by the turning aside of a stream. Here was a cliff dwelling two-thirds of which had been swept away since the beginning of the twentieth century. Morris, an archaeologist who puts engineering skill to use, set out to save the remaining third of the unexplored ruin. To do this he built two conversion dams, each more than 300 feet long, made of sandstone faced with woven wire.

When he was satisfied that the rest of the ruin was not going to be washed down the stream he dug into the new site. Some of the rooms were piled with sixteen feet of refuse accumulated through centuries of not too fussy housekeeping. From the trash-heaps the archaeologist extracted sandals, squash and pumpkin seeds, the usual broken pottery, and, a very unusual find, bits of cotton lace. This oldest American-made lace is really heavy cotton goods, but it was made with lace technique, and represents the attempt of some Indian woman to create more delicate stuff than the ordinary weave of cloth.

The grave of a warrior at the White House ruin contained another unusual find. Cotton had been taken from the bolls and spread like a quilt to make a soft bed for this man. He was not to be cold, either, for beside him was laid his fire-making set, consisting of a hearth and drill. Interest centers, however, not on the luxury of the warrior's burial, but on the bow and arrows beside him.   Bows and arrows were standard Pueblo weapons, yet they are rarely preserved through many centuries.   This warrior's bow had been broken to fit into the small pit.   There was a sheaf of twelve arrows, six with stone tips and six with wooden tips, and on the man's breast lay a pouch containing additional arrowpoints.

The region which has produced the most ingenious and attractive of the Pueblo pottery is the Mimbres Valley in New Mexico.   Mimbres pottery is decorated with a wide assortment of humans, fishes, birds, beasts, and insects, as well as highly imaginative geometric figures.   Ordinarily, Indian attempts at depicting animal life fall short of the success with conventional patterns, but not so in the case of the Mimbres artists.

The Mimbres bowls are so striking that it is only as an afterthought that anyone inquires about the people who made them. Modern knowledge of the Mimbreños is shadowy, and what is known deepens the mystery of why they should have excelled in decorative art.   At Swarts pueblo, in the valley, Mr. and Mrs. Cosgrove from the Peabody Museum of Harvard spent five years digging out a ruin with a precision and delicacy that might be called excavation with a toothbrush.   They studied fireplaces, doors, and walls of the potters' two-story homes.   They found stone axes, knives, and arrowpoints. The Mimbres inhabitants were tireless bead-makers.   After an archaeologist has picked out thousands of tiny beads in his examination of a burial place, he grows a trifle weary of this ostentatious wealth.   Mimbres Valley Indians adorned themselves with stone and shell beads and their homes with fine dishes, but all in all they lived like other Pueblo groups of less esthetic sensibilities.   Their houses were substantial, not spectacular.   The burial of a child found by the expedition of 1928, sent out by the University of Minnesota and the School of American Research, shows a flash of the sentiment that we would expect in people with the Mimbres ideals of beauty.   Out of 157 graves, this child's contained the greatest number of gifts.   Following the usual custom, a beautiful pottery bowl was "killed" so that the spirit of the bowl might escape, and the bowl was laid over the child's head.   One arm of the child was still encircled by seven shell bracelets, and near the knee were eight shell tinklers.   Scattered about were broken strands of 1,500 red and blue-black beads.   A bone ring was another ornament or perhaps a toy.

A notable achievement of the Mimbres expedition of 1928 was the finding of hundreds of bowls and sherds of various types.   With this material, Bradfield, the ceramic expert of

Courtesy of the American Museum of Natural History, New York
POTTERY BOWLS
From Mimbres Valley, New Mexico.

the staff, was able to trace ceramic chronology of Mimbres tribes in almost complete sequence back to the beginning of the Christian era.

What caused the downfall of the Mimbres culture and why its beautiful pottery art was so completely forgotten are mysteries not yet fathomed.   The making of pottery in a good many other pueblos, fortunately, has survived the ups-and-downs of Indian life, survived even the white man's coming. To most eastern Indians, European brass kettles and iron pots made such an appeal that pottery lost favor.   Pueblo women did not acquire an inferiority feeling from the Spaniards' housekeeping, but after three centuries of the white man's influence the craftwork disappeared in this pueblo and that.   In the past few years the School of American Research at Santa Fe has conducted a campaign to revive the potter's art in pueblos where the old women still remember the technique.   Some of the women have gone to the museums to study  collections of prehistoric ware.   Some have come down to the ruins where the men of their families were helping at excavations and have examined with great care the designs on bowls and jars made by their ancestors.

The pottery industry now flourishes in about half of the inhabited pueblos, but not to replace the broken jars and bowls in Indian households.  The Indian woman has been shown that there is a demand for her art and she is learning to market her ware to advantage.  In some pueblos the income from pottery has become as great as the income from farm products.

A MAYAN PRIEST AND VOTARIES

A stucco relief from the "Palace" at Palenque, Mexico, showing Mayan profiles and elaborate headdress.

## CHAPTER TWELVE

## DIGGING UP A GREAT TROPICAL CIVILIZATION

TROPICAL regions have rarely been roused to produce note-worthy civilizations, for jungle lands are proverbially the places of the earth where life flourishes, but brain power stagnates. Yet tribes of Indians, known as the Mayas, conquered the American tropics, and their achievements outdistanced anything accomplished by the tribes of the temperate United States region.

In evidence of the conquest, Mexico and Guatemala and Honduras are dotted over with ruined cities, now buried in forests. The temples and rulers' homes and priests' houses were pictures in stone. No modern city can boast of such buildings, adorned with carvings and paintings of wartime victories and religious rites. Against the setting of tropic trees and sky, these buildings stood out like brilliant jewels. Statesmen of the Mayan cities ruled orderly groups of people who must have numbered tens of thousands. (In pronouncing the name Maya, it should be explained, the first syllable rhymes with "try.") The scholar-priests in the temples had a knowledge of astronomy and mathematics. These people alone, of all the old Americans, solved the difficult problem of perfecting a calendar. Our modern calendar is but slightly better adjusted to the traveling of the sun and moon. Mayan genius invented a system of hieroglyphic writing by which dates and other important records could be preserved everywhere the same. The Aztecs of Mexico, who also had a system of writing, borrowed heavily from the Mayan invention.

But while we marvel at the Mayan conquest of the tropics, which lasted for more than a thousand years, we must reserve some of our admiration for a conquest now in progress. This is the discovery and restoration of Mayan ruins by archaeolo-

235

gists and native workmen. Scientists, struggling with heat, insects, and thorny, deep plant growth, and led by native guides or by traditions of forgotten cities, find their way to some metropolis that has lain for centuries under a tangle of vegetation. Roots and branches have twined into the stones of the temples and have pulled them to earth. To cap the ruin, natives from near-by places have hauled away stones as they

*Photograph by Carnegie Institution of Washington*

WHERE MAYAN PRIESTS HELD RITES NINETEEN HUNDRED YEARS AGO

The beautiful white pyramid at Uaxactun, Guatemala, discovered in 1928.

needed building material. A number of the temples, palaces, and other public buildings have been pieced together as far as scientific knowledge and the remaining stones would permit. They stand today as the most magnificent architecture in America.

We can look at a single picture of a Mayan temple and learn enough about the builders to marvel at them, but not enough to understand them. Archaeologists are not content to wonder. They are determined to know what caused this flowering of thought and energy into a civilization that is sometimes compared to that of Greece. They wish to write Mayan history from the dim archaic beginnings up to the arrival of the Spaniards.

In the soil of the plateau of Mexico and in Guatemala have been found relics of the oldest known inhabitants of the regions. The finds are simple pottery and grotesque figurines like a child's clay men. The tribes who made these oldest objects were not savages. They raised grain — that standard achievement test of a social group. In fact, it was presumably in the highlands of southern Mexico that the wild plant teocentli was crossed with some unknown plant to produce the first maize. And whether those budding farmers knew it or not, that was one of the great events of the world.

In Mexico, too, the building of pyramids had an early start. A grassy hill at Cuicuilco, near an old volcano, was supposed to be a natural landmark until Gamio, a Mexican archaeologist, speculated that it might hold secrets. At his suggestion, Cummings of the University of Arizona excavated this hill in 1922. Digging through layers of vegetation, lava, and mud, he struck sloping walls of stones. Thus, the core of the "hill" turned out to be, not literally an angular pyramid, but a cone one hundred feet tall, built of chunks of volcanic rock covered over with lava blocks. Judging by the simple pottery and unpolished stone weapons buried about the place, and considering the changes wrought by volcanic upheavals, the pyramid is very old, possibly several thousand years older than our era. It appears to have been one of the first big experiments in stone, built to meet a desire for a high place on which to worship, as an altar on its summit attests. There are mounds of the archaic period in Guatemala, too, but cruder and simpler than the big cone at Cuicuilco and less predictive of great architectural achievement.

The oldest Mayan cities have been found in countries south of Mexico. Gamio, who perhaps has spent more time hunting down the forerunners of the Mayas than anyone else, thinks that the Mayan civilization did not grow up in these countries unaided, but that immigrants from Mexico adventured south, and that here a fortunate mingling of tribes took place. Earth-

quakes and volcanoes, he believes, may have played a major
rôle in shaping the destiny of these people. Some of the Mexican Indians left their homes in order to escape a neighborhood
where every time the earth grumbled, huts came tumbling
down and rocks flew like birds. They wandered south and es-

THE REGION OF THE STONE CITIES

tablished themselves in the stable lowlands of Guatemala and
Honduras, and their skill in building found an opportunity
here to express itself.

Whatever their origin, the inhabitants of the stable lowlands found time on their hands after providing food and shelter. Stone suitable for construction was plentiful. Religion
and the ambition of priests and rulers were powerful stimuli
to produce bigger and finer structures, and the cities grew in
number and magnificence. Starting before the Christian era
— no one knows exactly how far back — and ending about
600 A.D., the Old Mayan Empire flourished, with such cities
as Palenque in southern Mexico, Copan in Honduras, and Quirigua, Tikal, and Uaxactun in Guatemala.

In 1928 the jungle gave up important information at the
oldest Mayan city known — Uaxactun. (The letter "x"

which is sprinkled liberally through Mayan names is pronounced "sh." With this clue, Uaxactun becomes tame
enough as Wah-shack-toon. Accent the last syllable.) The
city's claim to special note came with the discovery that it
was in existence in 97 A.D., a century earlier than any Mayan
settlement hitherto known. The reason why Mayan dates
can be set down glibly in contrast with vague speculations as
to the age of other Indian ruins is that in most Mayan communities the priests regularly set up date stones every 1,800
days. The pictures and symbols of the Mayan writing system dealt chiefly with the recording of days, months, seasons,
years, and cycles of time. About thirty per cent of the symbols have been deciphered. There are several ways of corre-
lating the dates, but the translation most widely accepted
would give Uaxactun credit for existence within a hundred
years after the birth of Christ.

Prominent in the ruins of Uaxactun rose a steep pyramid-
like hill fifty feet high. Bits of the rubble slopes stuck out
through the forest mantle. The top was a platform of plaster painted red. It was a high place of sacrifice, but it was
more that that. As the archaeologists worked and camped
about the ruins, they caught the idea that this pyramid was a
huge sun-dial. Eighteen hundred years ago, astronomer-
priests in their regalia of fine clothing, feathers, jade, and stone
mosaics, were accustomed to mount the steps of the pyramid
to its summit to watch the sun rise. Their eyes were on three
temples located exactly near by. When the sun rose behind
the northern front corner of Temple One, the priests knew that
it was the summer solstice, June 21. When the sun rose
exactly behind the middle of Temple Two, the spring and
autumn equinoxes, March 21 and September 21, were at hand.
And when it rose from the southern front corner of Temple
Three, it was the day of the winter solstice, December 21. So,
at the proper time of year, they communicated to the people,
with ceremony and mystery, no doubt, the news that the gods
commanded the crops to be planted or the harvest gathered,
or the new fire to be made.

Ricketson, the leader of the excavations, was still fascinated by the pyramid.  It had the look of a pointed box, covering something.  Cautiously he dug experimental trenches into the sides, and scientific curiosity was justified.  There was a pyramid inside a pyramid.  Just as old masterpieces of painting have been covered over with mediocre art to conserve canvas, so the inner pyramid had been sealed up at some time before that oldest date stone, 97 A.D., was set up in the plaza.

The rainy season came on and the tantalizing discovery had to be left for another year.  Then the expedition workmen removed most of the rubble shell, leaving a sample bit at one corner for scientific reference use, and revealed a pyramid only twenty-five feet high, built of stone and covered with glistening white stucco.  A stairway on each side leads to the top, and guarding the steps are huge masks carved like grotesque human faces and serpents.  It is beautiful, and it is pronounced not Mayan at all in style, but pre-Mayan.  In other words, the founders of Uaxactun appear to be one of the missing links in the evolution of the Mayan people.  How far back into the pre-Christian centuries the city really was founded is uncertain.  Buried in the floor of the plaza were broken clay pots, small clay figurines, and parts of old house foundations, all older than the carved pyramid.

There were many other cities in the Old Empire; almost twenty rather large ones are known.  They were more remarkable for their sculptures than for their architecture, for the great age of building was to come later in Yucatan.  Of these cities, Palenque has long been famous as an encyclopedia in stone, narrating in its own way the Mayan achievements.  When Palenque was explored by travelers shortly after the time of the American Revolution, as many as fourteen stone edifices were found in the dense undergrowth.  Homes of the general population are never found in these cities.  The public buildings filled an impressive civic and religious area, and out from this hub radiated the thatched huts of the people, and their farms and garden patches.  Descendants of the Mayas today build the same kind of homes for their families, though they have forgotten their heritage of grander architectural projects.

Palenque's public buildings were covered with stucco, on which elaborate bas-reliefs and designs were carved. These impressed early travelers deeply, and gave rise to the first enthusiastic reports in appreciation of Mayan art. About 1840, the American traveler, John L. Stephens, was inspired by the fragments of marred sculptures to declare: "In justice of proportion and symmetry they have approached the Greek models." Since then the Mayan art style has become famous in its own right. Later discoveries of better preserved sculptures and paintings show that the Mayan beauty is based on a different conception of the universe from that of the Greek. This American art is not graciously curving and friendly, but fierce and exotic and brilliant. The portraits of the gods show them with grotesque features, sometimes with masks symbolizing their powers and fear-inspiring attributes. The hook noses and squint eyes and open-hanging mouths of these faces were to some extent exaggerations of the features seen in Mayan crowds. We know that Mayan mothers hung dangling objects before the eyes of the babies to make them squint. Ear plugs made sugar-bowl handles of Mayan ears, and noses were pierced so that jade ornaments could decorate the Mayan faces.

The elaborate detail of the carvings and painted friezes in the old cities makes it clear that though the Mayas lived in a Stone Age state of civilization, they had admirable accomplishments. The pictures show Mayan priests wearing robes decorated with beautiful patterns. Artisans worked the plumage of tropical birds into soft feather capes and into tall red, green, and yellow headdresses for the adornment of important tribesmen. Gold and copper were hammered into delicate jewelry. Until recently, the cloth of the Mayas was known only from pictures and from a few charred fragments. But in 1928, Blom of Tulane University discovered well-preserved samples of woven cotton goods, hidden in a cave together with some pottery. The type of the pottery indicates that the cloth dates from the Old Empire, about the fifth century A.D.

After a few centuries of energetic progress in the Old Empire, strange events happened. The inhabitants began moving northward into untamed forests, moving in waves of migration. By 600 A.D. the last workman had carved a stone date in a city of the Old Empire — at least that is the latest that has been found — and the temples were left to the jungle and the owls, and finally to the archaeologists. Northward in Yucatan, a New Empire was being built. This is as if the population of the eastern coast of the United States were to pick up and move several hundred miles west into the Ohio Valley, leaving New York, Baltimore, Boston, and other cities deserted.

Almost every specialist in Mayan culture has his own theory as to the cause of this migration. Some believe that an epidemic drove the people from their homes in panic-stricken hordes. Famine induced by an improvident system of farming which left the ground finally in such a state that it could produce no crops, is another explanation. A different idea, suggested by modern plagues of grasshoppers in Mexico: insects in some terrible years might have eaten the food supply before the eyes of the helpless inhabitants. Civil war between the groups is another speculation; and still another is that an overpowering theocracy set such heavy demands on the workers that the crops were neglected and the people were starving.

In native writings there is a reference to the discovery of Yucatan between 471 and 530 A.D. So, it was a surprise when in 1926, Gann, the British archaeologist, emerged from a trip into southeastern Yucatan with news that he had found a carved date stone showing that Mayan adventurers were established in Yucatan in 333 A.D. This old northern monument, set up when the southern Empire was rising to the height of its glory, means that the southern cities were not forsaken in a sensational overnight move of an entire nation, as it has sometimes been pictured. On the contrary, the people were moving for several centuries.

The same year of Gann's discovery, the Carnegie Institute unearthed more proof of the "Pilgrims" in Yucatan, at the city of Coba. In the heart of Coba, now dense forest, they traced the ruin of a religious center. There is a terrace covering four acres on which stand the remains of three buildings and a number of mounds. The place bears the name Macanxoc, meaning "You cannot read it." At the site were found eight large hieroglyphic monuments which the scientists scrubbed free from mud and proceeded to spell out, in spite of any challenge to their reading ability. The oldest of the monuments bears a date which Morley, head of the expedition, read as 350 A.D.

The Mayan colonists in Yucatan found streams scarce. Immigrants clustered thickest near lakes and natural wells and at these sites grew such cities as Coba and Chichen Itza. The New Empire became architecturally finer than the Old, and it was more progressive. The eagerness of the educated Mayas toward progress is after all the most impressive feature of their panorama of civilization. The saddest factor is their selfishly restricting wisdom to the favored few. The workmen who carved the date stones probably could not read them. When the Spaniards came, it was comparatively easy for them to wipe out the accumulated learning by disposing of the priests and rulers and by burning the books in the temples. Modern descendants of the Mayas speak the old language, and some use a calendar of the old type; but the higher learning is all gone — unless some priest's tomb should yield some of the paper books sufficiently preserved to be read. Only three Mayan manuscripts are known to be in existence, and these, which are treasured in European libraries, deal chiefly with magic formulae and rituals and the calendar.

A progressive project of the New Empire was the construction of smooth white stone roads, 30 to 60 feet wide, straight through the forest for miles. When Gann discovered the first of these roads, a few years ago, he injected something new into our pictures of Mayan life. There were no horses in Yucatan, no wagons. Dirt trails were satisfactory for foot travel. What, then, was the purpose of highways built several feet above the ground and representing a great amount of labor?

The answer presumably is the same that explains the temples and sculptures — religion.  Coba, where the first of these roads was found, was a staunch promoter of road construction.  The roads are sometimes lost in the underbrush and their course today is hard to follow, but one road is believed to have run east from Coba to the coast toward a place of religious pilgrimages, Cozumel Island.  Another prob-

Photograph by Carnegie Institution of Washington

THE TEMPLE OF THE WARRIORS AT CHICHEN ITZA

A side view of the temple as it stands on its terraced pyramid after careful restoration.

ably led from Coba to Chichen Itza; 50 miles away, ending at the temple of the sacred well.  Along the entire fifty miles from Coba to Chichen Itza, it is supposed, went processions of dignified priests with their attendants and with the victims and offerings destined to be sacrificed on the altars or to be flung into the sacred well.

Chichen Itza (pronounced Chee-chen-eet-zah) was a holy city dedicated to a favorite Mayan deity, the Feathered Serpent.  The scope of such a deity's power can be imagined from the combination of bird representing the sky and snake representing the earth.  Chichen Itza was founded in the fifth century by a Mayan tribe called the Itza, and the name means the "Mouth of the Wells of the Itza." In Yucatan a place endowed with two fine wells, as this was, might be expected to advertise the fact proudly through its name. The Itza kept one well for a water supply; the other was held sacred. The sacred well is a pit about 140 feet deep and 180 feet in diameter. Underground streams keep the water at a level of about 70 feet from the surface.

Evidence of sacrificial rites held at this mysterious well was obtained by E. H. Thompson, longtime owner of plantation land near-by. Mr. Thompson used to descend daily into the well in a diving suit to search for relics in the mud floor. But not until 1923 did he announce his discoveries. Then it was revealed that he had a collection of Mayan jewelry, broken pottery vases, weapons, and the bones of young men and girls. The offerings had been flung into the well centuries before, in order to induce the god to send rain to make the crops grow. Flower-decked maidens hurled into the sacred well are sometimes brought into the stories of these old Mayan rites, as the dramatic climax of sacrifice. It was only later, however, after Mexican tribes came into Chichen Itza, that the gods demanded offerings more precious than material wealth. The Mayas rarely, if ever, had shed human blood in the name of religion. The ceremony of the maidens which they adopted is not precisely in the class of Toltec and Aztec human sacrifices in which the heart of the victim was torn out and other gruesome spectacles were devised. In the Mayan rites if the privileged victims who dived into the rain god's dominions were still alive after a time, they were drawn up from the well and were expected to report whether the god would save his people from famine.

In Yucatan, the Mayas were closer to Indian tribes of Mexico than they had been in the south and complications were multiplied. The downfall of the Mayas seems to have been vaguely foreshadowed when Chichen Itza joined forces with two other powerful Mayan city-states, Uxmal and Mayapan. Before the twelfth century, civic rivalry led to quarreling.  The ruler of Mayapan engaged foreign allies — Toltec soldiers from the northwest in the valley of Mexico.  The Toltecs invaded Chichen Itza.  It has been generally believed that the Toltecs slowly usurped power.  Scenes depicted on buildings at Chichen Itza, however, record a desperate and bloody struggle between Toltec and Maya which took place at some time — unless this art represents an exaggeration of the real state of affairs to please Toltec vanity.  Tozzer of Harvard has pointed out that in the Temple of the Jaguars at Chichen Itza it is possible to differentiate Toltec victors and Mayan captives joining in a rite in honor of the Feathered Serpent, a deity dear to both tribes.  Metal plaques dredged from the sacred well also show the two types.  The Toltec wears a bird on the front of his headdress, and his face is decorated with a jade nose-button.  In his hand is his atlatl, or spear-thrower, and a padded shield protects one arm.  The Mayan prisoner, usually shown groveling in the dust, is distinguished by his artificially flattened forehead, elaborate headdress, a long nose-bead, and leggings.  It must have been a sad turn of events for the proud and not very warlike Maya, if they were not only subdued by violence, but were forced to paint such scenes under the direction of gloating Toltec conquerors.

The beautiful temples which rose in Chichen Itza under Toltec rule owe a great deal to Mayan craftsmanship.  A new kind of pillar was introduced by the Toltecs in honor of the Plumed Serpent, and as you recall the three famous Greek types of column, you can see that a new type is an architectural event.  The Toltec invention was a column carved to represent the body of the Feathered Serpent himself.  His head was bent, thus giving the column an angular effect.  Chichen Itza by this time was impressively beautiful.  There was the Caracol, or Snail-Shell, which stands today like a round spiraling tower on its hill, and is believed to be an astronomical observatory.  The great Ball Court, where athletes played the difficult game of tlachtli, suggests our modern basket-ball courts though built with stone walls and carved stone rings set vertically high in the walls for "baskets." Most sacred, perhaps, of all the temples was the one known today as El Castillo, the Castle. Its pyramid base is high, and from it a road leads to the sacred well. Grander than this sanctuary was the "Court of a Thousand Columns," a religious plaza with a group of temples.

In this plaza, at the Temple of the Warriors, some of the most recent unexpected discoveries have been made. In 1925 Morris, in charge of Carnegie excavations at Chichen Itza, began digging at a hopeless looking hill of dirt with trees sticking out of it and carved stones jumbled in the earth. After the season of 1928, he brought back to Washington the report that the Temple of the Warriors was completed as far as he could return the stones to their rightful places. Today, on the summit of four receding stone terraces, it stands as the most elaborately decorated building in the city. Modern visitors may mount the stone stairway with its carved balustrades and walk through the two rooms of the temple, even up to the carved altar. The visitors can stroll about in the main hall and see on twenty columns the figures of eighty warriors, probably real heroes of unknown American battles. The sun beats down on the carved and painted figures, for the roof could not be replaced.

The problem of restoring the temple would have been difficult enough without extra handicaps, but while the expedition staff was excavating, it found traces of an older temple like a basement beneath the ruins. This early temple had been partly demolished to make way for a more imposing edifice on the site. The painted pillars, even the altar of the old temple, had been piled in as filling material or used as ordinary building stones for the new place of worship. Unlike the builders, the archaeologists wanted to keep both temples. By use of concrete piers to support the upper walls and floors, they succeeded in making the place safe. Then the rooms of the inner temple could be cleared.

A persistent search for the ceremonial treasure of the temples, which would naturally have been hidden near an

altar, led Morris to an altar site in the older temple.  Here in
the floor he unearthed a limestone jar containing the bones of
a bird, a polished ball of jadeite used in divining events, and
a mosaic plaque as big as a plate, made up of 3,000 fragments
of turquoise.  The wood on which the mosaic was mounted

A PYRAMID THAT WAS HIDDEN BY THE AZTECS

When the Spaniards began destroying the old gods, frightened Aztec priests
at Tenayuca ordered that their temple and its pyramid base be covered with
earth, and it was not until 1925 that this impressive structure came to light
again.  The coiled snakes that surround the pyramid still bear traces of red,
blue, and green paint.

had turned to dust, but two-thirds of the pattern lay in place
— if it could only be kept from jarring!  To save this fragile
art work, a museum expert came to Yucatan from New York
and patiently remounted the mosaic picture on wood.

Chichen Itza under Toltec influence was brought into civic
quarrels and battles.  Disease seems to have dragged down
the weakened population, and the whole fabric of Mayan civilization began to be torn apart, never to be patched together
again.

Meanwhile, it must be remembered, there were scattered Mexican tribes, more or less well known, which had their stone cities and their own variants of Middle American civilization. Of these, the Aztecs are the most famous, partly because it was the Aztecs who met Cortés when he landed on the Mexican coast. Letters sent home by the Spaniards made the wealth and manners of these Mexicans as sensational talk as the tomb of Tutankhamen was not so long ago. Recent publication by the Museum of the American Indian of a letter written by a Spanish servant to his master back home suggests the impression that these people created.

"It is the richest land in the world where were found the following things," he wrote in part. "It has so much gold innumerable or without comparison, and has much silver and precious stones, namely, turquoise, garnets, rubies, and many other necessary things according to people who knew it. There are many clothes of cotton richly woven with figures sewed with a needle. One can hardly tell what wonderful things one finds in their houses; their bedsteads are covered with canopies and other costly cloths. The people of this land are honest and have extraordinarily beautiful women. One cannot estimate the value of the houses of the great lords, neither are they comparable with those in our land, because it is a great sight to see the buildings of these countries, the large halls, the entrances to the doors, the courtyards, are built with much marble and are decorated; all buildings are painted in various colors. They have many buildings so that the king with all his retinue may live comfortably therein. It is hard to tell what curious things one finds; their gardens are decorated with trees, with tables for banquets wonderfully wrought. The cities are larger than Seville; more than half of them have five miles of roads in length and breadth, wondrously beautiful, with splendid streets, all of them beautifully paved."

The Spaniards did not let their amazement interfere with the business for which they came. The first news reports declared that here was the world's richest country. They set to work to justify that announcement and prove the pecuniary worth of their expedition.

Spanish priests, meanwhile, went to the task of converting the natives and of wiping out all reminders of the old deities. How the Aztecs made frantic efforts to salvage one of their places of worship is shown at Tenayuca, near Mexico City. A pyramid here was covered entirely with

EVERYDAY LIFE OF THE MAYAS IN A SEASIDE VILLAGE

The scene includes three war canoes, each carrying two warriors; a woman watching a pot; another woman grinding corn; men carrying burdens; fish, crabs, and snails. Fragments of the mural painting were found in the débris of the Temple of the Warriors, and after they were pieced together a copy was painted by Ann Axtell Morris of the Carnegie Institution.

earth, so that it remained hidden for four hundred years. Mexican government archaeologists have worked for three years to dig out and reconstruct this buried pyramid. Reygadas, in charge of the excavations, pronounced the newly revealed monument as the most important example of Aztec architecture known. The great stone pyramid has a gigantic stairway. The steps are carved with hieroglyphs; and serpents' heads stick out at intervals from the sloping sides of the structure. Around three sides of the base are 138 stone snakes whose heads project facing the visitor. On top of the pyramid once stood a temple. Two altars may still be seen, and here again serpents of stone form the design.

All the efforts of explorers and archaeologists to restore the Mayas and their neighbors to their place in America's records and to reveal their stone cities are just a beginning. In Mexico alone there are twelve hundred registered archaeological sites. All these show vestiges of the prehistoric Mexican world important enough to warrant scientific interest.

From "Paleopathology" by Dr. R. L. Moodie          Courtesy W. B. Saunders Pub. Co.

## A PREHISTORIC SURGICAL OPERATION

This drawing, based on material found in Peru, depicts a Stone Age doctor treating a sick woman.  A hole has been cut in the skull, and hot oil, heated in the pot on the fire, will be placed in the wound.  To ease the pain the doctor will apply coca juice from a quid which he chews while he works.  The skull of this patient is preserved in the American Museum of Natural History.

CHAPTER THIRTEEN

## WHERE GARDEN SPADES WERE MADE OF GOLD

WHEN the Spanish adventurers reached South America, they discovered an Indian "empire" as large as two-thirds of the United States. It comprised Peru and part of Bolivia, and stretched up to include Ecuador on the north, and down into Chile on the south. The ruling caste was a group of powerful Indians known as Incas or "lords." The leader, the Inca, reigned amid such splendor and deference as few monarchs have ever commanded.

The Spaniards wrote again and again of Cuzco, the capital city of the Incas, a city magnificently set on a plateau of the Andes Mountains. Gold was used so lavishly about the palaces and temples of the capital that the eye of the beholder was dazzled. Metals had no money value in Peru; they were valued as beautiful materials. The nation worshipped as a major deity the Sun, god of light and warmth, and in the heart of Cuzco was a Temple of the Sun, plated with gold. An enormous golden sun disk, encrusted with emeralds and other precious stones, stood against the temple wall where it would catch the rays of the rising sun. Silver and gold were used to make the useful articles of the temple, even the garden spades. There was almost no end to the golden resources. When the Inca fell captive to the Spaniards, he gave orders to his couriers and they brought treasure until a room was piled high with gold — fourteen million dollars' worth, we are told — as ransom.

The ruler administered a remarkable communistic government. The people worked part time for the temples of the Sun, part time for themselves, and part time for the Inca. An outstanding achievement of their organized effort was a system of smooth stone roads, one of which traversed the mountainous country for 1,500 miles. The transportation problem was

253

handled by uniformed runners who carried messages and goods rapidly by relay. The Incas left no written records of their accomplishments. It is said that learned men were assigned the task of remembering important information. The Spanish writings are a curious blend of fact and imagination. It is left to the archaeologists to sort out the facts, and what is more difficult, to salvage any knowledge of the earlier, primitive cultures in Peru and of the tribes that went into the melting pot of the Inca Empire.

IMPORTANT ARCHAEOLOGICAL SITES
IN PERU

The search for Peru's prehistoric remains goes on in two types of country. About fifty miles back from the Pacific coast begin the great ranges of the Andes, which form ridges running north and south. In these highlands are lofty plateaus and mountain peaks lost in the clouds far above sheltered valleys. Between the ranges and the Pacific lies a strip of coast, sandy, and desert-like except where streams run across it to the ocean and bring to life the land they touch. The greater part of the area lies within the tropics. But the climate ranges from sub-tropical to sub-Arctic.

Early tribes that came into this region at some unknown time, certainly several thousand years ago, took up residence in sheltered sites. They came probably from the north or east and worked their way gradually toward the ocean. As their ideas of architecture developed, the highland tribes built monuments and buildings of massive stone. The coast people, lacking stone and wood, built their cities of adobe brick.

Excavations in graves many hundreds of years old show that the Peruvians were industrious weavers of cotton and fine

RUINS OF AN INCA PALACE

This sample of wall from a ruin in Cuzco shows how the Peruvians fitted stone blocks into massive plain construction, in striking contrast with the ornate architecture of Middle America.

woolen cloth. Modern textile manufacturers have discovered that these Indians had sound notions of design and color, and some of the silks and rugs in the shops today owe their charm to art from Peruvian graves. The pottery made for home use and for honoring the dead developed along unusual lines. The farmers learned some of the fundamentals of agricultural science, for they developed the potato from a little, runt-like plant and made of it a nutritious food. They terraced the hillsides to form flat strips of land, and in the terraced truck gardens they raised a remarkable array of American foods: maize; beans of many sorts, including Lima beans; peanuts; pods of cayenne pepper; white and yellow potatoes; sweet potatoes; manioc, and fruits of various trees and shrubs, such as chirimoyas, pepinos, and locumas; squashes and possibly pumpkins.

The doctors performed surgical operations on the skull and eye and knew how to amputate limbs. Many of the operations were successful, as the bones of the patients testify. The metal workers heated gold and silver and copper in furnaces and cast beautiful objects; in the course of time they learned to make bronze and to plate it with gold and silver.

*Photograph by Field Museum of Natural History*

POTTERY FROM PERU

The potato, which was first cultivated in Peru, is fittingly used as a subject for native art.

What the Peruvians accomplished is impressively clear. But when we look at the specimens of woolen cloth, the grotesque earthenware vases, the mummies, bronze axes and jewelry, we begin to ask questions that start with when, and how, and why. And there we come face to face with the difficult parts of the record that the archaeologists are trying to explain. Excavations show that many of the achievements for which the Incas have received praise were inventions and customs well developed in much earlier centuries. The Incas, by conservative estimate, started on their program of expansion no farther back than the twelfth century A.D.

Scientists seeking traces of the tribes who started the civilization on its upward climb have found the oldest man-made objects in the highland region. These are time-worn remains of stonework. Most worthy of note are the ruins of Tiahuanaco, lying scattered about a barren plateau, 13,000 feet above the level of the sea at the southern end of Lake Titicaca in Bolivia. There are enormous stones set on end as if to mark graves, and huge statues roughly carved in the semblance of stone gods or heroes. There are sections of wall and terraces built with altars on top for outdoor rites, and there are portions of temples. The great stones must have been pushed or pulled into place in much the same way as the Egyptians handled stone for their pyramid constructions. Workmen equipped with stone tools — no iron or steel has ever been found at the ruins — took the blocks brought to a building site and dressed the rough surfaces of the stones, so that they would fit perfectly without mortar. Sometimes copper clamps were countersunk in the blocks to hold them firmly together. One stone weighing about nine tons was cut out to form a gateway and then decorated with beautifully carved friezes. This monolithic gateway is regarded as one of the wonders of South America, and one of the puzzles, too, for the pictures cut into it have never been satisfactorily interpreted. A notable design in the carvings of the frieze and in other carvings about Tiahuanaco is the puma. This member of the cat family was worshipped on the plateau, and wherever the face or figure of the puma appears on a vase in some other part of Peru the idea is traced back to Tiahuanaco. No dates can be set for the ruins. Some seem to be much older than others, and some experts believe that two groups of men, widely separated in time, worked on the back-breaking stone walls and statues. The oldest of the ruins are undoubtedly several thousand years old.

Archaeologists speak more definitely about dates when they come down to the last thousand years of Peru's prehistory. Pottery made as far back as the early centuries of the Christian era has been found at ruins along the coast. The old vases and pitchers receive closer attention than any other type of Peruvian article, for they give the best criteria for dating the development of the country.

Numerous pottery specimens show that tribes of the northern coast region became dexterous at modeling and painting earthenware. Besides household pottery, special pottery for funeral use was made. All the high-lights of an individual's career, his occupations and interests, were illustrated in the clay objects placed in the grave. There are vases shaped like houses, portrait vases that represent individuals, even to showing their diseases and deformities, vases like vegetables, like fish, like guinea pigs. In fact, the panorama of life in a Peruvian community was accurately reproduced in clay. There is no doubt from the realistic representations, how the Peruvians worked their farms, how they danced, how prize fighters hammered clumsy opponents, how the surgeons worked, how the Peruvians looked in youth and old age. From this pottery we know more about the life of Peru than of any other culture in prehistoric America. In cities of the southern coast, less was known about modeling and reproducing nature than in the north, but more thought was given to use of beautiful colors and conventionalized designs.

Photograph by Museum of the American Indian

POTTERY FROM PERU

A graceful water jar of a type used in the Incan period. The carrier fastened the jar on his back by a strap which passed through the handles of the jar and was brought over the carrier's chest.

Long and intensive studies of the ware found at a single site have been made by Uhle of the Central University of Ecuador and Kroeber of the University of California. In 1925 Dr. Kroeber conducted explorations along the coast for the Field Museum of Natural History, and found no fewer than eight different styles of pottery in a comparatively small area in the north. Cycles of beauty and color changes, even degeneracy of designs, have been traced. Contacts of the coast with the highlands have been shown by jars such as were made in the distant mountains and that appear at one stage in the ruins along the coast. So valuable are these investigations that the government of Peru set aside one of its strict regulations and permitted Dr. Kroeber to take out of the country some of the archaeological specimens he collected.

It may be said here that the Peruvian deserts and jungles would be the goal of many an exploration party today if it were not for restrictions which the Peruvian government has deemed necessary in order to preserve the antiquities. For years there was so much reckless digging at old ruins and graves by people bent on finding gold or curios that could be sold to museums that the government was driven to putting a lock and chain, figuratively speaking, on the ruins. The field at present is open to local scientists and to an occasional foreigner in whom the government has confidence. But in spite of regulations there is unauthorized digging about the sites associated with the magic passwords, "Inca gold."

Among the finest of the prehistoric cities is Chan-Chan, a northern coast settlement, where the naturalistic pottery flourished. Chan-Chan means Sun-Sun, and the city was the headquarters of a ruler known as the Gran Chimu. The edifices in his city were of adobe, decorated with plaster relief designs gaily painted.

Chan-Chan has become a lifeless wilderness. Archaeologists who have partially excavated the site can trace the walls of palaces, tombs, and fortifications, and can locate streets and gardens. But earthquakes have shaken the region several times, and treasure-hunters have naturally taken an interest in a city that once yielded four million dollars to Spanish coffers. The figure is no exaggeration; for in the days of the Conquest a fifth share of all metal taken from the Peruvians was claimed by the Spanish crown, and Chan-Chan's contribution was duly recorded. Gold-diggers at various times have done serious damage to the site, and as a final touch to the destruction, there have been years when heavy rains beat on the ruins.   In the record-breaking rain of 1925, gauges recorded a foot of rain instead of the usual eighth of an inch. The city became a mud-washed desert of humps and depressions that on closer inspection could be seen as walls and streets. Some of the most famous mosaics of stucco were practically destroyed or badly damaged.

Chan-Chan in the north and Nasca in the south were great cultural centers of the coast.   But up and down the coastal strip are evidences of abandoned towns and graveyards buried in sand; disintegrated, forgotten — except when some archaeologist comes seeking new material to fit into the Peruvian puzzle.   The best evidence comes from the graves in the desert, for the dryness and the nitrous character of the sand have acted as excellent preservatives.

At Paracas, one hundred miles from Lima, Tello has unearthed three hundred mummies, swathed in colorful robes. The old custom was to wrap a body in a compact bundle.   If the family was prominent, many layers of finely embroidered robes and blankets were used to enfold the remains.   On top of the bundle was sometimes attached an artificial head made of cloth filled with stuffing.   Eyes, nose, and mouth were cut out of silver or some other material and fastened in place, making the face very like that of a child's rag doll.   The bundle, head and all, was laid in an artificial cavern in the sand or in a little vault of adobe and rushes.   With it went the usual pottery and possessions and a generous supply of food.

When mummies obtained at Paracas several years ago were unwrapped, the discoverers were surprised to find some of the skulls deformed in a way that the highlanders used, but that had not been previously observed among coast inhabitants.   The coast tribes sometimes flattened their heads, but this other fashion was a binding of the head as grotesque as the lily-feet of the Chinese lady.   The Peruvian child destined for the distinction of a deformed head was bandaged about the forehead at an early age.   As the child grew the head pushed up, lengthening in its desperate attempts to grow.   Headaches can be imagined!  Eventually, the man or woman possessed a high-brow skull in the most literal sense of the term.

In Peru traditions of lost cities are almost as insistent as traditions of buried gold, and it is not to be wondered at, considering the practically inaccessible desert places and mountains where some of the cities were situated. When such settlements were abandoned by their last inhabitants, they were soon lost in wind-blown sand, or else covered by tangled growth of vines and woods.

Faith in lost cities was justified when such a city, never seen by the Spaniards and almost forgotten even by the natives, was discovered in 1911 by the Yale Expedition, led by Bingham. This city is Machu Picchu, a ruin hidden in the heights of the Andes. A native of the mountains led the explorers through the jungle and up hazardous cliffs, and at last, on the flat ridge of a mountain top and down over its terraced side lay the city he had promised to reveal. This discovery gave science an unparalleled opportunity to study an Incan city that had never been sacked by the Spaniards or by later men. Dr. Bingham returned to Machu Picchu with a group of scientists several times, leading joint expeditions of the National Geographic Society and Yale University.

The houses found were for the greater part one-room affairs with gable ends. No roofs appeared, for the Peruvians did not know how to fit stone roofs on their buildings, nor did they need house coverings more substantial than wooden beams and thatch. The masonry of the old Peruvian walls is what always amazes visitors. The buildings were not ornate in the styles approved by Mayan and Aztec architects. The Peruvian buildings command awe by their sheer bulk and solid perfection of stone fitted to stone. And the walls stand today so perfect that a knife blade cannot be fitted between the building blocks. Some of the stone houses at Machu Picchu have windows, a rarity in most of the ruined cities. One temple with three large windows in the walls has been named the Temple of the Three Windows. The plan of the mountain city was traced carefully. It had two strong walls for defense against enemies, and a dry moat between the walls as an added protection. The stone houses stood at different levels up the side of the ridge and it is evident that every spare patch of earth in the city and between the city walls was used for gardens and farms. The streets that climbed from one terrace to another had more than one hundred stairways of stone.

Excavations in the neighborhood of the hidden city revealed more than one hundred burial caves, and traces of an elaborate system of highways that led to the stronghold. Ruins discovered in the surrounding country show that this was a center of dense population in its prehistoric day.

Objects obtained at this lost city of the Andes have shed much new light on native life. Not a trace of gold was unearthed, but a great many bronze axes, knives, and ornaments. The most valued find of metal, however, was a fragment that seems trivial until its meaning is understood. This is a little roll of tin. The Peruvians knew something about bronze, for specimens have been found at Machu Picchu and elsewhere. But it was a matter of controversy whether metal workers knew how to produce bronze or whether they occasionally chanced to find a piece of native copper containing an alloy of tin. The roll of tin is supposed to be the material used by some shop worker who cut off small bits as he needed them. In other words, this prehistoric artisan must have been intentionally manufacturing bronze. The find assumes especial significance because nowhere else in America is the Indian positively known to have advanced from the Stone Age into the Age of Bronze.

The Peruvians did not completely master the art of hardening metal. Axes, chisels, and bits of jewelry from Machu Picchu have been analyzed by Matthewson of Yale, and his report states that the largest amount of tin occurs in a spoonlike object with a hummingbird handle. This dainty bit of bronze was fortified as if for hard use by thirteen per cent of tin, whereas everyday knives which might have been effectively strengthened by such a mixture had only three to nine per cent. The metal workers had probably learned that a greater amount of tin formed an alloy better for casting bronze articles. That the articles at the same time became stronger for use they apparently did not realize.

Skulls unearthed at Machu Picchu and in other parts of Peru have revealed wide use of surgery; and as the collections increase, we become more and more respectful of the operations the Peruvians attempted. Coca leaves were used as an anesthetic. Even so, some processes would have been extremely painful as the doctors used instruments no more delicate than sharpened chisels and saws of stone, bronze, and obsidian. Several hundred skeletons and mummies obtained in cemeteries not many miles from Machu Picchu have provided enough material for MacCurdy of Yale to report that these burial caves seem to represent a period of strife which tended to develop the art of surgery. Clubs and slings were wielded freely, judging by the fractured bones and operations on the skulls. Of 273 skulls, seventeen per cent had been operated on at least once, and one had been operated on five times. The cranial operation known as trepanning was frequently practised. The large percentage of successful operations found among the skull collections suggested to Dr. MacCurdy that the surgeons must have possessed effective means of combatting infection.

In the summer of 1928 a new lost city was found by Peruvian scientists while they were visiting Machu Picchu. From the vantage point of the city, they scanned the ranges with powerful field glasses and spied what appeared to be ruins on Huayna Picchu, a near-by mountain. And thus a new mountain retreat awaits exploration.

As the various prehistoric Peruvian cities developed their distinctive customs and arts, the local influences spread over the surrounding country. In the centuries leading up to the Inca conquest, there were a number of such city-states with strong rulers. The Gran Chimu of Chan-Chan, for example, extended his power over a five hundred mile strip of coast and when the Incan armies added this city-state to the empire there was a great siege.

The chief contribution that the Incas themselves made to Peruvian culture was along the line of government. Through their efforts, tribes worshipping different gods and speaking different languages were drawn together in one great communal system and their lives were regulated with a daring completeness seldom attempted by a government in any age. Fascist Italy offers the closest modern parallel to the Incan organization. But Italy has no problem of initiating foreign groups into the Fascist regulations. Nor has Italy gone so far in regulating the existence of its people as the Incas achieved.

Photograph by American Museum of Natural History

OTHER PRODUCTS OF THE REALIST SCHOOL OF PERUVIAN POTTERY

Vessels representing a disease of the lip and amputated limbs.

The greatest deficiency in the Peruvian culture, at least from the point of view of those who would like to understand that culture, is the lack of an alphabet or glyph system of writing. The Peruvians solved the problem of records in their own way, and efficiently enough for their own purposes. Certain men were assigned to remember important facts, thus constituting a system of human government files. For figuring, some ingenious Peruvian invented the quipu, a device made of strands of cord. By tying different kinds of knots in the strands and by using different colored cords, it was possible to keep census records, time records, and other statistics needed for official

business. Modern herdsmen of Peru who still use the quipu
have explained the theory of the device. But the old quipus
that have been unearthed cannot be interpreted, because no one
knows the key to the various colors and arrangements of knots.

As Mexico has its modern descendants of the great Mayas,
Peru likewise has its representatives of the Inca line, and its inhabitants who might trace ancestry to the officers, soldiers, and
laborers of the Incan régime. These Indians recall a little of
the ceremony and traditions of the ancient glory. They make
use of some of the farming knowledge developed by their ancestors. They take pride in the massive ruins and fine pottery
art that proclaim the attainments of their race. But they have
made little effort to win back the old heritage of skill and enterprise. The spirit of Inca leadership, which once welded similar material into a precise and highly productive concern, is
missing.

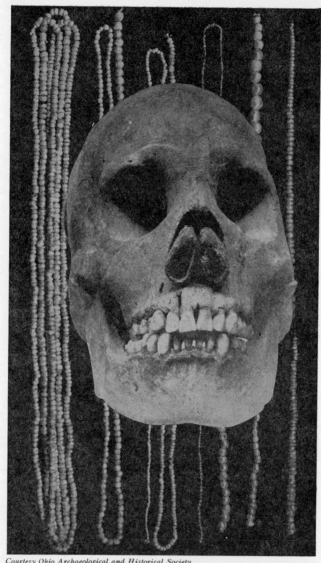

### LUXURIES OF THE MOUND BUILDERS

Pearls; also a copper nose, warranted durable, for funeral purposes.

## CHAPTER FOURTEEN

# THE MOUND BUILDERS OF PREHISTORIC AMERICA

IF this chapter were a motion picture film it would start by unreeling an endless procession of little black ants scurrying along with numberless grains of sand to build an ant-hill. Presently, the black thread of moving ants would grow large and blurred before our eyes and turn into the forms of endless Indian workmen of strange appearance and dress, carrying baskets and skins filled with earth to pile on a great, growing mound. The scene would be the Mississippi Valley, and the time one of those misty centuries before Columbus.

This prelude picture would present to you the North American Indian in a rôle rather different from that usually assigned to him in imagination. The red man in stereotype is independent, romantically lonely, and not inclined to the grind of manual labor. But several thousand large mounds and uncounted smaller ones scattered over two-thirds of the states testify to Indian industry. The hand-made hills rise above the land here and there from the Great Lakes to Louisiana, from Georgia and Florida westward to Texas, and north to New York State. They are our most familiar prehistoric American monuments, and they have been surrounded by the greatest haze of mystery.

The first settlers venturing westward were curious about the earthworks so frequently observed. The pioneers asked some of the Indians if they built these artificial hills, and were told no. So, the theory flourished that the mound builders were an ancient and unknown race which came to America bringing with them the custom of mound building and knowledge of a higher type than the Indians had. These unknown ancients, so the story went, vanished before the Indians arrived. Pearl necklaces and copper armor found in the mounds have supported the theory of an un-Indian race which held advanced ideas of what is valuable in jewelry and had learned how to use metal.   The Indians' apparent eagerness to accept glass beads for what the Europeans regarded as an exchange for their lands will always stick in the white man's mind as evidence that the typical red man had no sense of values.   And here were American burials with real gems which in their day must have been regal.

More than a century ago, scientific attempts to unravel the mysteries began.   But it is only of late that the mounds have begun to tell their story in connected fashion, and to respond to the determination of archaeologists to learn who the mound builders were, how long ago they lived in the country, and why they disappeared.

It is now known that mound building was a custom of some of the tribes of Indians who planted settlements along the Mississippi and its far-flung tributaries during probably the last thousand years that the natives had this country to themselves.   The blood of these tribes must flow in some Indians today, though the line of descent has not been proved.

To gain a mental picture of these prehistoric Americans we can see them best at the highest point of their development.   They were different in dress from wandering plains Indians in feather war-bonnets and gay blankets.   A typical hero of the Hopewell region in Ohio is reminiscent, strangely enough, of his contemporary across the Atlantic, the medieval knight clad in bright mail.   From objects unearthed in burial mounds, we can picture the warrior or ruler of a mid-western mound settlement wearing a shiny copper breastplate and wide copper bands on ankles and wrists.   Deer antlers branched from his copper helmet and added to his height and dignity. His scant woven skirt was gaily colored, and probably was decorated with glittering spangles of mica, for many cutouts of mica have been found.   Around the warrior's neck dangled strings of bear teeth, jingly shells, and softly shining pearls. His weapon was a stone axe or a copper hatchet, bound on a wooden handle.

The people led and protected by such a man were grouped in a community of wigwams, each made of a pole foundation set in a circle and presumably covered with bark for walls. The household pottery was shaped in original forms but there was no display of design to compare with the best art of the Southwest. Personal decoration was more important to the mound builders, as their ornaments and possessions indicate. The principal food crops of the gardens were corn and beans, and to vary the menu these Indians went to the forests to hunt and to gather nuts and berries and to the rivers for mussels and fish. In the villages there was good craftsmanship in weaving, carving, and the making of weapons. Cotton and wool were unknown, but cloth was woven with threads of plant fiber dyed crimson, orange, yellow, tan, and other colors. Rare pieces of this Indian goods have been found clinging to copper breastplates and preserved in the original colors by the verdigris on the corroding copper. In cold weather, skins of mink, beaver, and other animals were prehistoric equivalents of the modern fur coat. The stone weapons were well shaped, and were manufactured with painstaking care. The making of pipes inspired the highest efforts in carving, and artists of the Hopewell mound region turned out pipes in the form of practically every bird and beast of the

A PREHISTORIC WARRIOR, COPPER–SKINNED AND COPPER–CLAD

A drawing based on objects found in Indian mounds of Ohio.

prehistoric American forest. Stone frogs, squirrels, crows, racoons, rabbits, perched on top of pipe-stems, show what these craftsmen could do when they cared to.

The chiefs planted their settlements in rich valley country to insure the food supply. Above these low-placed villages the mounds rose conspicuously. Some were raised over graves of rulers or other important tribesmen; some covered the burials of many people, forming vast cemeteries. On the summits of other mounds, high and flat-topped, were temples. Many of the high places served also as signaling towers. In cleared country a fire signal might thus be read miles away, and among villages strung fairly close together a message relayed in code and telling of war, peace, or conclave could be spread with impressive promptness.

A STONE PIPE CARVED BY PRE-HISTORIC INDIANS

In the "dark ages" before the white man's arrival in the New World, midwestern Indians smoked tobacco in such pipes as this. The frog represents unusually fine carving.

Another use of the highest mounds in the Mississippi Valley was better understood following the great flood of 1927. During that catastrophe, thousands of terror-stricken people and herds of cattle climbed up on the old Indian mounds to escape the rushing water. As many as 500 individuals could take refuge on some of these artificial hills. It has been suggested that some mounds may have been built with just such an emergency in mind, for Mississippi floods are no new story in America's history.

Strangest of all the mounds are those in Wisconsin and nearby states, shaped in outlines of such animals as the eagle, deer, or bear. From the air, one of these earthen forms appears like a huge toy animal cutout, lying on its side. The effigies generally represented the totem animals of the clans and were connected with religious ceremonies. To the confusion of some students, a few of the animals have lost their original clean-cut outlines in the course of weathering, and in their modified appearance have been taken for beasts that Wisconsin Indians never knew — camels, for instance, or mastodons. One of these mounds by the trickery of washed-down soil developed a clearly defined trunk, elephant-like. This caused some insistent speculation as to the possibility that shaggy mastodons roamed the Great Lakes region in comparatively late Indian days. But a more careful survey revealed that the elephant must be a buffalo in disguise, having lost a couple of horns by the same flowing of soil that endowed him with an elongate nose.

That some of these effigies were planned as dug-outs for refuge in wartime has been learned by Miss Frances Dens-

*Courtesy Ohio State Archaeological and Historical Society*

A GREAT HILL BUILT BY INDIANS AT MIAMISBURG, OHIO

more. An old Winnebago Indian, John Thunder, was talking to her about the group of mounds at the site of a battle where his ancestors and the Sioux had fought until both sides were nearly wiped out. John Thunder said that his people had built these mounds. The "dream animal" that protected a man told him to make a mound in its likeness, and to hide inside in time of danger. He added that there was space inside for storage of food and for several persons to remain in hiding and that the entrance was concealed. Other members of the tribe verified this explanation.

Ohio has two serpentine mounds, the only earthen snakes of this sort in the United States. These have attracted much attention, because they bear on the theory that the serpent worship of Mexico was introduced into this northern region. The serpent-shape mound in Adams County winds along the

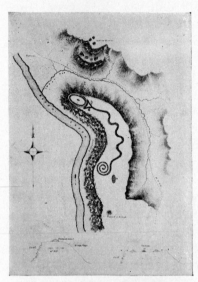

PLAN OF THE SERPENT MOUND
OF ADAMS COUNTY, OHIO

edge of a cliff beside a river to a length of 1,254 feet. An oval mound, perhaps an altar, lies at the head like an egg about to be swallowed by the big snake. This strange mound has been incorporated in a public park.

That many of the artificial hills conceal objects of great historic interest is only beginning to be understood by the public. Some of the mounds stand on private property, and when they are in the way they are usually leveled off by steam shovel or plow with never a thought of the loss to America's knowledge of itself. At times, curiosity seekers and vandals, stirred by vague tales of buried treasure, have dug destructively into the hillsides. At the end of the short, feverish digging, skeletons have been scattered and graves disarranged in the vain search for gold or fine pearls, and random objects have been carried off to be displayed on mantlepieces as curios. An entire site has thus been spoiled as a historic document.

Attempts are now being made in a good many states to save the important mounds that have so far escaped plows and construction gangs. Indiana archaeologists and historians, for instance, have been making a survey throughout their state as a first step toward finding out exactly what material of this sort the state possesses. In 1925, Illinois bought the biggest of all the American mounds, the Cahokia mound near East St. Louis, and converted the site into a park. Fortunately,

Cahokia has been protected from vandals and amateur excavators by the vigilance of the hereditary owners of the property, and it appears today very much as it looked to the first white explorers. This man-made hill, one of a very large group, covers sixteen acres and is 104 feet tall.

An Illinois business man, George Langford, was roused to engage in serious digging at the Fisher mounds, sixty miles from Chicago, when he discovered that these mounds were being plowed over. In his first year of systematic excavation, 1926, Langford's trenches and tunnels revealed 500 skeletons and a vast quantity of implements.

The great number of burials uncovered here is of significance because at least three successive groups of people, separated by nobody knows how many centuries, inhabited this same site and added to the same mounds. The oldest, most primitive group had laid their dead beneath the original ground level and covered them over with a heap of earth. These people had no possessions buried with them, except flints of such crude shape that they may not have been hand-made weapons at all. That life was a struggle and birth extra-hazardous among these oldest residents may be imagined from the fact that every woman buried here is accompanied by a new-born infant. They were a long-headed people as measurement of the skulls showed.

Above them, in another layer of earth, were many burials of a group that succeeded them. The skulls of these were round, indicating a different physical type. They were not very tall or sturdy of frame. Well-made copper and stone weapons were buried with the warriors, and jars of food were lying beside the women and children. The men could expect to take their spears and arrows and hunt their own meat in the next world, but the women and children were not to be dependent on the luck of shadowy hunters. A pathetic touch to the burial of the children is that in almost every case someone had placed the child's fingers in the jar, so that the baby might be in close touch with its food supply if it became hungry. Mothers of this community died valiantly protecting their children in time of war. One young mother, buried with her baby, had an arrowpoint in her forearm and another under her left shoulder-blade. She had shielded the child with her arm as long as she could, but a well-aimed shot to the heart had ended the struggle.

Over these round-head warriors and their wives came a blanket of earth, and above this were the burials of the last Indians to occupy the site and use the mound cemetery. Here was a still different physical type, a tribe with skulls broader than any of the others. These were living in the time of the white man's appearance, for their possessions include silver buckles, bits of European cloth, and, buried with one child, some glass and china beads. This discovery and the finding of mounds containing European articles with every burial from top to bottom show plainly that the mound builders did not entirely vanish or abandon their customs before the explorers and settlers came.

A new and unusual method of mound exploration was introduced in 1928 by Shetrone of the Ohio State Archaeological and Historical Society. Assembling dirt-handling machinery, workmen, and a corps of student aids, this archaeologist set out to slice the great Seip mound, one of the Hopewell group, as if it were a loaf of brown bread. The impressive old cemetery had already been dug into here and there, and it had attracted exceptional popular interest because of the great strings of pearls that were found. Now, slice after slice, every cubic foot of earth was removed and each thin cross-section of the hill carefully examined. This technique revealed the method of building the mound. The first Indians started with a small burial heap. Then a thick layer of earth was added to make it a tall, pointed pyramid. Over that, later, was piled a new layer of earth to convert the pyramid into a rounded hill, and finally a layer of river gravel was spread over it. Having demolished the Seip mound as thoroughly as he could, Shetrone reassembled it, that it might stand again as a famous landmark.

The Middle West did not have a monopoly of the advanced skill and industry typical of certain mound-building tribes of the Mississippi Valley.   For example, fine craftsmanship flourished at a mound settlement on the Etowah River in northern Georgia, known today as the largest prehistoric Indian town in the Southeast.   Etowah has attracted excavators for years, but the site is large and its secrets until lately were only sampled.   Recently, Moorehead, an authority on the moundbuilder culture, has returned again and again to the Georgia site as if drawn by a magnet, and finally has extracted the main points of its story.

Mounds in other regions have shown the fighting life of the people and the pomp and ceremony which attended officials even in death.   But at Etowah may be found the finest evidence of the everyday life of these Indians.   Most of the mounds that rise in the center of the settlement hold graves. Around these were huts and ceremonial houses.   Bits of the clay walls of buildings have been excavated, and the old foundations of wigwams still can be found by digging beneath the present surface of the soil.   In these are scattered bone sewing needles, shell hairpins, and other useful articles, and in addition there is copper hammered into thin plates and delicately ornamented.

De Soto, making his way to the Mississippi, passed through northern Georgia about 1541, and it is possible that he and his followers visited Etowah.   The first trace of contact with the Europeans was found in 1928 when the hilt and part of the blade of an iron sword came to light during excavation of a big mound.   The foreign sword had been stuck upright into the ground beside the body of an Indian warrior.   It is not unreasonable to fancy that here lies a chief of Etowah who played host to the Spaniards, and that the sword was a gift from Spanish leader to Indian leader, for this man was buried apart from the others.   Besides the sword, he was provided with a supply of fine arrowpoints for use in future battles. Over him was a shelter of cedar and pine posts, well preserved.

The South had another progressive center of Indian mound culture in the marsh country of southern Louisiana.   This was discovered in 1926 when Collins of the Smithsonian set out to do some archaeological pioneering along the Gulf coast. The only Indians ever known to inhabit the undesirable swamp land were the Atacapa, or "man-eaters," a primitive tribe which survived until recent times and held white men at a respectful distance by their reputation for cannibalism. Collins returned with news that mound builders, no relatives of the crude Atacapa, had inhabited the reefs along the Gulf in earlier centuries. They had skill in handling copper and other materials and they made good pottery.

In these investigations into the life and times of mound-building groups, copper has turned up with astonishing frequency and in distant places: copper ornaments in Louisiana, copper breast-plates and celts in Georgia, copper plentifully scattered in the Mississippi Valley. The source of practically all of this copper would be the shore of Lake Superior. The explanation which springs into your mind, and yet may seem incredible, is the only possible answer — trade over hundreds, thousands of miles, with no beasts of burden. If the mound builders made no other great contribution to our realization of prehistoric America, they have shown us more distinctly the far-flung network of commerce that spread over this country long before the white man came to bewilder the Indian into bartering the use of his land for bead jewelry.

Mississippi Valley communities were particularly cosmopolitan in their imports. Traders, journeying overland afoot — as all Indians did before the Spaniards brought horses — and perhaps carrying canoes to take them down the rivers, came over trails from as far west as the Rockies, bringing eye-teeth of the grizzly bear, which were much prized as ornaments or as charms. From the West, too, was brought black obsidian for making spearheads and knife blades. The nearest deposit of this volcanic glass is in Yellowstone Park. The trading was not necessarily a direct process of carrying an order of bears' teeth to a waiting chief on the banks of the Mississippi. Long-distance trade must have been more haphazard than that, proceeding often by relay. But the existence in the mounds of so many articles and substances foreign to the region is clear proof of some established trade routes and organized activity.

The West had no monopoly of the commerce. Copper nuggets, already mentioned, were "shipped" southward from the mines near Lake Superior to be hammered into breastplates, combs, and axes. Mica came from the Appalachian highlands. Galena, which lately entered our everyday language as a radio crystal, was a product of the Illinois region, and treasured for its pleasing sheen. Meteoric iron was used, too, when it could be hacked off some meteorite that providentially landed from the sky. But with all this use of metal, the Indian artisans had no idea of smelting it or converting it into a more potent, tempered tool. It was merely material to be hammered or chipped like a chunk of stone.

From the Gulf of Mexico the mound settlements acquired barracuda and alligator teeth, tortoise-shell, large conch shells, and beads made of tiny marine shells. Pearls were desired, and to meet the demand workers harvested quantities of these gems, not from oysters, but from the fresh-water mussels in streams of the Mississippi Valley. Sixty thousand pearl beads were taken from one Ohio mound alone. Some of these win the admiration of experts, who can see that the long-buried pearls, though now discolored from acid soil or fire, must once have been beautiful. One remarkable chain from the Hopewell mounds contained 300 pearl beads which added to the splendor and prestige of some chief or his wife. The Indian jeweler's technique of converting pearl globes into beads was not so different from modern methods. Some were bored for stringing by means of a fine stone splinter, but a slender stick and a little sand and water were the usual equipment.

The Spaniards cast an interested eye on the pearl jewelry of the Indian. Garcilasso de la Vega, writing perhaps of Etowah, referred to a gift of pearls as large as hazelnuts, made to De Soto by a cacique, or priest-chief. Describing De Soto's acceptance of the gift, the historian continues:

"He wished to learn, however, in what manner the pearls were extracted from the shells. The cacique replied that he would send out people to fish for pearls all night, and on the following day at eight o'clock his wish should be gratified. . . . In the meantime much wood was burned on the bank, producing a large quantity of glowing coals. When the boats returned, the shells were placed on the hot coals, and they opened in consequence of the heat. In the very first, ten or twelve pearls of the size of a pea were found, and handed to the cacique and the general, who were present. They thought them very fine, though the fire had deprived them of their lustre."

Even the artificial jewelry trade flourished in prehistoric America. Plentiful as pearls were, artificial pearl necklaces were worn, perhaps by less affluent Indians. The synthetic gems were made by wrapping wooden beads in a coat of mica. Eye teeth of the grizzly bear, much rarer than pearls, were also imitated. Artisans in the Ohio region went further in their efforts to manufacture something as good as nature could make. They supplied copper linings for the noses of some of the more distinguished men and women for funeral use. Why a dead Indian should need a copper nose more than copper eyes or ears is a fine point of reasoning that we may not appreciate. Perhaps the fundamental importance of breathing is indicated. A copper nose would assure the possessor that he would be able to draw the breath of life in the next world.

Extensive trading operations may have brought some of the mound builders into contact with distant races of Mexico. This is suggested by the discovery in the Mississippi Valley and the Gulf areas of pottery and copper and shell objects covered with designs distinctly Mexican. Even the early mound investigators, especially Thomas and Moore, found such things. The recent excavations at Etowah brought new objects of this sort to light, and among thousands of relics gathered these were the most intriguing question marks. Men portrayed on the copper shields resemble the striking figures of Aztec or Mayan art. The most likely explanation of the Mexican objects is that traders or adventurers from Yucatan brought samples of art from the country, or else vivid descriptions of what they had seen, and that artists of the mound

settlement proceeded to copy the style, just as decorators today have become enthusiastic over Mayan designs for modern applied art.  Moorehead last summer found additional
evidence in Illinois that the Mexican border was no barrier
to immigration in early days.  Out of a mound along the Illinois River came pottery jars beautifully decorated with the
sun and the serpent, both of which were prominent religious
symbols of the American tropics.

Etowah in Georgia and Hopewell in Ohio stand well in the
foreground of perspective as we look back mentally at the prehistoric map of the eastern United States area.  These two
might be called the New York and Chicago of their time, if
we do not draw the comparison too closely.  There were no
teeming millions of population in these ranking towns, but
such places were favored spots where art flourished and material progress reached its best heights east of the Mississippi.

To the scientist, there is equal interest in any number of
the less spectacular mound settlements.  Most of these were
occupied by less advanced groups of Indians.  The pottery
often is primitive.  The stone weapons lack finish.  But the
mounds fill in the picture of the prehistoric East.  They show
the spread of agricultural settlements, for each mound means
that here a group tarried more or less permanently.  They
also show the strikingly diverse types of anatomy represented
among the tribes.

In 1924 Fewkes went to Weeden Island in Florida, and dug
into a shell mound in a palm-tree grove.  Inside the heap he
found two different layers of burial.  The lower layer contained small-boned Indians, of medium height.  In the upper
level, piled up by the tribe which later took over the grove,
were sturdy big Indians with round, thick skulls.  Now it
might be supposed that the big-boned people would have been
the active and inartistic group, in contrast with the more delicately built people.  But the reverse was the case, as the pottery shows.  The big Indians were the good artists who made
beautiful cups, bowls, vases, and trays.  The little people
were tyros at the Indian's favorite art.  The story of what

happened cannot be learned definitely, but it would seem likely that the smaller men were some of the oldest Floridians and that they came to Florida by way of Cuba. Their clay and stone possessions are similar to those of Cuban natives. The huskier individuals must have come from the North, perhaps

*Photograph by Bureau of American Ethnology*

A BOWL FROM THE MOUND AT WEEDEN ISLAND, FLORIDA

Such attractive ware as this shows that southeastern Indians could rival southwestern tribes.

some of the first tourist tide seeking southern sunshine. Apparently, there was a controversy over land in this pleasant island, and the newcomers won the argument and remained in possession of the grove including the mound cemetery, which they found useful.

Why did the building of mounds cease almost entirely before the white explorers arrived? There was probably a variety of factors involved. Plagues perhaps; there was such wide trading with distant parts of the country that diseases must occasionally have been introduced into communities not able to fight them off. Wars with wandering tribes or with other mound-building tribes must have weakened the groups. A good many of the skeletons were injured in ways that indicate violence. Flood, famine, and pestilence may have come all three together in some years. The frequent burial of families—a man and woman with a baby between them — indicates an agent of wholesale death, with some survivors left to honor the dead in the approved ceremonial manner. Those mound builders who were left to meet the white men abandoned old customs and arts, even as other Indian tribes, and took to European goods as rapidly as such things could be acquired. And the white man's diseases, also acquired in the trading process, hastened the decline and disappearance of the entire culture.

*Photograph by Canadian Department of Mines*

## A RARE SIGHT THESE DAYS

A group of totem poles at Kitwanga saved from falling into decay. A Canadian government archaeologist, aided by old Indians who recall the method of painting the poles, has set these wooden biography records back in place, and re-painted them.

CHAPTER FIFTEEN

# ESKIMOS, INDIANS, AND MYSTERY IN THE AMERICAN NORTHWEST

THE main highway of the prehistoric American continent was the great Northwest. In the course of centuries groups of new Americans who entered the Yukon Valley of Alaska turned their faces toward the Canadian wilderness. They camped where food was good, and then advanced along cleared places of the ocean shore or followed the rivers. If hidden traces of the original Americans might profitably be sought anywhere, it would surely seem to be along this main highway and its eastern branch leading eastward across Canada.

But when archaeologists set out to explore the Alaskan-Siberian borders for clues to the old immigrants, they found nature less helpful in the far Northwest than in other regions. The air is chill and damp. The wooden-walled houses and wooden bowls made by the inhabitants fall into mouldering decay in the span of a man's lifetime. And, as if there were not trouble enough for science in struggling with such a climate and in puzzling over the highly specialized objects used in an Arctic existence, the tracks and trails of the old inhabitants look as erratic as the mazes that psychologists set in their laboratories for rats and students to solve. Paradoxically, when the difficulties of the climate become sufficiently accentuated, they turn into aids to science. If the chill dampness actually freezes the objects lying in the soil, they are preserved as in a refrigerator, and in these circumstances remarkable discoveries have been made.

The baffling problem of the North always has been: What kind of Indian, if any, is an Eskimo? There are Indians in Alaska and Canada, and there are Eskimos in both countries. By observing the groups and by digging up the relics of the old

283

inhabitants, differences and similarities are made evident. The Indians, for example, preferred tanned skins for garments, but the Eskimos wore their coats with the fur on. The Indians lived along the upper reaches of the streams and rode in bark canoes. The Eskimos chose the bays and ocean beaches for their homes and devised that admirable skin boat, the kayak, which carries them so satisfactorily through iceberg traffic, and which is so flexible a piece of hunting equipment. And besides the one-man kayak, the Eskimo had big skin boats for family transportation and whale hunting.

The Eskimo used stone lamps, and these were so important that we may well pause to consider what Dr. Walter Hough of the United States National Museum has said about them. Among his conclusions are: "that one of the most important functions of the lamp is for melting snow and ice for drinking water; that the lamp is employed for lighting, warming, cooking, melting snow, drying clothes and in the arts, thus combining in itself several functions which have been differentiated among civilized peoples; that the architecture of the house is related to the use of the lamp — the house is made non-conducting and low in order to utilize the heated air; that the lamp is a social factor, peculiarly the sign of the family unit, each head of the family (the woman) having her lamp; that the invention of the lamp took place on some seacoast, where fat of aquatic animals of high fuel value was abundant, rather than in the interior, where the fat of land animals is of low fuel value; that the typical form of the lamps arises from an attempt to devise a vessel with a straight wick edge combined with a reservoir, giving the vessel an obovate or ellipsoidal shape."

The snow house, inevitably associated with the Eskimo, is a comparatively recent development confined to Canada and Greenland. Alaskan Eskimos lived in heavy wooden pit houses; in older times eastern Eskimos did the same. The northern Indian, too, built his home of wood with a pit foundation. Both the Alaskan Eskimo and Indian depended on

wood from which to carve dishes and tools.   The Eskimo had
some pottery in addition to wooden and stone receptacles.
The only earthenware dishes that northern Indians made were
gouged out of clay blocks.   Neither Indian nor Eskimo was
able to make the soil yield grain or vegetables in the far north.
So far as we know, they never tried.   Alaskan strawberries
and truck gardens just below the Arctic Circle are white man's
magic.

The standard explanation of the Eskimo has been that
some of the primitive northern Indians in the caribou coun-

*Photograph by U. S. National Museum*

A HOUSE OF WHALE JAWBONES AND RIBS

Ruins of an Eskimo dwelling at St. Lawrence Island, Alaska.   The room
was about twenty feet square, the floor was three feet below the ground, and
the inhabitants entered by way of a long tunnel.

try, northwest of Hudson Bay, turned into Eskimos in the
course of racial evolution, and that their descendants scattered
east to Greenland and west to Alaska.   The most primitive
Eskimos today live in this caribou land and hunt the caribou
for food.   But recent discoveries are raising controversy and
causing some scientists to doubt that the Eskimo Garden of
Eden really was in the wilderness of central Canada.

Between 1921 and 1923, the Rasmussen expedition went
into this Hudson Bay region.   The inhabitants of the igloos
told the Danish explorers of a tradition that before them there

was a people in their land who lived in whalebone houses, a people they called the Tunit. Following the clues offered, the archaeologist of the staff, Therkel Mathiassen, poked around the most favored sites for settlements along Repulse Bay, and found the ruins of a village of twenty houses, surrounded by underground caches for storing meat and by cemeteries and refuse heaps. The houses were circular and half underground. The walls were of stone, turf, and whale skulls, and the roofs were of whale jawbones and ribs covered with turf. These strange homes, abandoned centuries ago, were so overgrown with grass and moss that the arrangement of the rooms could no longer be traced. But out of the tangle of ruins Mathiassen dug more than two thousand objects showing the ways in which the departed people lived.

From this prehistoric village and from other ruins on Southampton and Baffin Islands were brought very many objects proving that the old inhabitants were not like the primitive modern caribou hunters who live in this region now. Their livelihood had been gained from Hudson Bay. They lived more prosperously and more comfortably. In evidence were the knives, cups, and bows of whalebone, by-products of the sea hunter's catch. There were ivory points for harpoons and lances, ivory ice picks and ivory salmon decoys. There were arrowheads made of antler, and lamps of soapstone. These discoveries struck a blow at the old theory of the origin of the Eskimos. It is possible that the caribou Eskimos are not what they were taken for — remains of the old primitive régime surviving unchanged in the original Eskimo homeland. Instead, they may be examples of what happens when evolution allows a race to slip back instead of pushing upward.

After the Danes at Hudson Bay, Jenness of the National Museum of Canada came to Alaska in 1926. He chose to dig among ruins at Cape Prince of Wales and the Diomede Islands. This is a strategic point, because Bering Strait is narrowest at Cape Prince of Wales; and the Diomede Islands, which lie in the middle of the strait, are like two stepping stones cutting into halves the fifty-mile gap between Asia and

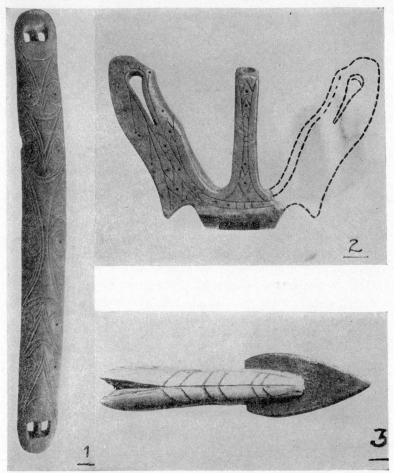

*Photograph by U. S. National Museum*

THREE STAGES OF ESKIMO ART

1. A box handle from St. Lawrence Island, found in 1928, decorated with fine carving of concentric circles and dots and curved lines. This is typical art of the oldest known Eskimos. 2. Later Eskimo handiwork, still gracefully designed, but less elaborate. The use of this object is unknown, but it is surmised that it may have decorated a helmet or may have adorned a ceremonial staff. 3. A recent Eskimo product — a harpoon, very simply carved, and equipped with an iron blade.

America.  Surely some of the early wanderers must have found this short cut.

When Jenness landed at Wales, he inquired for help in digging and learned that all the native men were off with the reindeer herds or at work in the tin mine.  An old man and six Eskimo boy scouts were the assistants he enrolled in the hunt for prehistoric inhabitants.  The digging revealed no news of any people that might definitely be called original Americans.  But the efforts of the little squad of workers turned up the same sort of good Eskimo craftwork that had been found by Mathiassen two thousand miles away to the east.  A more surprising discovery appeared when Jenness dug into deeper layers of hard earth below these relics, and found broken objects of bone and ivory that set a still higher standard of what the Eskimo could once accomplish.  If only one of these ivory objects had been displayed a few years earlier, the suggestion that it had been made by an Eskimo would probably have been regarded as interesting but incredible.  No Eskimo had ever been known to plan such graceful curving designs for his ivory or bone harpoon heads, nor could any known Eskimo have executed the design, if he had been able to conceive it, with the precision of these unknown artists.  Yet here were the bits of fossil bone and ivory in impressive array.

While Jenness was making his discoveries, Hrdlicka, that same summer, was traveling hundreds of miles down the Yukon and along the coast of Alaska north of the Arctic Circle. From this expedition he reported traces of the same skill that the Eskimos had once possessed and had somehow lost.  On one island he learned that numerous prehistoric implements could actually be seen frozen in old trash-heaps.  Several bushels of broken articles and fossil ivory had been carried off that year by enterprising townsfolk who worked them over into beads and pendants and sold them to tourists as Alaskan souvenirs.

The evidence thus accumulated has convinced scientists of the strange fact that the Arctic had its golden age, like old Greece, when the people of the North were busy, prosperous, artistic, and very much interested in living. In those days Eskimo hunters spent long winter evenings close to the stone lamps, working to make their weapons beautiful. The large number of sea creatures represented in the remains of the settlements show how successful the hunters were. And then, instead of continuing to become more inventive, artistic, and wealthy, these people lost interest in self-betterment. They dropped back, perhaps through disease and hard times — who knows? They fell into the less admirable state that we associate with the Eskimo race.

In 1928, Collins of the Smithsonian, following Hrdlicka's route to the Bering Sea, camped on a tiny islet off St. Lawrence Island, where he set to work digging intensively into a frozen refuse-heap sixteen feet high. This mountain of rubbish contained the most extensive Eskimo village thus far excavated. The mound was composed of sweepings from the housekeeping of a village through many centuries. Animal bones, broken tools, pottery, and ornaments were all mixed with a binding of earth, and the whole frozen permanently stiff. The archaeologist who undertakes this sort of a summer-time job expects to work in wind, fog, and chill rain. His spade and trowel dig into earth so hard that after he has taken off a few comparatively soft inches of the top layer, he must wait until the air thaws out the newly uncovered surface before he can go at it again; and this is not within the Arctic Circle; it is sub-Arctic.

The most surprising moment of the digging arrived when the bodies of six of the oldest inhabitants were found encased in ice. Six children had been buried in the refuse-heap. Three were dressed carefully in their best clothes of fur and bird skins. The place where they lay happened to become filled with water which froze, and so these children were preserved in a fashion unique in Arctic records. On first hearing of this, we are likely to be appalled at the thought of a village dump being chosen for burial purposes. But after that shock, we realize that this is a logical development of a Stone Age point of view. Prehistoric men and women in practically every country have had little of the very modern aversion to refuse piles. Sight and smell of dinner remains had no emotional effect whatever. The island mound no doubt was picked as quite satisfactory as a burial place for the simple reason that it was safe above the tide and was easily dug.

Another surprise was found at the bottom of the mound. Here were ruins of the homes of some of the first inhabitants of the island. The houses lay buried six feet below the present beach, indicating that the shore line on which they were built has been slowly sinking for centuries. After these homes were abandoned, people from nearby huts had continued to use the site for a kitchen midden, until there was no trace of the original settlement in sight. The age of the settlement can be vaguely estimated from the fact that the latest homes, built on top of the mound, were abandoned before the white men came.

In the settlements at St. Lawrence Island, three stages of Eskimo development were found. There was the work of the oldest artists, who had the keenest sense of beauty and wrought many circles and flowing curves in the fossil ivory. Then followed a simpler, but still very graceful style of carving, and finally the simple geometric designs of lines and dots and circles with which Eskimos of historic times have decorated their possessions. These discoveries are paralleled by similar finds unearthed in northeastern Siberia. It now remains for archaeologists to trace the ancestors of the skilful ivory carvers, and so to approach the main stem of the Eskimo racial line. Some scientists who have visited the region believe that the stem will be found in this Bering Sea region on one side of the Strait or the other.

Almost anyone who pores over a map of Bering Sea to study the likely migration route is struck by the curving chain of Aleutian Islands that swing out from Alaska toward Asia. They look like fine landing stations for people who might try to get from one shore to the other. But a boat from Asia would have three hundred miles of difficult sea to cross before reaching the Commander Islands, the first island link. It is more plausible that early wanderers found their way to the islands from the Alaskan side. If early groups of immigrants did settle in this by-path, off the main traveled route, it is possible that they have left a long succession of buried clues to show what many generations of old Americans were like.

The tribe that lives in the islands is a good exhibit of how life changes when conditions change. These slant-eyed, round-faced folk are held to be offshoots of the Eskimo family. When they took up residence on the islands they found that the sea about their homes did not freeze when winter set in. Their snow-shovels, snow-goggles, and ice-picks for hunting were all worthless trappings, and they had use only for their harpoons and throwing-lances for fishing and their bows and arrows for hunting. Changes of this sort and the lonely desolate life on the rocky islands made the inhabitants a strange group with strange ways.

Of all their customs, the manner of disposing of the dead has attracted most attention. Russian explorers sent out by the Empress Catherine struck a note of climax in their reports of the Aleutian Islands by mentioning Arctic mummies, similar to the Egyptian, wrapped in furs and hidden in cavern tombs. No scientific explorer was able to find these tombs among the precipitous cliffs until the eighteen seventies. Then Dall of the Smithsonian discovered one of the cavern tombs and saw the packages wrapped in seal skins and woven grass mats. Natives who could remember the traditions of their grandfathers helped interpret the finds. Not every islander got such a burial. The honor was reserved for a great chief and his family and for the best whalers of a tribe. A whaler, even his tools and weapons, were mascots. It was believed that they would bring success in whale hunting to anyone who possessed them. Hence, the dried body of a whaler was bundled in furs and mats until it was as proof against the unfavorable weather conditions as it could be made. Then the family carried it secretly to a cave and hung it up to protect it against contact with the damp earth. After that, they returned home, hoping that robbers would not steal the family luck.

A type of mummy rarer than those wrapped in bundles has never been brought away from the islands. These are said to be placed in caves in positions resembling life. Dead men clad in wooden armor stiffly grip their spears as they wait to fight the enemies of a shadowy world. Dead women sit

*Photograph by Smithsonian Institution*

A "MUMMY" OF THE FAR NORTH

Aleutian Islanders swathed their dead in such fashion and hid them in cavern tombs.

holding embroidery and bone needles. Old men sit posed beside their drums, waiting to play again for the winter dances. If they do not moulder away, some of these strangest cavern burials may yet be the trophies of an explorer's summer, and may provide new material evidence of the complete accoutrements of an Aleutian Island family.

While some tribes made themselves thoroughly at home in the North and took on new appearance and new customs and became Eskimos, other tribes were becoming typical Indians. Eskimo and Indian borrowed very little from each other, except where their territories joined. Even when they lived in neighboring land, they were as apt to become enemies as friends. Indian traditions tell of battles with the Eskimos, a condition that can be readily understood if both tribes chose to hunt in the same bays or rivers when food was scarce.

Several years ago, Krieger of the Smithsonian picked up the trail of the Indians who followed the main highway through British Columbia to the northwestern states and on into the south. His hunt was for the ruins of circular houses with foundations underground that the old northwestern Indians had built. He also sought their cremation burials. These were the two outstanding signs of their particular culture. Through Washington and Oregon, down the Snake River into Idaho, he traced pit houses and cremation burials. In a canyon of central Idaho the trail finally was lost. But he had found pictographs on the rocks that suggested the art of the southwestern Basket Makers, and even a dart with a charred wooden stick, exactly the sort of weapon the old Basket Makers fitted into a dart-thrower and hurled at their enemies. How the Basket Makers found their way into the Southwest more than three thousand years ago has never been demonstrated. It is a significant clue that the art technique of these old Southwesterners has been found along the

*Photograph by U. S. National Museum*

DANCING MEN PECKED IN HUGE ROCK NEAR LEWISTON, IDAHO

The wedge-shape shoulders, bent arms, and horned headdresses of the figures are after the Basket Maker style of art, and therefore suggest contact between the Southwest and the Northwest several thousand years ago.

Snake River as far north as Idaho. In these pictographs, the figures of men have square shoulders and round heads with ears or horned headdresses. This is the manner in which Basket Maker artists portrayed the human form, whereas the later Pueblos drew men in a simpler style as jointed figures. These pictures may be evidence that the Basket Makers spread into a broad area, and that their scouts or colonists left these rock records. Or, there is a possibility that the pictures were left by men from the north advancing southward to establish the Basket Maker régime. When more clues come to light, a new "oldest" chapter may be fitted into western America's prehistory earlier than the Basket Maker age.

But the evidence may not wait until the archaeologists can get to it. In the West especially, field workers feel the pressure of making every minute count. If a worker is fortunate, he arrives at a site before it has been spoiled by amateur souvenir collectors, farmers, floods, or the crushing fingers of time. If he is unlucky, he is a year or a week too late. In the Columbia Valley the Indian villages occupied exactly the locations that modern orchardists choose for planting. The fruit grower, like the prehistoric Indian, has an eye out for a sheltered, well-watered site. Modern plowing and tree planting activities bring up from the earth large quantities of antiquities, but these methods of excavating are not the methods of science, and the old Indian ruins are ruined indeed, from the expert's point of view.

At one prehistoric village which Krieger reached in time, at Wahluke, Washington, he found the ruins of thirty pit houses in a row along the river. The people of this river village made stone bowls for kitchen purposes. No clay pottery or wooden dishes appeared. They made spoons from horns of mountain sheep, their pipes were long stone tubes, and their stone weapons and tools are pronounced among the most beautiful examples of Stone Age craft. They ate clams and saved some of the shells to wear as pendants. Elk furnished them all sorts of useful things, including meat, antlers for making bowstaves and weavers' tools, bones for gouges, and teeth for charms or jewelry. In fact, every creature and every plant of the Northwest woods was a potential source of food or fabric for these observant, ingenious people.

The picture of isolated, self-dependent Indian tribes does not fit this Northwest country. Complex trade and travel existed. Rivers were the best roadways, and the Columbia was the chief route from the North. Hence, tribes seeking food or special trade objects passed up and down that river in their canoes very often. Almost one hundred different types of articles, such as pipes, headdresses, stone clubs, pottery, and arrowpoints, have been found at the prehistoric graves in these neighborhoods. The specialist sorts out the objects he has unearthed, and arranges in the collection old pipes from Pueblo towns of the Southwest, jade celts from Alaska, shell beads from the California coast, and even pipes from across the Rocky Mountains.

The age of the Northwest Indian villages is still vaguely pre-white man. Some scientists have tried to fix the lifetime of a settlement by figuring how long it would take the clams in a shell-heap to accumulate. The problem resolves itself into: If we know how many shellfish an Indian would eat in a day, how long would it take for a village the size of the one in this particular neighborhood to consume a mountain of clams ten feet high and one hundred feet long? The answer is bound to be approximate, for no one knows how many calories a prehistoric Indian might require, nor what quantities of other edibles he added to the fish. But the clam-shell arithmetic is useful in terms of round centuries.

Archaeologists are sometimes asked why the rock-carving and totem poles left by the Indians do not show events that happened in the old days. Rock pictures are particularly plentiful in the West, so much so that strong efforts have been made to solve their meaning. It was hoped that here were records of great battles and conquests and migrations. The largest series of petroglyphs in Canada is 250 feet long, and it is a reasonable supposition that such a monument has a message worth reading. All together, there are thousands of pictures, carved, scratched, or painted on boulders.

Steward of the University of California recently made a broad study of these prehistoric art exhibits.  His conclusion was that many of the gaily painted animals and crude lines were magic wrought by the Indian to make his herds and game animals increase and thus insure food for his people. Some of the moon-faced, angular human beings painted on the rocks with brown and red pigment have been pronounced dancers in ceremonial rites.  Others are believed to be deities. Some are clan symbols, or marks of individuals to show that they had passed by that place, and some may have been marks to identify important sites such as water-holes.  The wealth of designs that the Indian artists concocted in their heads and drew on the rocks is taken as proof that no system of recording language was devised for standard use.  The artist seems to have been almost as untrammeled in his inspirations as the schoolboy when he draws a picture of the teacher or his best girl on a fence.  No way to determine the age of the petroglyphs has been found, and it is difficult to identify any of the tribes that made them, because costumes, tools, and weapons are rarely shown in such form that they can be recognized.

Totem poles, those other Indian monuments that were made to record important facts, are not ancient relics for all their battered and ancient appearance.  The longest life of one of these carved cedar posts is threescore years and ten. Still, a scientific meeting was a trifle surprised recently when Barbeau of the National Museum of Canada stated that the fashion of carving these big, ambitious signposts is entirely modern, that the most intensive period of totem pole carving was no longer ago than from 1830 to 1890, and that the few house posts older than that are primitive samples.  The Alaskan art of wood carving and the use of totems or clan symbols is older than this.  But the pole fashion was a transitory one that grew and improved like any fashion, and finally was discarded, all in plain view of the white man.

The totem poles, contrary to popular notions, were never idols.  They were crests or heraldic devices of a family and clan.  If there was room on a pole, after the genealogy was recorded, the space was filled in with designs suggesting family history or distinctions. A Secretary of the Interior visited an Alaskan Indian's home some years ago, and soon thereafter the Secretary's figure in frock coat and stovepipe hat appeared on the Indian's pole as a badge of his social attainments.

Within recent years, the carving has become less artistic, and has finally ceased. Some of the finest old poles have been laid down as sidewalks. But as the poles became antiquarian exhibits, and museums and parks began bidding for them, the Indian villages were cleared of their supply of the stiff wooden

A HOUSEHOLD BOX CARVED BY INDIANS OF THE NORTHWEST COAST

badges of honor, and now a good pole in its native setting is as rare as a butterfly table in a New England attic.

An outdoor museum of fine totem poles has been established by the Canadian government along the Skeena River in British Columbia. Under the guidance of Harlan I. Smith, the Indians of the region were won over from reluctance to assent to such a project, and finally they gave active help toward the cause of preserving the art of their forefathers for modern travelers to admire. Since 1925, forty-two poles have been placed where they can be seen from the railway.

A MASTERPIECE OF NATIVE AMERICAN ART

A shield of turquoise mosaic, consisting of 14,000 fragments of stone, made by
an Aztec artist.

## CHAPTER SIXTEEN

## THE RED MAN'S AMERICA — A POSTSCRIPT

It may be futile, but it is undeniably fascinating to speculate as to what America would be like today if Columbus' ships had turned back, if no other adventurous sailor had found the New World, and if the Indians could have had these last five hundred years to shape the continent's destiny.

Would the Incas with their gift for statesmanship have included wider and wider territory in their great South American civilization, until they met the armies of the Aztecs and of other Mexican tribes? What would have happened if Inca met Aztec? And would the powerful Iroquois confederacy have continued to conquer and weld together tribes until there was an Indian United States? Would Indian thinkers have devised an alphabet, so that the battles and the treaties and the destruction of cities and the deeds of rulers and heroes could all be recorded? Would some lazy, ingenious Indian have domesticated some tractable beast to draw his burdens? And would another efficiently lazy innovator have invented the wheel to open up new possibilities in transportation? Would Indian curiosity and keen observation have completely won the secrets of bronze and iron?

We must admit that these things did not come in the course of several thousand years of Indian life that have been recreated by the archaeologist's efforts. But then we recall that the Indian did make astonishing progress in some regions, and so we wonder if the turn of a century might not have brought some powerful statesman to make a nation of Americans, or an Indian genius to teach the people new possibilities of life.

As it was, the Indians left to themselves remained men and women of the Stone Age; only in Peru did they step forward into an Age of Bronze and begin an intelligent conquest of mining — so far as we know. That reservation means that some scientists have clung to the opinion that the stone carvings and the jade jewelry of the Mayas could scarcely have been made without aid of sharp metal. Traces of metal tools among tropical ruins have been argued over, because a few men hold that these were manufactured by prehistoric Indians.

It is not quite fair to the Indian to regard him as stupid or unseeing because he failed to think out the inventions that have led to our heights of civilization. Take the wheel, for instance, a simple device that the Chinese produced about 2700 B.C., and that was introduced into Egypt by the Hyksos about 2300 B.C. Why should the Indian see a particular need for wheels, when he had no powerful beast of burden that could be hitched to a cart? Dogs were used to drag sleds and other contrivances in the North and in the plains. But horses vanished from America before the end of the Ice Age, and there is no evidence of the Indians ever having seen such animals until the Spaniards brought horses on their ships. The Indian was not slow to appreciate the value of the horse, once he caught a glimpse of the Spaniards riding swiftly across the country. It was only a few years until the Indians not only were riding fast horses but breeding stocks for themselves. Cattle were unknown until the sixteenth century, when the Spaniards brought them to the New World. The llama in South America was tamed and used as a carrier of light loads. Perhaps in time the western Indian could have tamed the buffalo. It is hard to see what other native animal in the northern hemisphere could have been pressed into service.

Indians of the West Indies invented a sail boat, but so far as we know Indian adventurers never set out to sea to discover Europe or any other invisible overseas land. In the North-west was developed the kayak, which is waterproof, light in weight, non-capsizable, and altogether efficient for fishing in Arctic waters. The red man was just on the border of the machinery age; for samples of bow and strap-drills, continuous-motion spindles, and reciprocating two-hand drills are known. If there had been an interchange of ideas between the Indian and other races, to bring in foreign points of view and foreign inventions, much more might have been accomplished. When foreign influences did come, they were so overwhelming and so alien to the red man's entire world that he succumbed to them rather than gained benefit.

Reconstructing prehistoric American life, it appears that the natives came near to making the most of a difficult, isolated situation. Their arrow and javelin points were efficient enough for shooting game and killing one another. Their houses and tents were adapted to life in various climates and surroundings. Their art developed from crude clay figurines, worthy of the efforts of a five-year-old child, to such splendid mosaic work as the Aztec ceremonial plaques that contain thousands of tiny pieces of turquoise fitted into complex design. Indian medicine-men, with all their weird and alarming rites and their paraphernalia of fetishes and unholy remedies, nevertheless had some sound therapeutic knowledge. Miss Densmore has shown that their use of psychiatry to treat the mind of the patient was decidedly progressive.

And what the Indian thought of the white man's education can be seen from the trenchant criticism quoted by Franklin in his *Remarks concerning the savages of North America*. In 1744, the Virginia commissioners had offered to take six Indian boys to be educated at William and Mary. The Indians begged courteously to be excused. They said, according to Franklin:

"Several of our young people were formerly brought up at the Colleges of the Northern Provinces; they were instructed in all your Sciences; but when they came back to us, they were bad Runners, ignorant of every means of living in the Woods, unable to bear either Cold or Hunger, knew neither how to build a Cabin, take a Deer, or kill an Enemy, spoke our language imperfectly, were therefore neither fit for Hunters, Warriors, or Counsellors; they were totally good for nothing. We are, however, not the less obliged by your kind Offer, tho' we decline accepting it; and to show our grateful Sense of it, if the Gentlemen of Virginia will send us a Dozen of their Sons we will take great care of their Education, instruct them in all we know, and make Men of them."

The Indians might have blended some of the white man's fashions and inventions into their own native culture and might have held their ground longer, if the Europeans had not brought a Pandora's box filled with germs that were far more deadly to the Indians than muskets and swords.

It is believed that until the white man came there were no epidemics of scarlet fever, measles, or smallpox in America. Public health standards were kept high by a rude and radical system of eugenics which weeded out defectives, sickly babies, and the senile. In addition, many normal, but frail, babies must have died. When Sterling of the Bureau of American Ethnology explored ancient town sites in South Dakota he found three baby skeletons to every adult in the cemeteries. The Indian child that grew up was strong and vigorous, though not so perfect physically as has been popularly supposed: witness their long pharmacopeia. But foreign diseases communicated by sailors and colonists ravaged whole tribes before the eyes of the helpless Indian medicine men. Smallpox, in particular, swept tribe after tribe, from the Gulf States and Yucatan to Alaska. The Indians had no immunity to this new germ.

The European regarded the spread of diseases as the work of a favoring providence. Jedidiah Morse, describing the mortal sickness which reduced the Nantucket Indians in 1763, said: "The hand of Providence is undoubtedly in this surprising evidence of mortality among the Indians to make room for the English. Comparatively few have perished by wars. They waste and molder away. They, in a manner unaccounted, disappear."

Invisible disease germs, gunpowder, hard labor imposed by the white man, and the destruction of game herds, these put an end to the red man's America.

The surprising thing is that after three centuries it is still

possible to probe into the minds of living Indians and bring out
facts about that prehistoric America. Ethnologists who encounter aged, full-blood Indians who have lived not too close
to modern American institutions find that these types can often
tell a great deal that is recognizable as "real Indian." The
old people remember, because it was the elderly Indian's obligation to remember important information and to pass his
wisdom on to the younger generation. When questioned seri-
ously they are keen to feel the responsibility of making the
Indian ways clear.

These Indians have explained many a puzzling fact about objects dug up by the archaeologist's spade. They have helped
reduce the number of museum relics that are set up in collections with vague, guessing labels because no white man is able
to imagine any use for such contrivances. But the present
generation of scientists is the last one that will be able to explore the archaic layer of the Indian mind, at least in North
America. The Indian's memory for his past is running low.

## THE MAID OF CHIOS

A fourth century B.C. marble head from the Aegean island of Chios. An original of the best art of the early Hellenistic period.

A TEMPLE TO THE GOD OF THE SEA

At Paestum on the west coast of southern Italy stands one of the best preserved
of early Greek temples to the Greek god Poseidon (the Roman Neptune).

CHAPTER SEVENTEEN

## THE OBLIGATIONS OF SCIENCE

Archaeology is the new science of old things. That does
not mean that such things need be as old as Methusaleh;
indeed, they can be as old as only a generation ago.

When the words theology and geology and biology began
to be used in English, they probably looked strange and
sounded hard. But when it was known that in Greek *theos*
meant "god," that *ge* meant "earth," that *bios* meant "life,"
and that *logos* meant "word" or "study," the meanings of
the new words became plain and their use easy. When one
hears that *archaios* means "old," Archaeology becomes as
simple as the others.

Every new science with a strange name has to run the
gamut of jokes. To see real paroxysms of scientific language,
however, one must turn to other sciences rather than to

archaeology.  It would be no joke to run foul of many such chemical compounds as the new carbomethoxymethyl-tri-methylammonium-bromide.  What indeed are the pesca-lurious gyrations of a thyramb?  It is a matter of more than medical trepidation when one reads that the famous physician Sir William Osler said he "had had a pleopolymorphic-cocco-bacterio-bacillary-upper-respiratory passage infection."  Let us be thankful that we have only the simple terms of archaeol-ogy to face.

Archaeology has risen so rapidly in scientific value and has so widened its activities, that it is necessary already to limit the fields of its work.  A geologist, not long ago, was a scien-tific authority on general geology.  Now there are a dozen kinds of geologists, of which the petroleum geologist is the latest variety.  There is hardly an archaeologist who today would dare to claim authority as a general archaeologist.  There are, to name a few of the definite fields, Oriental, Indian, Mesopotamian, Mediterranean, Palestinian, Egyptian, Greek, Roman, British, American, Prehistoric, Classical, Early Chris-tian, Medieval, Renaissance, Modern archaeologists.  The archaeologist who knows all about the old tide-water colonial mansions in Virginia may not know anything about the pot-holes in the rocks up the Susquehanna river.  He, or she, who is an authority on spool-beds, Paul Revere silver, Duncan Phyfe furniture, Potowattomie head-dress, or early American money, may know very little about Sioux wampum, Congaree arrow-heads, great-grandmothers' samplers, pre-Whitney spinning wheels, Navajo blankets, candle-wick spreads, Siwash pipes, or mound builders' pearls.  But these things all belong to archaeology, as much as do the Maya pyramids in Cen-tral America or the Pharaonic pyramids in Egypt, as much as does the great wall in China or the Roman wall in Scot-land, as much as do the caves of the Buddhas or the Altamira cave in Spain, as much as do the seven wonders of the ancient world or the seventy times seven recently resurrected wonders of the ancient and medieval world.

Alexander the Great was an archaeologist as well as a sen-

timentalist when he carried with him on all his campaigns a
copy of Homer's poems and put it each night under his pillow.
The Roman emperor Augustus was an archaeologist when he
had fourteen obelisks brought from Egypt and set up in Rome
on the parapets (or *spinae*), built lengthwise in the stadia,
round which the chariot races were run.   Every one of these

*From an engraving by Piranesi*

### CIRCUS MAXIMUS AT ROME

In the centre of the *spina* rises one of the obelisks brought to Rome by the
archaeological emperor Augustus.  This obelisk now stands in the Piazza del
Popolo at Rome.   Around this embellished *spina*, or backbone, the chariots
ran the seven lap races.   The engraver has exercised the artists' privilege in
his reconstruction, and has left off the high wall that sustained the seats on
one side and the near end of the circus.

obelisks was cut and wedged out of the solid granite east of
the Nile, and carved with hieroglyphic writing more centuries
before Augustus' time than have elapsed from his time two
thousand years ago until now.   The emperor Titus was an
archaeologist as well as a conqueror when he brought back to
Rome after his capture of Jerusalem the marvelous seven-
branched candlestick of solid gold.   Lord Elgin was more of
an archaeologist than a diplomat when in 1802 he brought from

Athens to London the broken marble statuary from the Parthenon on the Acropolis. Many popes were good archaeologists when they took the 6,000 marble, granite, and alabaster columns from the Roman buildings fast falling into ruin, and set them up in various of the churches of Rome. Many of our own forefathers were archaeologists when they picked up the Indian arrowheads turned up by their plowshares, and brought them to their houses where they were treasured as keepsakes until they were given or sold to their ultimate proper habitat, a local, state, or college museum.

British Museum       *From a Greek Vase Painting*

ACHILLES

The painter's model for this great Greek leader in the Trojan war was a youth of the sixth century B. C.

It is a natural desire to try to find and then to cherish as mementoes the things that belonged to people who lived and died before our time. The act prompted by that desire is only another name for archaeology, even when the chief aim was curiosity, sentimentality, or simply pride of possession. When Rienzi, a few hundred years ago, found in the Roman Forum a Latin inscription on a marble monument that had preserved in engraved writing the power of the tribunes of the ancient Roman Republic, and when with its help, and with that of others which he found, brought about his election as a Roman tribune, he was acting for personal and national interest; but he was an archaeologist without knowing it.

It was a clever person who said that if Cleopatra's nose had been an inch longer, the face of the whole world would have been changed. But the discovery of the famous stone at the Rosetta mouth of the Nile, and the translation of the characters engraved upon it, was a more important and a more exciting affair than all the businesses Cleopatra could ever have stuck her nose into, no matter how long it might have been. The conquest of the Behistun inscription, those wedge-shaped, or cuneiform, characters cut into a cliff that bordered Persia, was a greater conquest and one fraught with more importance to the world in the long run, than all the conquests in that region made by Aryan, Babylonian, Mede and Persian, Macedonian, Arab and English. The names of Achilles, Hector, Ulysses, and Aeneas will never die; neither will the name of Heinrich Schliemann ever die. He was the German lad whose imagination was so fired by the Homeric story that his enthusiasm kept aflame until after nearly a half century he was

*British Museum          From a Greek Vase Painting*

BRISEIS

The girl over whom Achilles and Agamemnon quarreled. Note the straight ancient Greek profile from top of forehead to end of nose. She is painted on the other side of the vase on which is the Achilles.

able to carry out his plan of hunting for Troy. He found it and authenticated Homer. The name of Arthur Evans will still be alive when most of the kings of England will be forgotten. Evans brought to light the long-lost, almost forgotten, and quite incredible Cretan or Minoan civilization.

Tutankhamen, Carnarvon, and Carter each made the other famous in the annals of archaeology. Sir John Marshall and Sir Aurel Stein are going back into what were the mists of antiquity and clearing away with the white light of scientific research the uncertainties that have hung over the distant past of India. The Carnegie Institution of Washington is back of the work that is restoring the long-lost Mayas to their chief place in Central America. The School of American Research at Santa Fe is protagonist for the Pueblo Indian cultures.

People have always been archaeologists; they always will be. As an exact science, however, archaeology is not much more than fifty years old. It may well be that its rapid growth is to be attributed to the overwhelming fascination that attends the entire course of an archaeological enterprise. First, there is the fun or exploration before hitting upon a site. Secondly, there is the breathless excitement of the excavation during which at the most unexpected moments there are dug out or turned up the long-lost objects of former civilizations, objects all of which are of interest, many of which are of great importance, and some of which are absolutely priceless. Then thirdly, there is the interpretation, publication to the world, and the public exhibition for the world, of the various things which have been found. There are now thousands of museums in the world full of what we call archaeological objects. Children throng the museums abroad as well as here. In fact the intense interest of young pupils in the things in the museums has been capitalized, and now visits to the museums are part of the regular work of many schools.

No one would go to Egypt were it not for the pyramids, the temple at Luxor, the tombs in the Valley of the Kings, and the great Museum in Cairo. The first and the last place in Athens to which everyone goes is the Acropolis with its matchless ancient temples in their shattered glory, but much of everyone's time between visits to the Acropolis is spent in the National Museum. The Hermes of Praxiteles alone, that wonderful piece of sculptured marble, draws the world to Olympia. Delphi, Delos, and Olympia offer terraces of the ruins of the past, and offer them not in vain. In Rome the museums are nearly the *sine qua non*. The multitudinous archaeological display through the miles of rooms and corridors in the National, Vatican, Villa Giulia, Capitoline, Conservatori, Lateran, and Mussolini Museums makes the eager eye and mind forget the weary feet and tired body.

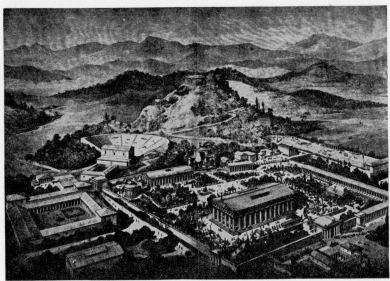

*Restoration by Thiersch*

OLYMPIA

A good restoration of the site of the ancient Olympic Games. The stadium is at the right. The statues of the Hermes of Praxiteles and the Victory of Paeonius were discovered by German excavators near the ruins of the temple.

Germany is perhaps prouder of the broken marble statuary in the Munich Museum that came from the gable ends of the Greek temple at Aegina and of the marble figures in relief in the recently opened new Asia Minor Museum in Berlin which once adorned the great altar at Pergamum in Asia Minor, than of anything else it owns. When one speaks of France, the Museum of the Louvre in Paris leaps at once into the mind. London without the British Museum would be unthinkable. Thousands of citizens and visitors enjoy the archaeological exhibits in our museums in Boston, Providence,

New Haven, New York, Philadelphia, Baltimore, Washington, Richmond, Charleston, Buffalo, Pittsburgh, Cleveland, Toledo, Detroit, Chicago, Milwaukee, St. Louis, Denver, Santa Fe, San Francisco, and San Diego. Archaeology has come to be a tremendous factor in the human side of the life of the whole civilized world.

*Photograph by R. V. D. Magoffin*

ROME, EAST OF THE JORDAN

Transjordania and Arabia are full of the monumental remains of Roman dominion. The Roman theatre at Amman, the ancient Philadelphia, is a striking memorial of show days of long ago.

An example of one of the latest of the startling discoveries of archaeology may not be amiss.

On the line of the Berlin to Bagdad railway at a big bend in the Halys river in Anatolia (that river which King Croesus made famous by misinterpreting the *double-entendre* handed out to him by the Pythia and the priests at Delphi that said a kingdom would be destroyed if he crossed the river), the Germans, some twenty years ago, made a great discovery of several thousand clay tablets. The place where they were found was the site of the ancient capital of the Hittite Empire, known to the Greeks as Pteria, now Boghaz-keui. It was an archaeological *tour-de-force* to have made the Hittite Empire rise from an unknown and lost identity to one of the great states of the second millennium B.C., along with Babylonia, Egypt, and Crete.

At the newly found old city were documents in plenty. They were found in two rose-colored rooms of a palace and in three grey-colored rooms of a temple. The tablets were of baked clay, about one foot high and eight inches wide, with double columns of writing on both sides. The writing was in small cuneiform or wedge-shaped Mesopotamian characters, running from 40 to 80 lines on each tablet face. It was soon seen that the historical inscriptions found in the temple dated after 1300 B.C., at which time it seems that the temple had been turned into a Record Office. If any document covered more than one tablet, the sequence was carefully indicated, and usually at the end of the documents the author gives his name, his profession, and his residence.

The Swiss scholar Forrer proved that there were eight languages represented in the tablets, although they were written in the same general cuneiform fashion.

The official but not the colloquial language of the Hittites is that in which two of the world's most famous letters were written. They were from Tel el-Amarna in Egypt and were edited as long ago as 1902, and then called the "oldest remains in an Indo-Germanic language." (Indo-European is the proper term outside of Germany.) One of them was from Amenophis III, the father of the heretic Pharaoh Akhnaton, written to Tarhundaraba, King of Arzawa. When it developed that several of the other languages represented in the Boghaz-keui tablets were translated into this official language, and that the scribes had given the names of the other languages, it became clear that Forrer was on the right track. He gave the name "Kanisian" to the official Hittite language, although he had no authority for doing so.

It is a sort of wizardry that brings out of a lot of broken tablets, inscribed with cuneiform letters, the proof that the Hittites taught in their schools the long-dead Sumerian language, because the cuneiform was a Sumerian invention, and because it was thought that charms sung in that old language were peculiarly effective. It may be wondered how such a fact can be proved. It is done in this way. On one tablet is a Sumerian text; in another column the pronunciation of the same text is given in the "Kanisian" cuneiform; and in two other columns are given a Babylonian and a "Kanisian" translation of the same Sumerian text. That is proof enough.

It then appeared that another language represented is the Babylonian, which is seen to be the diplomatic language. Then there are the Luvish, the Balaish, the Harrish, and the language of the Manda people. Most interesting of all is the one called "Proto-Hattic," which is the real Hittite, but it is so strangely formed that it could not have been identified had it not been translated into the official "Kanisian."

The reason the scribes do not give the name of the official language in which they write is because it would be supposed to be understood. But their reason for naming the others has in it an element of modern, as well as of ancient, psychology. The scribes give the proper names to the other languages because invocations of foreign gods would be more effective if they were made in the language of the peoples where the gods belonged. They were much afraid that the gods might not understand if they should be addressed in the official Hittite "Kanisian."

This is a brief story of one of the exciting possibilities brought to the philologist and historian by archaeology.

It was said by some one that "business is making people think they can't get what they don't want." Archaeology is making people want what they never expect to see and what they can't imagine exists.

The ancient Greek writer Pausanias was an archaeologist as well as a historian. In fact, the one text above all others that an excavator in Greek lands must have is that of Pausanias. He traveled widely and wrote much about the buildings and the statuary that he saw. He visited Olympia, the site of the ancient Olympic games. He mentioned, among other facts, where the beautiful Victory made by Paeonius and the marvelous Hermes sculptured by Praxiteles stood in reference to the great temple.

The architect Vitruvius and the scientific Pliny the Elder, both Roman writers, were they writing today, would be no less famous as archaeologists than as litterateurs. Two men of the middle ages known to fame for other reasons, Petrarch (1304–1374) the poet, and Mantegna (1431–1504) the painter, also well deserve to be called archaeologists. It was, however, the travels of various Englishmen and Germans in the East during the seventeenth and eighteenth centuries, and the sketches they made to illustrate their descriptions of the ancient things they saw, that gave the modern world its archaeological bent. The volumes on those travels are priceless archaeological treasures because many of the things described and sketched have either disappeared entirely or have been hopelessly shattered since even that seemingly short time ago. But relying on those sketches many monuments have been correctly restored, and many artistic compositions, particularly sculpture groups, have been realigned or restored from the broken pieces which were picked up by or sold to travelers and which later came to light, widely dispersed, in private collections or public museums.

There seems to be general agreement that historical research is scientific and valuable only when it builds on these two bases: (1) consciously transmitted information, *i.e.*, Literary Sources, and (2) unconsciously transmitted testimony, or Relics (*reliquiae*). With the coming of the new archaeological sciences it became evident that no one science can stand up against, or even apart from, the rest. The more important of these new sciences that constitute ARCHAEOLOGY are anthropology, ancient architecture and art in their many forms, ceramics, epigraphy, numismatics, palaeography, topography, and toponomy.

The Greeks gave us the word *archaiologia*. By it they meant "information about the past." The Romans translated the Greek word with their word *antiquitates*. We may translate both words approximately if we say, giving to both their widest significance, "antiquity" and "antiquities." In its broadest sense, therefore, Archaeology is the scientific study of the remains of past civilizations "that branch of knowledge which takes cognizance of past civilizations and investigates their history in all fields by means of remains of art, architecture, monuments, inscriptions, literature, language, implements, customs, and all other examples which have

Royal Ontario Museum of Archaeology.                    Courtesy of Director Currelly

TYPES OF GREEK VASES

survived." (Century Dictionary.) Ancient civilization was not centripetal; it was centrifugal. Both sets of ideas are important, because in the one we may find the undisturbed strata, such as an unbroken line of broken pottery, against which a chronological yardstick may be placed with inestimable potentialities of cross measurements. In the other we are forced to make comparison to balance valuations, to weigh evidence, to discover influences, in the prosecution of which only the care of the trained scientist can ultimately be tolerated.

Archaeology has become a science because there is material on which to work, laboratories where the work can and must be properly done, places where material after proper treatment can be safely left or safely housed, and publications where every detail of the work from first to last can be, or is, illustrated, historically illuminated, and scientifically explained. Past civilizations offer an almost inexhaustible mine of material, the excavation sites are the laboratories, protected sites and museums are the housing desiderata, and the scores of accredited archaeological Bulletins, Revues, Monumenti,

Notizie, Denkmaeler, Jahrbuecher, Mitteilungen, Annals, Memoirs, and Journals furnish faithful hostages to future assessors of past results.

The ownership of material is certainly local, perhaps national. Excavations or archaeological laboratories may be local, but only at the cost of probable accusations of self-interest and the certain charges of un-scientific methods. Scientific excavators must visit other excavations even as noted surgeons visit one another's clinics, as chemists and physicists watch the experiments of their rivals, as geologists or botanists accompany the expeditions of their famous confréres.

Excavation should be discouraged unless proper care can be given at once to the objects found. Certain monumental material must remain where found (*in situ*); unique finds of a movable sort should find proper lodgment in safe museums; duplicates, or if that is an untenable term, commonly acknowledged replicas, might best be treated as other interchangeable commodities.

Ny-Carlsberg Glyptotek, Copenhagen.
Courtesy of Director F. Poulsen

AN ATHLETIC COIFFURE

A beautiful marble head with the long hair bound up after the fashion of the athlete. Professor Caroline Galt has written about a bronze statuette at Mount Holyoke College, the hair of which offers noticeable similarities, facts which help to assign a date for the work.

Publication must be complete and absolutely honest; it should be approximately immediate. Criticism will correct unscientific work, rather than delay publication, because in most countries national pride is not confined to those who are excavating its antiquities. Pride in honest and adequate publication already exists. Excavation without publication is worthless, but excavation apart from scientific knowledge and without a proper publication is inexcusable.

It is quite proper to resent the damage done, however unwittingly, by a Schliemann or any other entrant in a field destined to become a place of science. It is perhaps only proper to lament the state of society where irreparable damage has been or can be done. It is very hard to blame a man for not knowing what he could not be expected to know. But methods and means are now both known and recognized, and there should attach some measure of disgrace to any nation which will not take a definite stand, both a national and an international stand, for the proper exploration for, and the excavation, preservation, and publication of, the material with which scientific archaeology claims to deal.

Italy, as being more hospitable to artistic enterprise than any other place in the Mediterranean world in the eighteenth century, holds primacy in the history of modern archaeology. About the middle of that century many ancient tombs were found and explored in Tuscany and hundreds of beautiful painted Greek and Etruscan vases were taken thence, mostly to the Vatican, but many came into the possession of persons of wealth in nearly all the countries of Europe.

The German writer Winckelmann with his *History of Ancient Art* in 1763 startled a somewhat sodden world out of self-satisfaction and took its basic aesthetics back to its Greek foundations on the strength of the recent archaeological finds of Greek works of art or Roman copies of them. Thomas Bruce, Lord Elgin, Ambassador to the Porte in 1799, saved to the world many of the sculptures from the Parthenon and brought them back to England. The world calls them the Elgin Marbles and they are the brightest of the many gems in the British Museum. In passing it should be said, in the light of occasional questions as to the propriety of having taken them from Greece and as to the timeliness of restoring them to their local habitat, that had those marbles been left in Greece they would have suffered irreparably, as did those pieces which were not taken. The time has not yet come to restore them to the Acropolis. The British Museum is still the proper place for the Elgin Marbles.

Systematic excavation began first in Babylonia and Assyria in 1811, and until 1860 practically all archaeological work was carried forward in the territory called the non-Greek Near East.  Smith and Porcher began to work at Cyrene in Africa in 1860, Cesnola was in Cyprus from 1867 to 1876.  In 1870 Heinrich Schliemann discovered the ancient city of Troy, and became the miracle man of archaeology.

A CRETAN PANTRY

Two of the many storage magazines beneath the floor of the Minoan palace at
Cnossus in Crete.

In 1873 Austria entered the archaeological field.  Its first work was on the island of Samothrace, where the Victory, now in the Louvre, was found.  The Austrian concession was in Anatolia, and its main work was done in Lycia and Caria, and at Ephesus.

Germany has just celebrated (April, 1929) the hundredth anniversary of the founding of the German Archaeological Institute in Rome.  It began in 1875 at Olympia in Greece, the excavations there until 1880 ranking high in the annals of the science.   Germans also excavated the sites of the cities of Pergamum, Miletus, and Priene in Asia Minor, and of Thera on the island of the same name.

The French carried through two of the greatest of excavations beginning in 1877 on the island of Delos, and in 1893 at Delphi, both ancient seats of the worship of Apollo.   England chose the Peloponnesus for its work, and the discoveries at Sparta and Megalopolis testify to their great success.   The British have also done good work in prehistoric Thessaly and Macedonia, and at Phylakopi on Melos.   In 1900 Arthur Evans, made Sir Arthur for his splendid work, began his career in Crete.   His discoveries at Cnossus, the palace of the fabled King Minos who had the Labyrinth and the Minotaur, ran a close second in fame to Schliemann and Troy.   As the former gave back to the world the Mycenaean civilization, so did the latter fill in the gap between then and the civilizations of Egypt and Mesopotamia with the entirely forgotten Minoan, Cretan, or Aegean civilization.   Greece excavated at Epidaurus, where the best-preserved of ancient theatres is still to be seen, but confined its work mostly to Eleusis, the site of the famed Mysteries, and to Athens, the greatest spot of all.

The United States was the last of the great nations to enter the field of Mediterranean excavations.   The European nations took excavations out of the category of esthetic pastime and made them scientific enterprises under properly subsidized national Schools of Archaeology.   They got far ahead of us for that reason.   We might never have arrived on the scene but for private enterprise.   It was the foundation in Boston in 1879 of the Archaeological Institute of America that gave our scholars the opportunity to engage on equal terms with their European colleagues in the new and entrancing science of archaeology in the Old World.   The work at Assos (1881–1883), at the Argive Heraeum (1892–1893), at Corinth, beginning in 1896, and elsewhere, has shown that our archaeologists are the equals of those of any other nation.

Since 1870 the amount of work that has been done is amazing.   The chief temples of Greece, south Italy, Sicily, and Asia

Minor have been dug out and measured. Modern architecture in the civilized world shows the influence of that phase of excavation. On the sculptural side the results have been no less startling. The history of ancient art, the development of its canons of style, and the full realization of its matchless and inimitable beauties, have been brought out by the discoveries of such pieces of archaic sculpture as the Apollo of Tenea, the metopes from the temples at Selinus in Sicily, and the pedimental groups from the temple at Aegina. The Elgin marble, the frieze from Bassae, and the Lycian marbles in the British Museum have given us those magnificent examples of the Greek work of the fifth century B.C., and the sculptures from the Mausoleum at Halicarnassus and from the temple of Artemis (Diana) at Ephesus have done likewise for the work of the fourth century.

*Courtesy of the Royal Ontario Museum of Archaeology, Toronto*

A MARVEL IN MARBLE

The sudden enlargement and the increased fame of the British Museum, the Louvre in Paris, the Vatican in Rome, the Hermitage at Leningrad, and the museums at Berlin, Dresden, and Vienna, because of the wealth of the new finds made by archaeology, are contemporaneous phenomena with the rise of new museums at Athens, Olympia, and Delphi in Greece, the Terme (now National) in Rome, the Metropolitan in New York, the Museum of Fine Arts in Boston, the Imperial Ottoman Museum in Constantinople, and the Ny-Carlsberg in Copenhagen.

It should be repeated that real scientific excavation began with the German work at Olympia in 1875, with the French at Delos in 1877, with the Greeks at Eleusis in 1882 and on the Acropolis in 1855, with the Italians at Falerii in 1887, and with the Americans at Corinth in 1896. Better and better methods were employed as these excavations progressed.

Since 1900, however, beginning with the work of Arthur Evans at Cnossus, and the Italians at Phaestus, in Crete, with

*Courtesy of the British School of Archaeology in Jerusalem*

THE PALACE OF AHAB

Clearing away the débris from the palace of King Ahab at Samaria in Palestine.

that of Winckler in 1906 at Boghaz-keui, the capital of the newly discovered empire of the Hittites, with that of the English at Sparta in 1907, and the Americans at Samaria and Sardis since 1910, the field has suddenly broadened to a world-wide area. The Western Hemisphere also has taken its place in the front rank of archaeological opportunities; the countries of Europe both in their home lands and in their colonies are driving ahead with state appropriations and private concessions; India, and most important perhaps of all, China, are clamoring for scientific archaeological investigation. Opportunities are decidedly

greater and more numerous at present than are funds
and trained men.  There seems clearly to be an opportunity
to push the work.  With that comes the privilege of insist-
ing upon ever better scientific methods.  Is it not possible to
say that there is even more now than opportunity, that there
is also duty?  No country is better able in every way to assume the lead in archaeological science than the United States
of America, no country is more generally welcome.  If we

*The Art Institute of Chicago*                              *Gift of Alfred E. Hamill*

A FIGHTING GREEK

A fine Hellenistic copy of a fifth century B.C. marble relief of a fighting
Greek warrior.  The technique shown in the treatment of the hair, beard, and
muscles is worthy of the art of the best Greek period.

shall continue to insist upon correct methods, unselfish work,
and honest, adequate, and immediate dissemination of results, in a word, upon science without spoils, we may confi-
dently expect to gain and hold an international leadership in
the archaeological world, eminent, unquestioned, and wise.

The accomplishment of this consummation so devoutly
to be wished, this expectation so worthy to be realized, may
not be immediate.  Much has been done by some of the greatest nations, but the idea that antiquities, whether actually
found or politically acquired, are "spoils," is still much in evi-

dence.   It should not be hard to convince nations that the sale of spurious antiquities has worse than no justification. It may take time, but it should not be difficult to extend quite universally the present exchange of objects for museums and exhibits; it will be much harder to curb the enthusiasm of the private collector.   It will be hardest of all to stop monopolistic concessions, because they are political in nature, and political protests stir up national animosities.

But the scientists of the world exert an influence which is commensurate with the single-minded, disinterested, and honest attitude they assume for the elimination of discredited materialistic or nationalistic pseudo-science, and toward the extension of pure science in its every form.   Science is international, and must prevail.

# MUSEUMS AND THEIR BEST ARCHAEOLOGICAL OBJECTS

## AUSTRIA

VIENNA.　*K. K. Kunsthistorisches Hofmuseum:* Giölbashi Frieze; Bronze statue from Ephesus; ancient objects found in Austria.

## CANADA

TORONTO.　*Royal Ontario Museum:* statue of Aphrodite; head of Meleager; important Greek vases.

## DENMARK

COPENHAGEN.　*National Museum:* rich in Scandinavian, especially Danish antiquities.

*Ny-Carlsberg Glyptothek:* the Jacobsen head of a pugilist; standing and seated statues of Anacreon; Meleager; Borghese Juno; splendid collections of busts; copies of Etruscan wall paintings.

## EGYPT

CAIRO.　*National Museum:* art objects from the tomb of Tutankhamen; Sheikh-el-Beled; every type of objects from Egyptian tombs.

## FRANCE

PARIS.　*Louvre, Musée national du,* comprising Musée Napoléon I (1801), Musée Napoléon III (Campana collection from Rome), and Cabinet des Médailles: Victory of Samothrace; Aphrodite of Melos (Venús de Milo).

## GERMANY

BERLIN.　*Asia Minor Museum:* Pergame altar, and other objects from Anatolia.

*Neues und Altes Museum:* archaic seated goddess; earliest European polychrome standing statue; bronze praying boy; remnants of library of Asshur.

*Museum fuer Volkskunde:* antiquities from Troy.

COLOGNE.　*Museum:* the richest of German museums in objects from the Roman occupation.

DRESDEN.　*Albertinum:* Dresden lady known as *Grande Herculanaise;* the *Petite Herculanaise;* Zeus; Lemnian Athena; Bearded and Beardless Athlete.

FRANKFORT A.M.　Myron's Athena; Head of Alexander.

MUNICH.　*Glyptotek:* Aeginetan sculptures; Apollo of Tenea.

## GREAT BRITAIN

### ENGLAND

CAMBRIDGE.
*Fitzwilliam Museum:* Cretan stone statuette of Minoan goddess; Greek vases.

LONDON.
*British Museum:* founded by Charles I with objects obtained from the Sloane collection, willed to the nation in 1749; Parthenon (Elgin) marbles (1816); Hamilton collection of vases (1772); spoils from Egypt (1801); Townely Roman collection (1805); frieze from Bassae (1814); Phigaleia frieze; mausoleum of Halicarnassus; Nereid monument; Egyptian papyri; Greek and Roman coins; remnants of royal libraries of Ashurbanipal and Nebo; extensive collections of Stone, Iron, and Bronze Age objects.
*Lansdowne House:* Heracles; Amazon.

OXFORD.
*Ashmolean Museum:* Pomfret and Arundel marbles; head of Demosthenes; Evans collection of Bronze and Stone Age implements.

### IRELAND

DUBLIN.
*Museum of the Royal Irish Academy:* Irish antiquities.

### SCOTLAND

EDINBURGH.
*Royal Scottish Museum:* important Roman silver ware.
*National Museum of Antiquities of Scotland:* Scottish collection.

## GREECE

ATHENS.
*National Museum:* Mycenae and Cnossus finds; Anticythera bronze statue; copy of Polyclitus' Diadumenus from Delos; archaic "Apollo" figures; Victory of Delos; sepulchral vases and stelae.
*Acropolis Museum:* archaic poros pedimental groups; the "Old Maids"; balustrade of Nike Temple.

CANDIA.
Snake goddesses, frescoes, etc., from finds in Crete.

DELPHI.
Delphi sculptures; Agias of Lysippus; bronze charioteer.

OLYMPIA.
Hermes of Praxiteles; Victory of Paeonius; pediments of Zeus temple.

SALONIKI.
Venus Genetrix; Greek and Roman sculptures; the 1928 finds from D. M. Robinson's excavation at Olynthus.

## ITALY

BOLOGNA.
*Museo Civico:* head of Lemnian Athena; fine Etruscan and Greek vases; famous bronze *situla.*

BRESCIA.
Bronze Victory of Brescia.

FLORENCE.
*Museo etrusco (archeologico):* François vase; Idolino; Etruscan bronze orator; Etruscan tombs.
*Uffizi:* Niobid figures; Medici Venus; several pieces of Augustus' "Altar of Peace"; gems, coins, cameos.

NAPLES.    *Museo Nazionale (Borbonico)*: Farnese bull; Alexander mosaic; Harmodius and Aristogiton statues; Doryphorus of Polyclitus; Pompeian wall paintings; Campanian vases.

PALERMO.   *Museo Nazionale:* archaic metopes from Selinus.

ROME.      *Antiquarium of the Forum* (formerly the church of S. Francesca Romana): objects from prehistoric cemetery in Forum.

*Antiquarium of the Palatine:* objects found on the Palatine Hill.

*Capitoline* (1650): dying Gaul; marble Faun; Amazon.

*Conservatori* (1471): Spinario; Esquiline Venus; marble plan of Rome; terra-cotta pedimental figures.

*Lateran:* Sophocles; Poseidon; marble altars.

*Museo dell' Impero Romano:* casts and reproductions to illustrate extent and character of the Empire.

*Mussolini:* Hercules altar base; objects of early Italic art; Marius Curtius relief; portrait head of Domitian.

*Nazionale (Museo delle Terme):* wounded Niobe; "Maiden" of Antium; bronze boxer signed by Apollonius; Venus of Cyrene; bronze Hellenistic sovereign; Venus Genetrix; Augustus of Via Labicana; inscriptions; late finds from Tripolitania and Cyrenaica.

*Pigorini:* objects from the Bernardini tomb.

*Vatican:* Apollo Belvidere; Laöcoon; Apoxyomenus of Lysippus; Galleria lapidaria; Greek and Etruscan vases; objects from Regulini Galassi tomb; Scipio tomb; Prima Porta Augustus; "Aldobrandini marriage" painting.

*Villa Giulia:* objects from Barberini tomb; Ficoroni cista.

Private collections.    Villa Albani, Barberini (mostly sold); Borghese, Campana (in Paris and Leningrad), Castellani (mostly sold to British Museum), Farnese, Giustiniani, Ludovisi (from ancient gardens of Sallust), Odescalchi, Ruspoli, Torlonia.

SYRACUSE.   Landolina Venus; Greek coins.

## MEXICO

MEXICO CITY.    *National Museum:* Mayan and Mexican antiquities; "Aztec calendar stone."

## PERU

LIMA.    *El Museo de Arqueologia Peruana:* contains nearly all the private collections which existed in Peru.

## RUSSIA

LENINGRAD.    *Hermitage:* Greek jewelry including two gold medallions with heads of Athena Parthenos; Greek ivories (IV cent. B.C.); Greek vases, including one signed by Euphronius; gold and silver decorations of chiefs from tombs at Kul Oba.

## SPAIN

MADRID.    *Prado:* copy of Athena Parthenos; puteal with birth of Athena; statue of Sleep.

## SWEDEN

STOCKHOLM.    *Naturhistoriska riks-Museum:* Scandinavian collection.

## SWITZERLAND

GENEVA.    Heads of Alexander and Augustus; Hermes; Greek and
Roman sculptures and vases.

## TURKEY

CONSTANTINOPLE.    *Ottoman Museum:* Alexander sarcophagus; sarcophagus of
the Mourners.

## UNITED STATES OF AMERICA

BALTIMORE.    *Walters Art Museum:* marble head of Eros of Lysippus; copy
of Cyniscus by Polyclitus; Roman sarcophagi.
*Johns Hopkins University Museum:* only signed vase of
Epictetus in America; signed vases by Nicosthenes and
Phintias; Greek and Latin inscriptions, coins, gems, vases,
sculptures and terra cottas; Etruscan antefixes.
*Museum of Art:* part of the Cesnola collection from Cyprus.

BOSTON.    *Fenway Court:* Roman sarcophagus with satyrs and maenads.
*Museum of Fine Arts* (1870): Ludovisi throne; marble head
from Chios; Cretan snake goddess; alabaster Chephren;
Roman portrait in terra cotta; portrait of lady, in bronze.

BRYN MAWR.    Greek vases.

CAMBRIDGE.    *Peabody Museum of Archaeology and Ethnology:* Southwestern,
Mexican, and Central America antiquities.
*Fogg Art Museum:* Narcissus; Meleager; head of athlete;
Greek vases.

CHICAGO.    *Art Institute:* Greek cylix by Douris; relief of fighting war-
rior; Chinese memorial stela of 551 A.D.; Greek stela of
IV cent. B.C.; bronze sacrificial vessel of Chou dynasty;
Near East lustre jar, Samarra type, IX cent. B.C.
*Field Museum of Natural History:* well-balanced archaeolog-
ical collection; type exhibit of the Hopewell mound culture.

CLEVELAND.    *Museum of Art:* archaic female Greek head; Hellenistic
marble head; head of Heracles; statue of young man.

DETROIT.    *Museum of Art* (inc. 1885): draped Attic female torso of IV
cent. B.C.; torso of Aphrodite; heads of Augustus, Sept.
Severus, and M. Julius Philippus; Chinese Celadon vase
of Sung dynasty; painting by Ricci of Camillus rescuing
Rome.

INDIANAPOLIS.    *The John Herron Art Institute* (ded. 1906): Cypriote sculpture and pottery; Chinese and Japanese pottery and metal
work.

LOS ANGELES.    *Southwest Museum:* Southwestern and California collections.

MINNEAPOLIS.    *Institute of Arts* (opened 1915): life size marble lion, Greek,
IV cent. B.C.; Cypriote, Etruscan, and Roman vases; stone
figure of Kwan-Yin; Chinese jades.

NEW HAVEN.    *Stoddard Collection:* Greek and Roman vases.

NEW ORLEANS. *Tulane University Department of Middle America:* antiquities of Mexico, Central America and Northern South America.

NEW YORK. *American Museum of Natural History:* extensive Indian collections, especially fine exhibits of Peru and Middle America.

*American Numismatic Museum:* important Greek and Roman coins.

*Metropolitan Museum of Art:* Egyptian collection, tomb of Perneb; Etruscan chariot; painted room from Boscoreale; Cesnola collection from Cyprus; Greek vases; Greek and Roman glass, gems, and pottery.

*Museum of the American Indian, Heye Foundation:* comprehensive exhibits.

*New York University Archaeological Museum:* Roman inscriptions; Roman marbles; Egyptian papyri.

PHILADELPHIA. *Museum of the University of Pennsylvania* (1889): Attic grave stela; seated Dionysus; Roman head; Greek and Roman vases; Hellenistic head of Menander type; Peruvian material; excellent collection of Central American vases.

PITTSBURGH. *Carnegie Institute:* Costa Rican and Colombian collections especially good.

PRINCETON. *Art Museum:* a Praxitelean faun; III cent. B.C. Athena; statuette of Athena Parthenos; Greek vases; Roman mosaics and frescoes.

PROVIDENCE. *Rhode Island School of Design* (inc. 1877): marble statuette of a youth, IV cent. B.C. Greek; bronze statuette of Aphrodite, II cent. B.C., Greek; marble head of Amazon; torso of Dionysus; black-figured amphora signed by Nikosthenes; Roman sarcophagus portraying slaying of the Niobids; Graeco-Egyptian portrait head of II cent. A.D.

RICHMOND. *Valentine Museum:* splendid collection of Indian arrowheads.

ST. LOUIS. *Washington University Museum:* reproductions of objects found at Roman camp at Saalburg, Germany; fine collection of *aes grave.*

SMITH COLLEGE. *Hillyer Art Gallery:* torso of Eros by Lysippus; head of athlete; marble faun.

SAN DIEGO. *Southwest Museum:* objects illustrating Indian life of Southwest, Mexico, and Peru.

SANTA FE. *Museum of the School of American Research:* vases and objects made by the Pueblo Indians of the Southwest.

SAN FRANCISCO. *Museum of Anthropology:* Hearst collection of Greek marbles and vases.

TOLEDO. *Toledo Art Museum:* marble ram of time of Augustus; magnificent collection of ancient glass.

WASHINGTON. *United States National Museum:* type exhibits from each of the states and Alaska. Tuxtla statuette.

WELLESLEY COLLEGE. *Farnsworth Museum:* Greek statue of Polyclitan type; torso of Heracles.

WORCESTER. *Art Museum:* statue of Aphrodite; head of Julius Caesar.

# IMPORTANT ARCHAEOLOGICAL EXCAVATIONS AND PUBLICATIONS

| | |
|---|---|
| **1506.** | Discovery of the Laöcoon group in Nero's Golden House in same room with painting of Hector and Andromache. |
| **1606.** | Discovery of wall painting "Aldobrandini marriage," on Esquiline hill at Rome. |
| **1711.** | First discoveries at Herculaneum; more in 1738. |
| **1722.** | *Account of Statues, Basreliefs, Drawings and Pictures in Italy*, J. Richardson. |
| **1748.** | Digging begun at Pompeii. |
| **1753.** | Discovery at Herculaneum of 100 marbles and bronzes and 3,000 rolls of charred papyri. |
| **1761–'62.** | *Antiquities of Athens*, Stuart and Revett. In 1751 these painters made for England the first expedition to Greece. |
| **1764.** | *Geschichte der Kunst*, Winckelmann. |
| **1788.** | *Voyage du jeune Anacharsis en Gréce*, Abbé Barthélémy. |
| **1792–'98.** | *Doctrina numorum veterum*, Eckhel. |
| **1797.** | Roman antiquities given to France by Treaty of Tolentino. |
| **1798–1801.** | Napoleon's expedition to Egypt accompanied by archaeologists. |
| **1799.** | Rosetta Stone discovered in August. |
| **1799.** | Championnet excavates at Pompeii. |
| **1801–'03.** | Thomas Bruce, Lord Elgin, ambassador to the Porte, collects Parthenon marbles in Athens. |
| **1801.** | London receives antiquities from Egypt. |
| **1808–'15.** | Excavation at Pompeii under Queen Caroline. |
| **1811.** | Excavation begun by Rich in Babylonia and Assyria. |
| **1811.** | Discovery of pedimental groups at temple on island of Aegina. |
| **1812.** | Discovery of temple frieze at Bassae in the Peloponnesus. |
| **1812.** | Discovery of Petra by Burckhardt. |
| **1812.** | Aeginetan sculptures acquired for Munich by Crown Prince Ludwig of Bavaria. |
| **1812.** | *Grecian Remains in Italy*, John Izard Middleton, of South Carolina (son of Arthur, one of the signers of the Declaration of Independence), the first American archaeologist. |
| **1814.** | Bassae temple frieze acquired by London. |
| **1814.** | Traces of Old Stone Age Culture found in Central Caucasus. |
| **1816.** | Elgin marbles acquired by British Museum. |
| **1820.** | Aphrodite of Melos discovered. |
| **1821.** | A. Nibby identifies the groups of Galatians from the Altar of Pergamum. |
| **1821–'22.** | Voutier bombards the Acropolis at Athens. |
| **1826.** | Reshid Pasha bombards the Acropolis at Athens. |
| **1827.** | Discovery of Etruscan wall paintings at Corneto. |
| **1828–'29.** | Discovery of Etruscan vases at Vulci. |
| **1829.** | The French begin excavation at Olympia of the temple of Zeus. |
| **1830.** | Discovery of Roman silver from temple of Mercury at Berthouville near Bernay. |

1830.  Kul Oba (Hill of Ashes) tomb near Kertch in the Crimea opened by Dulrux.

1831.  Discovery at Pompeii of the mosaic of Alexander the Great.

1832.  Stone, Bronze, and Iron Ages delimited by Thomsen.

1833–'36.  Ross clears the Acropolis at Athens.

1835.  Reconstruction of temple of Nike Apteros at Athens.

1835–'45.  Discovery and copying of inscription on Rock of Behistun by H. Rawlinson, from which the cuneiform system of writing was later deciphered. Entire inscription completed and translated in 1856 by Edwin Norris.

1836.  Discovery of the Regulini-Galassi tomb at Cervetri in Etruria.

1838.  Archaeological work begun in Palestine by Edward Robinson.

1839.  Discovery of statue of Sophocles.

1840.  Work at Delphi begun by Germans (K. O. Mueller).

1840.  Stephens' expedition to Yucatan and Central America.

1841.  Discovery of Heröon at Giölbashi by Schoenborn.

1842.  Pediment groups of terra cotta discovered at Luna in Etruria.

1842.  Nereid monument of Zanthos acquired by British Museum.

1843–'46.  Excavation of Khorsabad by Botta.

1844.  Discovery of François vase at Chiusi in Italy.

1845.  Investigation of mound builders undertaken by Squier and Davis.

1845–'47.  Nimrud excavated by Layard.

1846.  Discovery of archaic statue of "Apollo" of Tenea.

1846.  Discovery in Egypt of papyrus containing three lost orations of Hyperides.

1846.  First discoveries at Hallstatt.

1846.  Ramsauer begins systematic excavation of Iron Age cemetery at Hallstatt.

1848.  *Cities and Cemeteries of Etruria*, G. Dennis.

1848–'56.  *Gli Edifizi di Roma . . . dei contorni*, L. Canina.

1849.  Discovery of Apoxyomenos (after Lysippus) at Rome.

1849.  Discovery of catacomb of St. Calixtus at Rome by De Rossi.

1851–'55.  Excavation by Mariette of Serapeum at Memphis in Egypt.

1852.  Excavation begun in South Russia.

1853.  Discovery of the necropolis at Villanova near Bologna.

1853.  Discovery of prehistoric caves in South France.

1854.  Discovery of lake pile-dwellings in Switzerland.

1855–'60.  Excavation at Pompeii of Stabian Baths.

1857.  M. Thenou finds first inscribed stone of Gortyna law inscription.

1857.  Uncovering of Mausoleum of Halicarnassus by Newton.

1858.  Silver medals of Roman officer found at Xanten in Germany.

1859.  Statuette of Athena discovered by Lenormant.

1859–'62.  Stoa of Attalus at Athens excavated.

1860–'75.  Excavation at Pompeii directed by Fiorelli.

1861–'69.  Excavation on the Palatine hill in Rome.

1862.  Heraeum on island of Samos investigated by Humann.

1862.  Excavations at Alesia in France conducted by order of Napoleon III.

1863.  Discovery of Victory (Nike) of Samothrace by Champoiseau. Sent to Paris in 200 fragments.

1863.  *Studien zur Geschichte des griechischen Alphabets*, Kirchhoff, from Chalcidian vases.

1864.  First discoveries at La Tène.

1865.  Discovery of necropolis at Marzabotto in Italy.

1866.  Establishment of Palestine Exploration Fund.

1866.        Discovery of portrait statue of Augustus at Prima Porta.
1867.        Five-year exclusive privilege for Delphi given by Greeks to French École d'Athénes.
1867–'76.    Discoveries of Cesnola in Cyprus.
1868.        H. Schliemann visits Homeric sites.
1868.        Discovery of silver treasure (dinner service) at Hildesheim in Germany.
1868.        Discovery of the Moabite Stone (stela of Mesa).
1868.        Cro-Magnon rock shelter at Les Eyzies discovered.
1868.        *The Primitive Inhabitants of Scandinavia*, Sven Nelson.
1869.        Discovery of "House of Livia" on Palatine at Rome.
1869–'74.    Artemisium (temple of Diana) at Ephesus excavated by Wood and Hogarth.
1870.        *Zur Geschichte der Anfaenge griechischen Kunste*, Conze.
1870–'74.    Discovery of terra-cotta figurines at Tanagra in Boeotia.
1871.        Dipylon vases found at Athens.
1871.        Discovery of Certosa necropolis near Bologna.
1871–'90.    Schliemann works at Troy, Mycenae, Orchomenus, and Tiryns (with W. Doerpfeld after 1882).
1872–'73.    Rayet and Thomas work at Miletus, Magnesia, and Priene in Maeander Valley in Asia Minor.
1872–'78.    Excavation of tombs in Cyprus by L. P. and A. P. di Cesnola.
1873.        Periods of Pompeian wall-paintings distinguished by A. Mau.
1874.        Schliemann at Mycenae.
1875–'81.    Germans excavate at Olympia and lay first correct foundations for the science of archaeological excavation.
1875.        Discovery of Victory of Paeonius at Olympia.
1876.        Excavations begun at La Tène.
1876.        Mycenae discovered by Schliemann.
1877–'94 ;   French excavations at Delos.
  1902–.
1877.        Hermes of Praxiteles found at Olympia.
1877–1907.   Excavations at Carnuntum.
1878–'86 ;   German excavations at Pergamum.
1900–'14.
1878.        Study of paleolithic implements in Thames bank at London begun, Worthington Smith.
1879.        M. Haussoullier finds fragments of Gortyna law inscription.
1879.        Stone Age paintings in cave of Altamira discovered by Sautnola.
1879–'81.    Fragments of *Ara Pacis Augusti* collected by V. Duhn.
1880.        Schliemann at Orchomenus.
1880.        Flinders Petrie begins work in Egypt.
1880.        Gogstad Viking ship discovered.
1880.        Bandelier begins first systematic archaeological work in Southwest.
1881.        Maspero begins work in Egypt.
1881.        *Ancient Bronze Implements of Great Britain*, Sir John Evans.
1881.        Maudslay's first archaeological expedition to Central America.
1881–'83.    American School excavates at Eretria.
1881–'83.    American School excavates at Assos (Clarke, Bacon, and Koldewey).
1881–1903.   Greeks excavate Hieron at Epidauros.
1882–'85.    Austrians excavate in Caria and Lycia (Giölbashi).
1882.        First painted terra-cotta sarcophagus found at Clazomenae.
1882–'90.    Greeks excavate at Eleusis.
1882–'90.    Rumanians excavate at Adamklissi.

| 1882–1903. | *Histoire de l'art antique*, Perrot e Chipiez. |
|---|---|
| 1884. | Italians excavate grotto of Zeus on Mt. Ida in Crete. |
| 1884. | Schliemann at Tiryns. |
| 1884. | Stamatákès begins excavations on Acropolis at Athens. |
| 1884. | Halbherr discovers Gortyna law inscription. |
| 1885–. | *The American Journal of Archaeology.* |
| 1885–'88. | *Denkmaeler d. Klass. Altertums*, A. Baumeister. |
| 1885–'91. | Excavations on Athenian acropolis directed by Kavvadias. |
| 1885. | *Sur la chronologie de l'âge du Bronze*, O. Montelius. |
| 1886. | American School at Athens excavates theatre at Thoricus. |
| 1886, '89, 1895. | Doerpfeld excavates theatre of Dionysus at Athens. |
| 1887. | Alexander sarcophagus discovered at Sidon. |
| 1887. | Discovery of archives on clay tablets at Tell el-Amarna in Egypt. |
| 1887. | First paintings on mummies found in Egyptian Fayum. |
| 1887. | Ludovisi "marble throne" found at Rome. |
| 1887–'88. | Stoa of Eumenes excavated at Athens. |
| 1887–'89. | Italians excavate at Falerii, Alatri, and Marzabotto. |
| 1887. | Excavations at Mas d'Azil begun by Piette. |
| 1887. | Exploration of Los Muertos by Hemenway Archaeological Expedition. |
| 1888. | Greeks excavate at Vaphio, near Sparta, and find the famous gold cups with bulls in repoussé. |
| 1888. | Discovery at Hawara of 1–2 cent. A.D. mummy cases with painted portraits. |
| 1888–'90. | Americans excavate at Nippur in Babylonia. |
| 1889–'90. | Americans excavate theatre at Sicyon in Peloponnesus. |
| 1889–1902. | *Biologia Centrali Americana. Archaeology; Vols. I–IV*, A. P. Maudslay. |
| 1890. | Flinders Petrie begins work in Palestine at Tell el-Hezy. |
| 1890. | Discovery of Gurob papyrus and one leaf of the *Antiope* of Euripides. |
| 1890–'91. | British excavate at Megalopolis in Greece. |
| 1890–'92. | *Final Report of Investigations among the Indians of the Southwestern United States, Parts I–II*, A. F. Bandelier. |
| 1891. | Discovery at El Hibeh in Upper Egypt of papyrus roll containing adventures of Wenamen. |
| 1891. | Honduras expedition from Peabody Museum starts ten years' exploration. |
| 1892–'95. | Americans excavate at the Argive Heraeum. Polyclitus made gold and ivory statue of Hera for this temple. |
| 1892–1903. | Germans investigate the *Limes*, the Roman wall between the Rhine and Danube. |
| 1892. | *Die Ruinenstatte von Tiahuanaco*, Alphons Stubel and Max Uhle. |
| 1893. | *Meisterwerke der griechischen Plastik*, Furtwaengler. |
| 1893–'94. | Doerpfeld excavates at Troy. |
| 1893–1901. | French resume excavations at Delphi (see 1840 and 1876). |
| 1893. | *The Cliff Dwellers of Mesa Verde, Southwestern Colorado, Their Pottery and Implements*, G. Nordenskiold. |
| 1894–'95. | House of the Vettii excavated at Pompeii. |
| 1894–'95. | Jewelry of XI and XII dynasties found by de Morgan at Dahshur. |
| 1894–'96. | Work on temple of Queen Hatshepsut at Deir el-Bahari. |
| 1894. | *Report on the Mound Explorations of the Bureau of Ethnology*, Cyrus Thomas. |
| 1895. | British work at Tell el-Amarna in Egypt. |
| 1895. | Grenfell, Hunt, and Hogarth begin to hunt for papyri in Egypt. |

| | |
|---|---|
| 1895. | Great silver treasure found at Boscoreale near Pompeii. |
| 1895–'99. | Germans excavate at Priene in Asia Minor. |
| 1895. | American Museum begins five years' work at Pueblo Bonito; valuable objects discovered. |
| 1895. | *Archaeological Studies among the Ancient Cities of Mexico*, W. H. Holmes. |
| 1896. | Americans begin to excavate Corinth in Greece. |
| 1896. | Austrians begin to excavate Ephesus. |
| 1896. | *The Historical Geography of the Holy Land*, 4th ed., G. A. Smith. |
| 1897. | Grenfell and Hunt begin work at Oxyrhynchus, 120 miles south of Cairo and find papyrus with sayings (*Logia*) of Jesus. |
| 1897–1910. | *Repertoire de la statuaire grecque et romaine*, S. Reinach. |
| 1897. | Jesup North Pacific Expedition begins investigation of prehistoric relations between Asia and America. |
| 1897. | *Ancient Stone Implements of Great Britain*, Sir John Evans. |
| 1898. | *Pausanias' Description of Greece*, J. G. Frazer. |
| 1899. | *Pompeii, its Life and Art*, A. Mau-F. W. Kelsey. |
| 1899–1907. | Deutsche Orient Gesellschaft work at Babylon. |
| 1899–1907. | Berlin Museum at work at Miletus. |
| 1899. | Classification of Peruvian Trujillo ware by Uhle. |
| 1900. | Bronze statues recovered from sea at Anticythera, off Peloponnesus. |
| 1900. | Arthur Evans begins work at Cnossus in Crete. |
| 1901. | Recovery of sunken shipload of marbles and bronzes off Cape Malea. |
| 1902. | Prehistoric cemetery found in the Roman Forum by Boni. |
| 1902. | French resume work at Delos. |
| 1902. | Code stele of Hammurabi found by J. de Morgan. |
| 1902. | *Troia und Ilion*, W. Doerpfeld. |
| 1902–'04. | Danes excavate citadel at Lindos. |
| 1902, '05. | *The Argive Heraeum*, C. Waldstein and others. |
| 1902. | Miniature bronze chariot, evidence of Scandinavian sun cult, found in Zealand. |
| 1903–'05. | Germans excavate at Megiddo. |
| 1903–'07. | Deutsche Orient Gesellschaft excavates at Assur. |
| 1904. | Discovery by T. M. Davis of sarcophagus of Queen Hatshepsut. |
| 1904. | H. C. Butler and E. Littmann begin work in Syria. |
| 1904. | *Griechische Vasenmalerei*, A. Furtwaengler and K. Reichhold. |
| 1905. | Discovery of tomb of father and mother of Queen Tyi, by T. M. Davis. |
| 1905. | *Archaeology and False Antiquities*, Robert Monro. |
| 1906. | Winckler begins work at Boghazkeui, capital of the Hittite Empire. |
| 1906. | On Jan. 13, Grenfell and Hunt find in Egypt a basket of broken rolls, among which were parts of *Paeans* of Pindar, of the *Hypsipyle* of Euripides, of Phaedrus and of a history of Greece. |
| 1906. | Discovery on June 13 of the Banca Commerciale Niobid on site of the Gardens of Sallust, Rome. |
| 1906. | Metropolitan Museum begins work at Lisht in Egypt. |
| 1907. | Recovery of sunken shipload of marbles and bronzes off Mahdia on coast of north Africa. |
| 1907. | British begin work at Sparta. |
| 1907. | School of American Research established at Santa Fe. |
| 1907–'10. | *Handbook of American Indians North of Mexico*, Edited by F. W. Hodge. |
| 1908. | Austrians excavate at Jericho. |
| 1908. | *The Acropolis of Athens*, M. L. D'Ooge. |
| 1908. | *A Century of Archaeological Discoveries*, A. Michaelis, translation by Bettina Kahnweiler. |

1908.  Fewkes' excavations at Mesa Verde started.

1909.  Americans begin work at Samaria.

1909–'12.  *Repertoire de reliefs grecs et romains*, S. Reinach.

1909–'14,  Germans excavate temple of Hera at Samos (Wiegand and Buschor).
1925.

1910.  Discovery of togate statue of Augustus on Via Labicana.

1910–'13.  Oxford University expedition in Nubia.

1910.  *The Archaeology of California*, A. L. Kroeber.

1910.  Americans begin work at Sardes in Asia Minor.

1911.  Discovery of ruins of Machu Picchu in Peru by Yale Expedition.

1912.  *South American Archaeology*, T. A. Joyce.

1913.  Discovery of the Venus of Cyrene, Dec. 1.

1913.  *Athens and its Monuments*, C. H. Weller.

1913.  *Repertoire de l'Art Quaternaire*, S. Reinach.

1914.  Discovery of treasure of Lahun.  Royal diadem with uraeus serpent.

1914.  Announcement by Hewett, based on Quirigua excavations, that Mayan culture was founded at least 2,000 years ago.

1914.  Peabody Museum expedition begins study of Basket Maker culture in Southwest.

1914.  Mural paintings in cavern of Trois Frères discovered by Begouin.

1915.  *Aegean Archaeology*, H. R. Hall.

1915.  Excavation of Tremper Mound by Ohio Archaeological and Historical Society.

1915.  *An Introduction to the Study of the Maya Hieroglyphs*, S. G. Morley.

1916.  Discovery of temple site and colossal head of Zeus at Aegira in Achaea by O. Walter of Austrian Institute.

1916.  Discovery of Uaxactum, most ancient Maya city known.

1916.  Excavation of Aztec ruin, New Mexico, begun by American Museum of Natural History.

1917.  Discovery of the Apollo of Veii.

1917.  Discovery of hypogeum near Porta Maggiore in Rome.

1917–'20.  Etruscan houses, remains of pre-Etruscan huts, and fragments of Villanovan vases, found at Capena, north of Rome.

1918.  H. R. Hall finds oldest Sumerian temple, near Ur.

1918.  2,000 amphorae found at Carthage.

1918–'19.  Harvard University and Boston Museum of Fine Arts send expedition to Sudan.  Tombs of all the kings of Ethiopia (750–250 b.c.) discovered by G. A. Reisner.

1918–.  Work in Iraq at Abu Sharein, Ur, and Tell Obeid (Thompson, Hall, Woolley).

1919.  *Handbook of Aboriginal American Antiquities: Part I*, W. H. Holmes.

1920.  Palestine Exploration Fund (Garstang).

1920.  English excavate at Mycenae (Wace).

1920.  G. Calza finds many sculptures and a store house, baths, and Mithraeum at Ostia.

1920.  *Manuel d'Archeologie Romaine*, R. Cagnat et V. Chapot.

1920.  Scientific classification set for pre-Mycenean pottery on Greek mainland by A. J. B. Wace and C. W. Blegen as Early, Middle, and Late Helladic.

1920.  Excavation begun by Swedish Mission under A. Persson at Asine in Argolis.

1920.  Discovery that remains of temple of Jupiter under former German embassy on Capitoline Hill in Rome are part of podium of the original temple built by the Tarquins.

1920.     *Discovery in Greek Lands*, F. H. Marshall.

1920–'22.     Discovery at Mycenae of a seventh shaft grave, and houses dating L. H. III (Wace).

1921.     American School begins to excavate Zygouries in Greece (Blegen).

1921.     French Archaeological School at Jericho.

1921.     Discovery and partial excavation of Neolithic type station in Honan, China.

1921.     Jewish Palestine Exploration Society at Tiberias.

1921.     Franciscans excavate at Capernaum.

1921.     University of Pennsylvania Museum at Beisan (C. S. Fisher and A. Rowe).

1921.     Harvard University at Samaria.

1921–'22.     Excavation of Ashkelon by British School at Jerusalem.

1921.     Inauguration of work at Pueblo Bonito by National Geographic Society.

1921.     Temple of Quetzalcoatl excavated at Teotihuacan.

1922.     Work at Gaza by British School at Jerusalem.

1922.     Thirty solid gold staters of King Croesus found April 13 in a pot at Sardes.

1922.     University of Pennsylvania Museum, under Alan Rowe, begins work at Beisan (Beth-Shan).

1922.     Discovery of hoard of 8,000 coins (81–268 A.D.) at Falerone in the Marches, Italy.

1922.     Odeum of Pericles located at foot of Athenian Acropolis by Kastriotis.

1922.     Discovery by Arvanitopoullos of three superposed temples of Zeus Thaulios (4th cent. B.C.) at Pherae in Thessaly.

1922.     Bronze Age settlement and Etruscan tombs discovered on Monte Mario in Rome.

1922.     Evidence of highest known Eskimo culture found in Hudson Bay region by Fifth Thule Expedition.

1922.     Excavation of prehistoric pyramid at Cuicuilco, Mexico, by Cummings.

1922–'23.     Third Asiatic Expedition of American Museum of Natural History finds Neolithic pottery and artifacts in Mongolia.

1923.     Excavation at Tel-el-Ful (Gibeah of Saul) by American School of Oriental Research in Jerusalem (Albright).

1923.     Professor Esther B. Van Deman proves (A.J.A.) that Nero made Sacra Via at Rome into an avenue 100 Roman feet wide, flanked by arcades, leading to vestibule of Golden House.

1923.     Discovery by W. Amelung of many fine fragments of sculpture in basements of Vatican.

1923–.     Excavation of Mohenjo-daro and Harappa in India (Sir John Marshall).

1923–.     Work on Mt. Ophel at Jerusalem by Palestine Exploration Fund (Macalister and Duncan).

1923–'24.     C. L. Woolley identifies oldest Sumerian temple as that of Aannipadda of first dynasty of Ur. King's name inscribed on gold bead, oldest piece of known Sumerian jewelry.

1923–'26.     Discovery of 200 pictographic tablets at Kish (Mackay).

1923.     Aztec pyramid at Tenayuca excavated.

1924.     Excavation of Forum of Augustus begun in Rome.

1924.     University of Michigan Near East Expedition works at Antioch in Pisidia, and finds over 200 fragments of local copy (Latin) of *Res Gestae Divi Augusti* (F. W. Kelsey and D. M. Robinson).

1924.     Discovery of Bronze Age "high place" at Bab ed-Dra (Kyle and Albright).

1924.     French resume work at Mallia in Crete.

1924.     *Villanovans and Early Etruscans*, D. Randall-MacIver.

Undated.    *A Century of Excavations in the Land of the Pharaohs*, James Baikie.

1924-'25.    Eutresis in Boeotia. Miss Hetty Goldman for Fogg Museum and American School at Athens proves occupation from Early Helladic to Byzantine times.

1924-'27.    University of Cincinnati and American School at Athens excavate at Nemea (C. W. Blegen). Discovery of earliest skeletal remains in the Peloponnesus.

1924.    *The Roman Occupation of Britain*, F. J. Haverfield, rev. by G. MacDonald.

1924.    *Air Survey and Archaeology*, O. G. S. Crawford.

1924.    *An Introduction to the Study of Southwestern Archaeology*, A. V. Kidder.

1924.    *Human Origins*, George Grant MacCurdy.

1925.    Germans finish work at Aegina with the prehistoric settlements, and resume work at Samos.

1925.    Germans on fifth expedition to Persia find palace castle of King Ardashir on mountain near Firuzabad (225–639 A.D.); also Christian catacombs in island of Kharg in Persian Gulf (E. Herzfeld).

1925.    Discovery of new fragment of Fasti Consulares in palace wall at Rome, left column with years 278–267, right 215–208 B.C.

1925.    *The Art of the Greeks*, H. B. Walter.

1925.    Blegen makes first discovery of Neolithic pottery in the Argolid.

1925.    The Palestine Exploration Fund lays bare the eastern wall of the Jebusite (Pre-Davidic) Jerusalem.

1925.    Discovery of 1,000 tablets in Assyrian by American School at Baghdad and the Iraq Museum (Chiera).

1925.    Discovery of Galilee Skull (Neandertal) in cave near Lake Genesareth by Turville-Petre.

1925.    Hellenistic discoveries in Afghanistan by the French (A. Foucher).

1925.    *A Century of Excavation in Palestine*, R. A. S. Macalister.

1925.    First Tulane Expedition to Middle America adds to known area of Mayan culture.

1926-.    University of Chicago expedition begins work at Tell el-Mutesellim (Megiddo) under J. H. Breasted and C. S. Fisher.

1926.    Swedes discover at Midea in the Argolid an unplundered *tholos* tomb with three skeletons and magnificent funeral treasure of gold vessels and jewelry.

1926.    *The Social and Economic History of the Roman Empire*, M. Rostovtzeff.

1926.    The joint expedition of the American School at Jerusalem and the Xenia Theological Seminary identifies Tell Beit Mirsim as the Biblical Kirjath-sepher.

1926-'27.    Work at Tell en-Nasbeh by Pacific School of Religion (Badé).

1926.    Evidence of Old Stone Age inhabitants in Scotland.

1926.    Discovery of Elden Pueblo by Fewkes.

1926.    Traces of early Eskimo culture found in Alaska by Jenness of the National Museum of Canada.

1926.    Corn and early pottery found in Nevada cave by Harrington.

1926.    Discovery of the ruins of Coba by Gann of the British Museum expedition.

1926.    Mason-Spinden Expedition explores ruins of eastern Yucatan.

1927.    American School at Jerusalem proves site at Beitin begun before 1800 B.C. Beitin is identified with Canaanite Luz and Israelite Bethel.

1927.    Italians under Della Seta excavate in Lemnos. 130 cremation ossuaries in Tyrrhenian necropolis.

1927.    *The Early Iron Age in Italy*, D. Randall-MacIver.

| | |
|---|---|
| 1927. | Excavation of Hippodrome at Constantinople (470 × 117 m.) shows that it had no *spina*. |
| 1927. | French work on sanctuary in Thasos, and on palace at Mallia in Crete. |
| 1927. | Germans resume work at Pergamum under Wiegand. |
| 1927. | Austrians find many pieces of sculpture at Ephesus. |
| 1927. | Italians under Maiuri resume work at Herculaneum. |
| 1927. | Swedes under Gjerstad begin work in Cyprus. |
| 1927-'28. | Field Museum expeditions in Labrador and Baffin Land. |
| 1928. | Work at Tell Djemmeh, south of Gaza, by British School of Archaeology in Egypt, under Petrie. |
| 1928. | Discovery near Metz of pair of splendid Greco-Celtic bronze flagons dating about 450 B.C. |
| 1928. | Palestine Exploration Fund resumes work on Ophel at Jerusalem. |
| 1928. | *Griechische Kleidung*, M. Bieber. |
| 1928. | D. M. Robinson excavates Olynthus in Macedonia for Johns Hopkins University and the Baltimore Museum of Art. |
| 1928. | *The Archaeology of Ireland*, R. A. S. Macalister. |
| 1928. | American School at Athens excavates in Odeum. |
| 1928. | Blegen of Cincinnati works at Argive Heraeum. |
| 1928. | *Babylonian and Assyrian Sculpture in the British Museum*, H. R. Hall. |
| 1928. | *Roman Coins*, H. Mattingly. |
| 1928. | *The Civilization of Greece in the Bronze Age*, H. R. Hall. |
| 1928. | Discovery of bronze Zeus, a jockey, and the forepart of a horse in the sea off Cape Artemisium in Euboea. |
| 1928. | Germans under Buschor at Samos find Roman portraits of Claudian family. |
| 1928. | Helleno-Danish expedition works on sanctuary of Artemis at Calydon. |
| 1928. | Etruscan necropolis with fine Greek vases found at Valle Treba. |
| 1928. | Drainage of Lake Nemi begun to recover sunken barges of Caligula. |
| 1928. | Extended reconstructions in palace at Cnossus in Crete. |
| 1928. | *Antike Plastik*, W. Amelung. |
| 1928-'29. | Tarkalan: Harvard University and American School of Oriental Research (Chiera). |
| 1928-'29. | Tel-Omar, near Ctesiphon: University of Michigan (Waterman). |
| 1928-'29. | Tel-O: Louvre and University of Pennsylvania (Père Legrain). |
| 1928-'29. | Cemetery of the Sacred Bulls at Armant, near Luxor: Egyptian Expedition Society (H. Frankfort). |
| 1928-'29. | Excavations of Vienna Academy of Science discover and excavate *mastabas* near pyramid of Cheops. The best of many finds is an inscribed offering plate of alabaster (H. Junker). |
| 1928-'29. | Butrinto in Albania: Italian Archaeological Mission (Ugolini). |
| 1928-'29. | Hazor: Marston Expedition (Garstang). |
| 1928-'29. | Roman Wall in north England: (Society of Antiquities of Newcastle-upon-Tyne). |
| 1928-'29. | Shear's fourth campaign in theatre at Corinth. |
| 1928-'29. | Italians in excavation of Roman theatre in Calabria find terra-cotta jars which had been used as amplifiers. Between Cumae and Sinnessa a fine stretch of lava paved Via Domitiana, mentioned by the poet Statius, has been found. Close to the temple of "Castor and Pollux" at Girgenti two archaic altars have been uncovered. |
| 1928. | Excavations at Caerlon in Wales bring to light a dedication inscription to Trajan. |
| 1928. | Pict village in Orkney Islands excavated by Childe. |

1928.    Excavation and repair of Temple of the Warriors at Chichen Itza completed by Carnegie Institution.

1928.    Evidence of transition between pre-Pueblo and Pueblo cultures reported from Colorado by Smithsonian expedition.

1928.    *Estado actual de los principales edificios arqueologicos de Mexico*, Dirreccion de Arqueologia.

1928.    Development of Mimbres pottery traced back to early stages by Bradfield.

1928.    Excavation in Mimbres Valley, N. M., by joint expedition of The Minneapolis Institute of Arts (Jenks) and the School of American Research (Bradfield).

1929.    *Neolithic Settlement at Olynthus*, G. E. Mylonas.

1929.    Germans excavate at Dipylon gate in Athens (financed by G. Oberlaender of Reading, Pa.).

1929.    *Daedalus and Thespis, Vol. I*, Walter Miller.

# INDEX

341